CAN RELIGION SAVE DEMOCRACY?

How More Faith—Not Less—Can Heal Our Public Life

MATTHEW KAEMINGK
AND SHADI HAMID

BrazosPress
a division of Baker Publishing Group
Grand Rapids, Michigan

Published by Brazos Press
a division of Baker Publishing Group
Grand Rapids, Michigan
BrazosPress.com

Printed in the United States of America

Library of Congress Cataloging-in-Publication Data
Names: Kaemingk, Matthew, 1981– author | Hamid, Shadi, 1983– author
Title: Can religion save democracy? : how more faith—not less—can heal our public life / Matthew Kaemingk and Shadi Hamid.
Description: Grand Rapids, Michigan : Brazos Press, a division of Baker Publishing Group, [2026] | Includes bibliographical references.
Identifiers: LCCN 2026013588 | ISBN 9781587436895 cloth | ISBN 9781493456444 ebook
Subjects: LCSH: Democracy—Religious aspects | Religion and politics—United States—History—21st century | United States—Religion—21st century
Classification: LCC BL2525 .K34 2026
LC record available at https://lccn.loc.gov/2026013588

Cover design by Paula Gibson

The authors are represented by Aevitas Creative Management, LLC.

Baker Publishing Group publications use paper produced from sustainable forestry practices and postconsumer waste whenever possible.

26 27 28 29 30 31 32 7 6 5 4 3 2 1

Contents

Preface

Our respective stories of faith and politics begin in college. We were both studying political science when the planes struck the Twin Towers on September 11, 2001. As the smoke was still clearing from Lower Manhattan, our own Muslim and evangelical communities became embroiled in heated debates around religion, politics, and violence. Both groups were discussing what it means to be a "good American." As young scholars of faith, we wanted to understand how our sacred texts and faith commitments should (or should not) show up in the public square.

In the subsequent years, we both moved abroad. Shadi studied the rise of Islamist parties in the Middle East amid the religious and political fireworks of the Arab Spring. Matthew spent time in Europe working alongside Muslim asylum seekers and studying European debates over Muslim immigration and the rise of right-wing Islamophobia across the continent.

We came of age in the 1990s, the placid years of Bill Clinton and Bob Dole. We were used to a form of politics that was relatively boring. C-SPAN discussions of marginal tax rates, budget deficits, and health-care spending were rather technocratic and wonky. But what we witnessed in the Middle East and Europe post-9/11 was something much more spirited—and frightening.

As waves of Muslim immigrants arrived in Europe, Matthew witnessed a continent locked in conflict over what it means to be truly French, Dutch, or Swedish. Europeans were asking themselves if devout

Muslims could ever truly be European. Political discourse was no longer about the size of the welfare state; it was about the very identity of Europe itself.

In the same vein, during the Arab Spring, Egyptians and Tunisians weren't fighting about unemployment, taxes, or trade policy. Shadi watched as Arabs vigorously debated which beliefs and practices should be preserved and promoted by the state—and which should be punished. This was an existential debate between Islamic and secular visions of the social order.

Before the terms *tribalism* and *identity politics* entered the American lexicon, citizens in Europe and the Middle East were becoming embroiled in questions that are as old as time: Whose tribe is best? Who are the outsiders? How might we assimilate—or expel—them?

Watching Barack Obama and Mitt Romney debate taxes and health-care policy before the 2012 presidential election, Americans didn't realize how lucky they were. The relative staidness of US politics was a historical aberration. The natural state of politics is much more tribal and apocalyptic, as we would soon find out. The conflicts in Europe and the Middle East foretold what was coming to American shores.

Having witnessed deep divides abroad, we both returned to the United States and watched as political conflicts shifted from policy to populism, from the economic to the existential. The right went from Tea Party tax cuts to Donald Trump's Muslim travel ban and Mexican wall. The left went from universal health care and minimum wage increases to defunding the police, wokeism, and debates over transgender surgeries for minors. The sleep-inducing C-SPAN discussions about marginal tax rates were a thing of the past.

This wasn't all bad. Every democracy needs a bit of polarization. In big, diverse, and unwieldy countries, it's only natural for citizens to disagree and even dislike one another. You should like your family and friends; liking random citizens you disagree with is a taller order. What's different today is that mere disagreement is giving way to disgust and even hatred. A growing number of Americans see their fellow citizens as both dangerous and deplorable. They see their fellow Americans as threats to be monitored and enemies to be vanquished.[1]

Fighting back against this development animates our research and writing. Our hope is that we can present another way for those who are hungry for an alternative. Our concern isn't only about politics, though. It's more than that. Having entered our forties, we are now approaching middle age. This unwelcome passage of time has us taking stock of the sweep of our lives and the role religion has—or hasn't—played.

On a recent holiday, I (Shadi) was home in Pennsylvania with my parents and brother. Some families avoid talking about the past. My family is different. We took part in various thought experiments about the past: Could I have turned out differently? Could I have ended up more religious? What would have happened had I gotten married in, say, my twenties? For so many Muslim parents of a certain generation, raising children in America while maintaining their Muslim identity was a novel experiment—a task that became more difficult in a secularizing society.

In the same vein, I (Matthew) and my wife are parenting three sons approaching their teenage years. How will we raise our boys to value Christian self-sacrifice and selfless service in a culture that increasingly values self-satisfaction and self-actualization? Moreover, in a culture that values speed, power, and success, how will our boys learn patience, humility, and grace?

For both of us, exploring the role of religion in America today is not simply an intellectual or political exercise; it's personal.

Despite being born and raised in the suburbs of Philadelphia, I (Shadi) never had much experience with Christians—at least not *serious Christians*. Some of my classmates had Christian backgrounds and perhaps occasionally attended church, but that was the extent of it. During and after college in Washington, DC, it was more of the same. To live among hyper-educated elites in major urban centers was to live in a largely secularized, disenchanted world.

In 2015, after living in the Middle East for four years, I was back in Washington, DC. One day, something happened that stood out to me while I was working at a coffee shop. Two young men, who might have otherwise been discussing their plans for the weekend, were engaged in

Christian prayer. I couldn't recall the last time I had seen people looking down, in intense contemplation, praying together—and in Washington, DC, of all places.

I (Matthew) grew up in the only American city that has never experienced a religious revival. Today, fewer than 5 percent of Seattle residents attend church.[2] As a Seattleite and a Christian, I was acutely aware that my faith marked me as "strange." When I heard Southern Christians claim that America was a Christian nation and a "city on a hill," I was quite confused. Christianity in Seattle was foreign.

But both of us found that we rather liked the strangeness of being a Muslim and an evangelical in a pluralistic America. And we didn't like people telling us religion wasn't strange when we knew full well that it was.

The strangeness of religion is at the heart of the case we hope to make in this book. We need more strangeness, rather than less, because the problems that the United States is facing are themselves quite strange.

Introduction

America has been losing its religion. As it turns out, this is a problem.

Religion is one of those things you might not notice until it's gone. This can be an individual loss of belief, a personal crisis of faith, or a "dark night of the soul." Or it can be a parting of ways between a whole nation and its religion. In the United States, more than forty million Christians have left the church in the past twenty years alone—a staggering and historic drop.[1]

It can be hard to make sense of this seismic cultural shift. We are living through a profound cultural change, and we will be dealing with its consequences for the rest of our lives. Our children and grandchildren will know and feel this loss of religion in their own lives. The cultural dominance of mainline American Protestantism is now in collapse, giving way to a public square that is increasingly secular, tribal, and polarized.

We millennials are old enough to remember Barack Obama's stirring address at the 2004 Democratic National Convention. The then largely unknown junior senator from Illinois offered a moving paean, declaring that the United States could transcend its divisions and gather around a shared purpose. It was a heartfelt vision of a nation unified. Obama reminded Americans that just as they did in the red states, "we worship an awesome God in the blue states."[2] In other words, religion need not divide us. The young senator was right, at least at the time.

Among Western democracies, the United States had long been uniquely, perhaps even suspiciously devout. From 1937 through 2000, religious participation in American churches, synagogues, and mosques hovered at 70 to 75 percent. Then something happened. Over the next two decades, that number plummeted below 50 percent, the sharpest decline in American history. Meanwhile, so-called nones—atheists, agnostics, and those without a connection to institutional religion—came to represent more than a quarter of the population.[3]

Why the religious exodus? Many Americans appear to have good reasons for losing their religion. Many cite religious hypocrisy, violence, and extremism. Who would want to join such a club? While the nones clearly have their reasons for leaving churches, synagogues, and mosques, their exit has serious cultural and political consequences.[4]

Some recent surveys suggest that the steep decline in religious attendance and observance is beginning to level off. Yet long-term trends are still moving toward less religion. According to Pew Research Center's Religious Landscape Study, American adults in all age groups are less likely to identify as Christian or pray daily as they get older. Only 51 percent of Americans age eighteen to twenty-four identify as Christian, and only 28 percent pray daily, compared to 80 percent and 59 percent of those age seventy-four and older.[5] This means that as older Americans pass away and younger Americans grow into adulthood, the overall decline in religiosity will be more acute. Short of a major religious awakening, membership and attendance within religious institutions will remain at historic lows.

This is the new reality. But what kind of reality is it really?

If there ever was a secular dream, it was that as traditional religions retreated, our politics would become more rational, reasonable, and inclusive. Religion, after all, creates divisions, extremism, and other social ills. If religion enflames our political passions, secularism will cool them.

According to this secular vision of the future, individuals can still be privately religious, but when they enter the public square, they need to slough off their superstitions and behave rationally. These enlightened citizens will sit quietly together and deliberate based on the shared truths of modern science, reason, and common sense. No longer beholden to dogmas of the past, they will find a secular common ground and spend their time improving people's lives instead of fighting about silly things like what God wants from us.

But that's not what has happened.

The dream of an America without God looks more like a nightmare. As Christianity's cultural grip on American public life has weakened, our society has become more fragmented and polarized. Tribalism is the new normal.

A paradox has emerged within the heart of American public life: The more secular the United States becomes, the more its politics resemble a holy war.[6] The public square has been transformed into a spiritually charged arena in which the ultimate forces of good and evil are locked in apocalyptic combat.

As Americans exit churches in droves, they're not leaving behind their religious passions. Instead, they're transferring those passions to the political battlefield. Citizens watch cable news and scan social media to discover which evil forces must be exposed and boldly confronted. School boards, college campuses, and legislatures are now arenas in which this holy war between good and evil plays out.

Houses of worship used to shape Americans' ultimate beliefs, identity, and ethics; today, our souls are formed in the battlefield of politics. The culture war is the new Sunday school.

Religion Without Religion

Like all human beings, Americans long for meaning, purpose, and belonging. In the past, they found those things in embodied and local religious communities. Today, they increasingly "find themselves" in and through political conflict mediated through social media feeds.

New York Times columnist Ross Douthat argues that our loss of religion has only worsened our divides. He writes, "Part of the nature of politics in a landscape where there's no religious consensus, there's no moral consensus, is that forces that appear to have energy behind them—world historical energy, perhaps—will draw people."[7] In other words, with the breakdown of religious authority, popular movements and charismatic personalities are filling the vacuum.

While religious Americans have, especially since the Bush era in the early 2000s, tended toward the right, today neither political party has any significant connection with traditional religion. As Douthat mentions elsewhere, "If you dislike the religious right, wait till you meet the post-religious right."[8]

Despite the enduring relationship between evangelicals and the Trump administration, Donald Trump is perhaps the most secular, irreverent, and irreligious president in American history. When the president posts an AI-generated image of himself as pope in the wake of Pope Francis's passing, we're seeing someone who is indifferent to religious traditions or morality.[9]

Even if one were to give Trump the benefit of the doubt on the grounds that we cannot know what is in the hearts of men, one need not be a Christian to take issue with the apparent glee his administration has expressed in deporting people without due process. The issue is not immigration per se—one may reasonably believe that immigration should be limited—but rather the *process* of deportation. Gone are the days of compassionate conservativism. Cruelty seems to be the point.

This, in short, is what religion without religion looks like.

Religious decline isn't the sole cause of our political problems, but it is a critical part of the story. The United States wasn't founded as a Christian nation, but Christianity is tightly intertwined with American history and identity. Without it, Americans—conservatives and liberals alike—no longer have a common set of values or morals to fall back on. However secular the left might sound today, its arguments for health care, education, freedom, and tolerance are indebted to the nation's long-standing religious imagination.

Religious undertones resonate throughout the Declaration of Independence, in lines we often learn by heart without fully grasping their implications: "We hold these truths to be self-evident, that all men are created equal, that they are endowed by their Creator with certain unalienable rights." The founders' moral and political imaginations were deeply shaped by the religious culture that surrounded them.

Signing their names to this declaration, the founders were not only betting their lives; they were saying something about the religious foundations of their wager. Every human being has inherent worth and inviolable rights. These rights were not created by the state; they come from a transcendent source. As a result, they're irrevocable. The great sociologist of religion Robert Wuthnow has called this America's "sacred umbrella."[10] Even Americans who weren't particularly religious had friends, colleagues, and neighbors who were, which meant that everyone gained a basic religious literacy and moral awareness.

The sudden decline of religion in American public life has not been equally distributed. It has mapped onto preexisting divisions around class, geography, and education. Today, it is common for highly educated elites in urban centers on the coasts to go about their lives with little exposure to Christians or Christianity. With the decline of mainline Protestant churches and the dwindling number of white religious liberals, Democrats and Republicans have grown increasingly estranged on questions of faith and religious practice.

Social scientists have identified a growing population of American secularists who openly distrust any form of public religion. This population is now a dominant force among Democrats, particularly among the class of professionals, activists, and advisers who shape the party's national message. White, nonreligious Americans overwhelmingly vote for Democrats.[11] Meanwhile, the exodus of white evangelicals from the Democratic Party is almost complete.[12] Each of these groups, fearing or hating the other, has become more assertive and uncompromising: They simply can't agree on the big cultural or political questions. The moderate religious center has not held; it has nearly disappeared.

But What About the Evangelicals?

At this point, you might be wondering about the evangelicals: What about their tremendous political power within the Republican Party? Their influence is indeed substantial, but a few emerging trends should serve as a caution.

The thing we call "evangelicalism" is being secularized and religiously hollowed out from within. Forty years ago, the term *evangelical* referred to a dense national network of believers who were embedded and invested in local churches. These evangelicals spent a serious amount of time studying Scripture, worshiping together, and growing spiritually within a network of Christian colleges, charities, camps, media outlets, and nonprofits. Back then, to be an evangelical largely meant to have a set of theological convictions and to be an active participant in an embodied church community.

This is not the case anymore.

Like all Americans, evangelicals today are walking away from organized and institutional religion. According to Pew researchers, the percentage of evangelicals who attend religious services at least monthly dropped from 74 percent to 60 percent between 2014 and 2024. In the same time frame, the percentage of evangelicals who read the Bible monthly or more dropped from 75 percent to 62 percent; those who attend a prayer group monthly or more dropped from 57 percent to 42 percent.[13]

Moreover, evangelical institutions have lost their influence over those who call themselves evangelicals. In 2019, *Christianity Today*, the flagship magazine of American evangelicalism, called for Donald Trump to be impeached and removed from office. Despite creating a media firestorm, the magazine failed to dissuade many evangelicals from supporting Trump. Likewise, Richard Mouw and Mark Labberton, former presidents of the evangelical bastion Fuller Theological Seminary (and Matthew's former employer), released a forceful joint statement condemning Donald Trump, using explicitly religious language to do so. Once again, there was no discernible impact.

Most tellingly, a 2021 Pew survey revealed an unexpected trend: White Americans who hadn't identified as evangelical in 2016 were more likely to adopt the evangelical label by 2020 *if they supported Trump*. This suggests that "evangelical" has become more a political identity than a religious one.[14]

In this new post-religious context, Christian faith and Scripture function less as moral constraints within evangelical circles and more as political cudgels to use against one's opponents. Evangelicalism is quickly becoming just another form of identity politics in America's culture war.

But evangelicalism isn't unique in this regard. Most religious denominations in the United States are dealing with institutional decline and the rise of individualistic forms of spirituality. The widespread decline of institutional religion and the rise of new spiritual and political movements that are increasingly radical, digital, and disembodied will have a long-lasting impact on the fabric of American life. What does the future of democracy look like in an America without God? The early signs don't look good.

An Unpopular Argument

The United States is at an impasse. Americans are increasingly lonely, anxious, and angry. Despite a culture that elevates self-care, younger generations of Americans are less happy and less hopeful than at any point in recent history.[15]

Scholars have started to name a new and frightening kind of mental illness: politically induced anxiety, fatigue, and depression.[16] Despite our focus on self-empowerment, many of us report feeling more vulnerable and fragile than ever. Perhaps it's time to try something new—or, rather, something old.

For us, that something old is religion.

Ours might be an unpopular argument, but as a liberal Muslim scholar and a conservative Christian theologian, we want to suggest that our respective faiths deserve a second look. As the United States enters its post-religious phase, Americans are asking many hard questions about how to live together amid deep divides and how to navigate a political environment that is increasingly passionate and apocalyptic. It turns out that both Christianity and Islam have centuries of experience with deep difference and political conflict. Who better to navigate people through the present holy war in America than folks who have gone through multiple holy wars throughout the centuries?

In the pages that follow, we don't offer our religions as ready solutions to all of America's problems. Instead, we offer our respective faiths as reservoirs of wisdom for navigating political differences. For centuries, Muslims and Christians have been grappling with tough political questions about conflict and peacemaking, trauma and healing, and reconciliation and patience. These lessons were hard won, and we want to share them with our fellow Americans.

We are aware that our case for more religion faces a serious uphill battle. The very idea of *more* religion in public life is likely to produce nervous laughter, raised eyebrows, or worse. This is the sort of argument that does not get a great hearing in polite company.

Trust us, we know.

Living in urban enclaves, many secular Americans have little personal contact with institutional religion. Their understanding of traditional Christian and Muslim communities has been filtered through a very particular media diet of television shows like *The Handmaid's Tale*. Media coverage of religion tends to focus on, even obsess over, this darker side of faith. When prestigious television shows have religious characters, they are often oppressed heroes or heroines finding a way to liberate themselves from the constraints of strict, stifling religion. After the September 11 attacks, hundreds of books on religion and public life warned against the dangers of Islamic extremism. After Trump's election victory in 2016, writers and pundits focused on the dangers of conservative evangelicals and Christian nationalism. Of course, uncovering the evils of radical religious movements is important. That said, many of these accounts give the impression that religion is, on the whole, a problem that needs to be solved.

Religious extremism is real, of course. This book will neither deny nor diminish violence and antidemocratic behavior in religion's name. The individuals who flew planes into the Twin Towers were shaped by what they believed to be religious ideas and commandments. Likewise, the people who stormed the Capitol, beat up police officers, and tried to overturn a democratic election were shaped and impacted by Christian nationalist beliefs. When we make a case for the democratic benefits of religion, we are not—in any way—denying the documented historical fact that many of our Muslim and Christian brethren have done terrible things in the name of religion.

Even still, we believe there is a more interesting story to tell about public religion. We believe that religion is actually far more complicated, rich, and beautiful than the two-dimensional picture we often receive in the American media.

A broader and more nuanced understanding of global faith would reveal how it has inspired citizens to volunteer, give, serve, and sacrifice for the common good. The disproportionate focus on Islamic and Christian extremism fails to note how both faiths can contribute in incredible ways to political reconciliation, peace, patience, solidarity, and generosity.

We believe our faith traditions can help us move beyond the simplistic fight-or-flight response of American politics. History is filled with stories of people either perpetrating or enduring ideological dominance. It can get boring after a while. What is fascinating to us are those curious moments when diverse people of faith actually discover a different way of being together—a way of peaceful coexisting and contesting one another amid deep disagreement. This book is about that. A different way of being together.

For Clarification

Obviously, any argument for the political wisdom of Islam and Christianity will require some qualification. For the sake of clarity, we present the following:

1. Christianity and Islam are infinitely complex global religions. There is no single or uniform political perspective in either faith or its sacred text. Moreover, neither of us is qualified to speak for all Muslims or Christians.
2. Christianity and Islam are two distinct faiths. They have serious theological and political differences. From time to time, we will speak about family resemblances between the faiths. While we have moments of agreement, this does not mean the two faiths are one.
3. The idea that one can use religion for its emotional, social, and political benefits is a dangerous game with diminishing returns. We believe that our faith traditions are indeed useful, but that's not the reason we have committed our lives to them. Shadi is a

Muslim because he fundamentally believes in God, the divinity of the Quran, and the example of the prophet Muhammad. Matthew is a Christian because he believes in the person of Jesus Christ and the testimony of the Bible. We believe our sacred texts contain useful wisdom for everyone, but more than that, we believe they are true.

4. This book is not an exercise in conversion or apologetics. While we would love for you to join us at church or mosque someday, that is not our aim. This book is an invitation to consider religious wisdom and practices that can help you navigate America's political differences and mend a democratic fabric that is tearing with each passing day.
5. While other religions (Judaism, Buddhism, Hinduism, Sikhism, to name a few) have much wisdom to share, we are hesitant to speak for faith communities that are not our own.
6. From time to time, we will critique perspectives we describe as "liberal," "modern," or "secular." These critiques come from a place of gratitude. We are sincerely thankful to have grown up in an American society with things like individual rights, constitutional protections, and the separation of church and state. Life in a modern, secular society, for all its faults, is far superior to life under religious authoritarianism.
7. Finally, at no point will this book offer a systematic theory or solution for democratic life. As we've said, we don't agree on various important political and theological issues. Together, we could never agree on a complete political vision. It's not happening, and that's okay.

Here is what you *can* expect. In the chapters that follow, we will examine eight critical challenges facing democratic societies in the West. After considering one specific challenge to democracy, each chapter will dip down into the ancient reservoirs of political wisdom found within Christianity and Islam. Drawing from these deep reservoirs, we will show how these ancient insights can help heal our democracy and common life.

The New (Ab)normal

In this era of polarization, even the most benign political questions become an existential battle over who we are and what it means to be American. Various scholars have argued that even the most educated citizens no longer vote based on policy; instead, they vote based on their belonging to a particular group. In *Democracy for Realists*, political scientists Christopher Achen and Larry Bartels make the case that "the most important factor in voters' judgments [is] their social and psychological attachments to groups."[17] Electoral campaigns are more about defending your own identity, your own tribe, and your own way of life. In this way, contemporary politics is beginning to resemble the holy crusades of the ancient world, cosmic clashes of religiopolitical tribes. Politics is explosive and no longer normal.

But what *is* normal?

Too often, we are beholden to the naive belief that with the right education, the right information, and the right intentions, we can reach political consensus around commonsense solutions. If we get enough reasonable people together, reasonable solutions will be found.

But reason appears to have reached its limit. As philosopher John Gray notes, "Reason can enlighten us as to our ethical conflicts. Often, it shows them to be deeper than we thought and leaves us in the lurch as to how to resolve them."[18] Common citizens don't agree on the common good. They have fundamentally different conceptions of what is just, right, and true.[19] Their ways of life can seem—and sometimes are—irreconcilable. Conflicts over identity are exceedingly difficult to resolve.

We call this phenomenon "existential politics": a heightened state of play in which political competition becomes anchored in identity rather than policy. This is a crisis of politics—but it's about more than that. It spills out into other parts of our lives. Our families, schools, businesses, and media outlets are all being torn apart by our politics.

Politicians and pundits thrive on fear. They tell us to distrust and even despise people in other political tribes. They tell us that each new election is the most important of our lives, and if the other tribe wins, it will threaten our very way of life. The authors of one study on political polarization note that "the presidencies of George W. Bush and Barack

Obama were so deeply divisive that each of the last three presidents was labeled, with empirical support, the most polarizing ever."[20]

This apocalyptic approach trains citizens for endless political warfare. We now experience existential politics as an enduring reality of American life. We experience tribalism in our schools and sports, our movies and music, our commercials and corporations. Every aspect of American life is a cultural battlefield.

During the 2016 presidential race, an essay titled "The Flight 93 Election," published under a pseudonym, went viral. (The author, Michael Anton, would later serve in the Trump administration.) The essay opens, "2016 is the Flight 93 election: charge the cockpit or you die. You may die anyway. You—or the leader of your party—may make it into the cockpit and not know how to fly or land the plane. There are no guarantees. Except one: if you don't try, death is certain."[21] In other words, Democrats are flying the country into certain disaster, and Republicans have no choice but to rush the cockpit and wrest control from the pilots. This election is a matter of life or death. Democrats constitute a clear and present danger, one that must be eliminated by any means necessary. Anton was comparing the Democratic Party to al-Qaeda.

This type of existential politics creates a permanent state of dread. Once citizens are taught to fear, they become much more susceptible to arguments that desperate times call for desperate measures. The notion that the rules of the game must be suspended is what makes great evils possible. When anything goes because everything is at stake, authoritarian behavior isn't far behind.

Politics Is Making Us Sick

We are experiencing a crisis of politics. But it is also a crisis of faith, meaning, and belonging. And it is making us sick.

In a 2022 study, political scientist Kevin Smith estimated that between fifty and eighty-five million Americans were suffering from politically induced fatigue, insomnia, loss of temper, and impulse-control problems.[22] Moreover, 40 percent of his sample of American adults reported that politics was a "significant source of stress" in their lives, while 5 percent—which would translate to roughly twelve million adults—reported suicidal thoughts due to politics.[23] Suicidal ideation due to politics is a completely new and troubling category.

The problem is especially bad for young people. In 2024, the Centers for Disease Control reported that depression and suicidal ideation were at their highest levels on record, with one in three teenage girls having seriously considered suicide.[24] Boys and men aren't faring well either.[25] In 2024, the United States registered its lowest-reported level of happiness in the history of the World Happiness Report. Its ranking dropped from the fifteenth happiest country in the world in 2023 to the twenty-third in 2024, largely due to a dramatic decrease in happiness among young people under thirty years of age.[26]

The coauthors of a study on the politics of depression argue that left-leaning adolescents have been particularly hard hit. After Trump's election in 2016, they "experienced alienation within a growing conservative political climate such that their mental health suffered in comparison to that of their conservative peers."[27] According to this line of thinking, liberals, because of their liberalism, have good reason to be depressed. After all, if America is bad, the world is bad, and therefore life is bad.

Without a sense of something *beyond* us, everything becomes *about* us. This creates an intense political landscape in which political tribes—invested with the belief that they are on the right side of history—want nothing less than total victory in the here and now.

If there is no afterlife, nothing beyond this world, the claim that this is "the most important election of our lifetimes" can start to feel true. This is a heavy burden to impose on an electorate. A finite election cannot bear this infinite weight. The fierce urgency of *now* makes political patience insufferable. As writer Kyle Orton puts it, "Tolerance might not be possible from the secular world, tinged as it is with utopianism and a drive for final victories."[28]

So how do we temper this longing for a victory that is immediate and decisive?

We believe Christianity and Islam tell us something important about learning to let go and accept defeat. At its best, religion is about loosening our tight grip on the temporal world, with all its imperfections. Religion can offer a sense of rest and relief by withholding final judgments for another time and place.

A key idea in these waning religious traditions is "delayed judgment." For the believer, judgment is real, but it comes later. A judgment will be made, but it won't be ours. If ultimate judgment belongs to God, a citizen can put down their sword and let down their guard just a little bit. In this life, we'll have political victories and political defeats, but they aren't final. For the religious, the final judgment will come, but it won't be now, and it won't be ours. For the exhausted citizens of existential politics, this should be a relief.

Political debates are important but rarely apocalyptic; they are of this world and this world alone. Political philosopher Samuel Kimbriel beautifully captures this distinction when he reminds us that "some days are for dealing with your insurance documents or fighting in the mud with your political opponents, but there are also days for solemnity, or fasting, or worship, or feasting—things that remind us that the world is bigger than itself."[29]

In this way, religion can help frenetic citizens to, well, chill.

Unfortunately, adherents of all faiths too easily forget this. The belief that one possesses God's exact truth can be intoxicating and dangerous. It can produce fanaticism and intolerance toward those who have failed to see the light. But this is true of all belief systems, religious and secular. Extremism is not a uniquely religious problem. Communist movements of the twentieth century show us the blinding ideological power of secular dogma. All those who disagreed with communism were said to be blinded by capitalism. Only when Marx was accepted as lord and savior could economic oppression be seen all around. Whether religious or secular, deeply held convictions carry within them the inherent risk of taking things too far.

The problem isn't religion, though. It's us. We are all tempted to play God: to condemn and judge, to cancel and cast out. If anything, secular politics—focused as it is on achieving tangible and decisive victories now rather than later—is even more prone to these pitfalls. Secular success depends on delivering immediate results; traditional religion is not results-based, at least not in the same way. It does not demand immediate and tangible proof of success.

Postponing judgment is critical to both Islam and Christianity, but anyone can adopt it. Judaism, Hinduism, and Buddhism contain their own rich variations of the concept. Regardless of their faith, citizens can decide to abstain on the question of whether a policy matter—an immigration quota, a particular approach to health care, a public-school curriculum—represents an absolute, incontrovertible truth. We might be confident that we're right, but there's always the chance we are wrong.

In practice, postponing judgment would mean that very few citizens are outside the fold or beyond the pale. For Americans, it means that, save for a relative few on the fringes, there are no "good" or "bad" Americans in an ultimate sense—or at least not in an ultimate sense that mere humans might be privy to. This is what an American public space friendly to religion could theoretically look like, and the good thing is that anyone can start to practice it.

Religion Is a Force for Good

Our proposed path out of the impasse might seem both strange and unwelcome, especially now. Traditional religion is often maligned as a wrench in the democratic gears, halting any hope for progress. Distaste for public religion is more pronounced among college-educated liberals and younger Americans more broadly. In other words, a large portion of the people who set the tone for our public debates believe that religion is a problem to be managed and mitigated.

The concern is understandable. Secularism became more attractive in part because of the uncompromising overreach of right-wing evangelicals in the 1980s and 1990s, and it has remained attractive due to the evangelical alignment with Trump over the past decade. If ambivalent Christians were looking for a way out of weekly church attendance, seeing their faith be manipulated to gain power made it a lot easier. After September 11, President George W. Bush made much of the fact that he was a born-again Christian in justifying his decision to invade

Iraq. He spoke of being guided by God. When he referred to the war on terror as a "crusade," it seemed less like a misstep and more like a harbinger of things to come.

As the world's two largest and most influential faiths, Islam and Christianity are often singled out. We have heard the arguments our entire lives: Muslims need enlightenment, and Christians need education. Only when they become more enlightened, modern, and secular will they become more rational and peaceful. The suspicion of Muslim migrants and conservative evangelicals is a stand-in for deeper fears. It's not specific people groups who worry secular liberals as much as it is the idea of public religion itself.

But what if this story gets things upside-down?

The dream of a secular public square is a fiction, and it's about time we accept that and act accordingly. For all our differences, the two of us agree on one thing: Religion is not a problem to be solved. Rather, it might be part of the solution.

Religion, on balance, is a force for good. For starters, it makes us happier. A 2019 Pew study found that in twenty-one out of twenty-six countries, the religiously active were happier than the religiously unaffiliated.[30] In times like these, happiness might seem like a luxury. But when political despair pushes young people toward vindictive ideologies, happiness becomes urgently necessary.

Religion, as we will see, is also a social good. Robert Putnam and David Campbell analyzed fifteen "good deeds" and found that frequent churchgoers were more likely to give to charity, volunteer, donate blood, spend time with someone who was a bit down, and (perhaps most remarkably) allow a stranger to cut in front of them in the grocery store. Even after controlling for a host of variables, the authors discovered that "not a single one of these 15 good deeds is more common among secular Americans than religious Americans."[31]

We also forget the positive role religion played in the great struggles of the modern age. The Christian belief in the inherent dignity of all people played an important role in the abolitionist movement. The great pacifist movements were often led by people of faith, who saw in Jesus's message an admonition to end all war.[32] America's labor unions find their origins in both Catholic and Protestant Christianity. Black churches were the central organizing force in the battle for civil rights in the 1960s. Today's secularized version of Martin Luther King Jr. makes it easy to forget that he was, first and foremost, a preacher and theologian whose religious commitments animated him and his followers in the most fundamental sense.

America's founders—including even deists like Thomas Jefferson, who didn't believe in the divinity of Jesus—recognized public religion as the lifeblood of American democracy. For them, religion was a clear source of moral energy and political renewal. The large number of small-town churches across a vast new country were everyday schools of communal belonging, volunteering, charity, debate, and political mobilization. The US Constitution includes vigorous protections for these little churches precisely because the founders—even if they did not go to church themselves—understood that communal and public faith was a source of vitality for the American experiment.

The America ideal did not suddenly emerge in Philadelphia in 1776. It had been developing for two hundred years in Protestant churches. These churchgoers did not want their pastors to become tyrants. Using a representative group of elders and a basic rule of law, these churches held their pastors in check for hundreds of years before Jefferson thought to do so with a king or a president.

But religion, in this context, wasn't simply about holding leaders in check. It was about cultivating in citizens a sense of duty, purpose, and social responsibility.

As we will show in chapter 7, belonging to a religious organization helps citizens develop democratic habits of participation and cooperation. In a church or mosque, citizens can learn how to be part of a small political community. They can volunteer, debate, serve, lead, fight, and forgive. As we will argue, these religious spaces can serve as critically important "schools of democracy."

But these traditional religious institutions are giving way to new forms of secular spirituality—think yoga, SoulCycle, CrossFit, mindfulness retreats, and book clubs. Unfortunately, these new forms of spirituality don't offer the same kind of democratic dividends. This is not to say that these communities aren't nourishing, but they are often focused inward, toward the self. Yoga groups don't establish homeless shelters. SoulCycle classes don't include marriage counseling. Mindfulness retreats don't organize neighborhood watches. Our democracy needs, and deserves, more than self-care. It needs selfless care.

An Invitation to Nonreligious Readers

Today, there is a real opportunity—and need—for secular Americans to reach out to their religious neighbors, to listen to them, and perhaps even to learn from them.

We're not asking you to convert. We're not asking you to bend the knee. We're asking you to be open-minded toward Christians, Muslims, and Jews who have been thinking hard about how to deal with social divisions, traumas, and hatred for centuries, even millennia.

Americans with higher education levels and incomes are less likely to believe in God, consider religion important, pray often, or look to religion for moral and ethical guidance.[33] As secular Americans distance themselves from their religious neighbors, they increasingly inhabit echo chambers in which religious literacy and curiosity suffer. They lose the capacity to understand, let alone empathize, with broad swaths of the public. Religious literacy might seem like an inconvenience, but we believe our democratic future depends on it.

Our heads aren't in the sand. At its worst, religion has motivated leaders and movements to engage in destructive acts. But the notion that religion is the primary cause of human violence is a myth. In fact, theologian William Cavanaugh calls it "one of the most prevalent myths in Western culture."[34] For starters, religion as something that can be separated into its own category is largely a modern invention. For most of recorded history, the categories we now call religion and politics were so intertwined that it was impossible to know where one ended and the other began. Not only that, but religion as we understand the word today didn't even exist. Its early English definition is unrecognizable to us today as "a state of life bound by monastic vows."[35]

As for the wars and genocides of the twentieth century—easily history's most violent century—they were not primarily religious wars. Hitler hated Christianity even as he occasionally indulged it. The killing fields of the Soviet Union, China, and Cambodia were justified in direct *opposition to* religion.[36] Humans are violent enough on their own, with or without this thing moderns now call "religion."

In short, the story we've told ourselves about public religion being the source of conflict is far too simplistic. Stories of religious extremism attract the most clicks, while too often religion's countless benefits get short shrift.

In addition, the democratic insights of Islam and Christianity have remained largely submerged and even unknown, including among believers. This book will attempt to change that, with the goal of communicating a vital message to Americans who are yearning for a different path out of our current crises.

A majority of Americans, while suspicious of mixing religion and politics, are still generally positive about the role religion can play in public life. Eighty percent say that religious organizations "bring people together and strengthen community bonds," while 64 percent believe that they "protect and strengthen morality in society."[37] In these pages, we will distill and explain just how religion can do these things and how ordinary citizens can apply these ideas and principles in their own lives.

A (Non-)Conversion Story

This book is not an argument about whether Christianity or Islam is true. Nonreligious readers don't need to convert for our arguments to hold weight. Readers can freely approach these ancient religious reservoirs, take a momentary drink of their political wisdom, then walk away. You don't have to believe that a faith tradition is true to grasp its insights about what it means to be human and to live amid challenging differences.

Our own unlikely friendship is a model. Shadi is a committed Muslim who has no intention of converting to Christianity. Matthew is a committed Christian who has no intention of converting to Islam. Neither of us believes that the other's religion is true. That might seem like a problem, but for us, that deep difference actually provided an opening. By sitting, discussing, and even arguing with each other over the past five years, we have come to see both Christianity and Islam as powerful, untapped reservoirs of political wisdom and insight.

Christianity and Islam—with around 2.4 billion and 2 billion adherents, respectively—spread so extensively and forged such sprawling multiethnic, multilingual, and multireligious empires precisely because they had something important to say about how to handle deep and challenging differences. To grow as they did, these two religions needed to contend with a complex range of human emotions and experiences. To spread themselves effectively, Muslims and Christians needed to pitch a big tent—and they had to do so quickly. As a matter of religious survival, these global faiths had to find ways to broaden their appeal and accommodate cultural, political, and ideological difference. They had no other choice.

Totalitarianism, of the sort we know today, didn't exist in the ancient world—because it couldn't. However despotic some Christian and Islamic empires were in the Middle Ages, these were still premodern states that were inherently limited in their size and scope. Christian emperors and Muslim caliphs simply didn't have the tools to dominate vast swaths of land like an autocratic leader might today. By today's standards, the imperial bureaucracies of early Islam and Christianity were tiny. Without modern technology and policing power, leaders couldn't reach into every remote rural area or track every move of residents. Without universal education, they couldn't turn children into "citizens." Without harsh immigration regimes or borders, there was no way to effectively assimilate or exclude people who weren't like them. Difference was everywhere. It was inescapable. More often than not, Christian and Muslim leaders had to develop political systems and cultural practices that were flexible enough to accommodate reality as they found it rather than as they wanted it.

These ancient religious skills and insights for how we might navigate deep difference have been obscured by history. The United States is losing these religious skills and insights. It's late, but it's not too late. We believe it is time to bring them back.

1

We Can't Quit Religion

KEY TAKEAWAY

Humans are hardwired for belief. Even as religion declines, the religious impulse doesn't disappear. It just migrates into our politics, making our democratic life more contentious and polarized. Recognizing this is a first step toward a healthier public life.

In 1980, fresh off a dramatic conversion to Christianity, Bob Dylan released a song titled "You Gotta Serve Somebody." The track makes a rather simple point: Human beings, by their very nature, serve.

Dylan's new track was an unwelcome message to his peers in the 1960s, who aimed to liberate themselves from religion in favor of a more enlightened spirituality. By contrast, "You Gotta Serve Somebody" insisted that human beings desire something more than self-actualization; humans want to worship, trust, and serve something or someone beyond themselves. Regardless of their wealth, education, or station, all human beings, Dylan was saying, long to offer themselves to something greater.

> But you're gonna have to serve somebody, yes indeed
> You're gonna have to serve somebody[1]

John Lennon hated the song. He rejected the idea that human beings were made to be servants and believed they were made for freedom and spiritual self-empowerment. Ultimately, Lennon elected to publicly parody Dylan's newfound faith, as well as religion as a whole, with the song "Serve Yourself." He ridicules Dylan's ideas in order to advance his own counternarrative.

Why We Can't Quit Religion

As much as we appreciate Lennon as an artist, his philosophical insights leave something to be desired. "Imagine," his most famous song as a solo artist, was unwaveringly optimistic at a time when the hope of the 1960s was dimming. In the opening couplets, accompanied by a gorgeous piano melody, the former Beatle intones, "Imagine there's no heaven. . . . Above us, only sky."[2] Throughout the song, Lennon envisions a new society, one without religion.

It wasn't too difficult for people in the 1970s to imagine a heavenless world in which citizens lived for today and not some imaginary, otherworldly heaven. During this period, the secularization thesis had come to dominate debates around the role of religion in public life. Scholars agreed that religion was a relic of a bygone era and that modernity—due to scientific progress, industrialization, and enlightenment—had made traditional religion less relevant. This wasn't to say that people would cease believing, just that their beliefs would become a matter of inward feeling rather than public expression. With few exceptions, scholars at the time assumed this was a positive development, because they thought that less religion meant less social division. These assumptions spilled into the popular consciousness, where they remain today, shaping how we speak about faith and facts, private and public, the sacred and the profane.

Today's leading scholars of secularization, such as Charles Taylor, Saba Mahmood, and Talal Asad, have thoroughly punctured the secularization thesis and many of its assumptions. Even still, secularist narratives about religion still dominate public conversation. Lennon's antireligious philosophy lives on in mainstream media, the arts, film, and the broader culture. There, a common plot centers on an oppressed individual who is trapped by the rigidity of their religious community.

They wrestle with and push back at the restrictions imposed upon them. They ultimately break free, and only then do they find happiness and an opportunity to be themselves, without religious shame and guilt.

Not all stories of oppressive religion are inaccurate, of course. The problem is that stories of religious oppression capture only one aspect of a much larger religious reality. But more than that, depictions of religion like that found in John Lennon's "Imagine" imply, rather naively, that without religion, everything would fall into place. Religion equals problems—or so the thinking goes. The admonition to avoid bringing up religion at social gatherings is so commonplace that we don't bother to question it. But what is it about this thing we call religion that provokes these fears and worries? What are we so afraid of?

The secularization narrative hasn't delivered on its promises of unity and peace. In fact, the gospel of secularism has only given us new things to fight about, with an alarming level of rancor and conflict.

The summer of 2020 was the most polarized of our lifetimes, with warnings of authoritarian coups, impending fascism, and even civil war. The aftermath wasn't much better and featured an insurrection backed by a former president that shook the nation. These are only the most extreme examples. Garden-variety polarization is everywhere, snaking its way into every avenue and artery of public life. As polarization continues to spread, Americans are dividing themselves up, not by religion but by their political ideology.

Younger Americans are more educated, more secular, and more left-leaning than their parents were, and they're unapologetic about drawing clear political battle lines in a way that will have profound implications for our democracy. For instance, a whopping 71 percent of Democrats now say they won't date someone who voted for the other candidate.[3] Mixed political marriages have become something close to nonexistent; only about 4 percent of marriages are between a Democrat and a Republican.[4] After retaking power in 2024, Republicans further fueled polarization, using the assassination of conservative activist Charlie Kirk as a cudgel against left-leaning Americans through cancellation efforts and politically motivated lawsuits and legal challenges.

Yet something has been happening beneath the surface of polarization—something that conventional political analysis has struggled to capture. Scholars and pundits typically explain our growing divisions by pointing to institutional decay, social media algorithms, or economic grievances. But these accounts, however compelling, miss a more fundamental truth: The religious impulse hasn't disappeared from American life; it has simply migrated.

Americans are still "believers" and "joiners," even if they are leaving organized religion and no longer regularly attending religious services. As more Americans abandon their churches, they're carrying their longing for belief and belonging into the political arena. Rather than gathering in religious institutions and houses of worship, citizens now find their identity in and through their political tribes. The ubiquity of social media and the decline of the old media gatekeepers fuel the quasi-spiritual intensity of these political fights. Social media doesn't create the existential need for belief and belonging, but it does inflame it by allowing more unbridled anger and frustration to come out into the open. Religious passion was always there; it has just been redirected and redeployed.

Believers and Belongers

Abraham Kuyper was the rare politician who was also a theologian. He served as the prime minister of the Netherlands at the dawn of the twentieth century, when the Dutch were in the early throes of secularization. He argued that secular passions, beliefs, and worldviews were ultimately just sublimated religion.

As a prime minister and a Christian, Kuyper led a nation that was deeply divided among the forces of socialism, liberalism, Catholicism, and Protestantism. He argued that all four of these ideologies were "faith-based" and that no human being or political movement could survive long without some ultimate point of belief, passion, or loyalty. Every person and every political movement, he believed, had some sort of ultimate trust or pivot around which they oriented their lives.[5] If that ultimate pivot didn't derive from traditional religion, it would come from some form of secular commitment, like capitalism, nationalism, socialism, or liberalism. Political theorist Samuel Goldman calls this "the law of the conservation of religion": In any given society, there is a steady supply of religious conviction and passion. What varies is how and where it is expressed. We can close all the churches and mosques, but some other passionate and zealous human community will emerge to take their place. Humans are believers and belongers.

No longer rooted in mainline Protestantism, understandings of the American creed have become richer and more diverse—but also more fractious. As our belief in America fragments, each side seeks to exert exclusivist claims over the other. Conservatives believe they are faithful to the original American creed and that liberals are betraying it. Liberals believe, with equal certitude, that *they* are faithful to the American idea and that conservatives are betraying it. As the chasm widens, each side becomes less intelligible to the other. Too often, the most bitter divides are within families.

For decades, conventional secular wisdom told us that this thing called religion produced dogmatism—an unfounded certitude in matters of opinion. But today we see dogmatism spreading far outside religious circles. As one recent study shows, "Irreligious people may be even more inflexible than their religionist peers [with] regard to two aspects of closed-minded cognition: tolerance and integration of contradictions, and readiness to consider and appreciate others' perspective."[6] In another study, religious people were dogmatic about moral concerns, while the irreligious were most dogmatic about analytical concerns, meaning they were less willing to understand other people's perspectives.[7]

If Kuyper is correct that all human beings desire ultimate belief and belonging, then erasing or sequestering religion won't extinguish our spiritual passions. They will simply shift elsewhere.

Secular Creeds

For all their faults, Christians and Muslims living in pluralistic countries like the United States are well aware that their particular faith is just that: particular. By this, we mean that they understand that their faith will never be shared or embraced by all their neighbors. They're aware that their faith is not provable by science or reason. They're aware that all faiths—including their own—require a level of, well, faith. But these believers understand, however reluctantly, that their particular religious community participates in a much larger American marketplace of religion. And, being a marketplace, it will necessarily feature some competition and even resistance. From its founding, the United States codified religious diversity and freedom. The colonies were home to a variety of competing religious communities. If American believers wish to wax nostalgic about a golden age of theological unity and uniformity, they will need to look to foreign shores.

Our point about the *particularity* of faith might appear simple and straightforward. But it's precisely at this point that secular individuals like John Lennon begin to struggle. Muslims and Christians understand this point; Lennon does not. He simply cannot concede that he too represents one more particular faith in a diverse religious marketplace. He cannot admit that he too is participating, indeed competing, in a great spiritual contest right alongside his religious neighbors. Why?

Embedded within Lennon's lyrics is the belief that people who reject religion have transcended faith and the human need for belief and belonging. Lennon was certain he had discovered a unique method to transcend all religious and political division, something that no one before had ever quite managed. According to his secular dogma, a new and matured form of humanity had emerged in the 1960s. Religious people were casting about in darkness, while Lennon and his ilk had stepped into the light.

The irony, of course, is that in a song carefully designed to mock and taunt Bob Dylan's desire to serve, Lennon has unwittingly proven Dylan's point. The song reveals that Lennon, in fact, does serve someone. He serves himself.

The idea that individuals might reach enlightenment with the right education, information, and insight is beguiling. It means that, at least in theory, we might be able to put aside our differences or, better yet, transcend them. This, so the thinking goes, is what makes progress possible. Because these ideas continue to have a profound social impact, we need to look at them with a critical eye.

Consider for a moment a new creed that has swept through the United States in recent years. A popular yard sign reads as follows:

In this house we believe:

- Black lives matter
- No human is illegal
- Love is love
- Women's rights are human rights
- Science is real
- Water is life
- Injustice anywhere is a threat to justice everywhere

This yard sign is not a list of facts. Rather, it features a list of fervently held beliefs about the world not as it is but as it should be. Yes, water is technically required to stay alive, but "Water is life" is making a broader argument about the need to combat climate change through aggressive policy interventions. "No human is illegal" is true in some ultimate sense—we are all God's children, after all—but, again, this is a broader claim about state recognition of noncitizens entering the United States.

There is a boldness to the yard sign. Displaying it demonstrates a high degree of public confidence and conviction. Like a Jehovah's Witness knocking on doors, this yard sign evokes a desire *to evangelize.*

And yet, after hammering this sign into the ground with great conviction, secular people can do something that no Muslim or Christian could possibly imagine. They can go out to lunch with a dear friend and declare with a straight face that they are spiritually uncertain, open-minded, and largely agnostic about the ultimate nature of right and wrong, good and evil.

Displaying this yard sign for all their neighbors to see, secular individuals aren't transcending religious dogmatism—they are extending it in a different form. They are mimicking religious confidence but without fear of a god who might also command that they communicate their beliefs with some level of humility or grace.

When Muslims recite the profession of faith that there is only one God and Muhammad is the last Prophet, they fully understand that they are making a particular religious choice. They recognize that their Christian neighbors, by definition, won't—indeed can't—share their belief. Muslims recognize that their faith is strange, particular, and open to rejection. As a result, they recognize something their neighbors with the yard sign do not.

The Myth of Religious Neutrality

Human beings believe in all sorts of things. Human beings love to make meaning and they long to discover it. Humans imbue meaning into stories and relationships, promises and commitments, and objects of trust. No matter how jumbled our belief systems and values might be, we all carry them. All human beings experience feelings of love and hate, joy and fear, longing and lament.

Over time, people begin to connect these experiences and beliefs. They begin to order their commitments. They start ranking the relative importance of family and work, justice and mercy, wealth and charity, self-indulgence and self-sacrifice. As finite beings, we can never fully justify the priorities we select, and yet *we do select them*. We make sense of the world. We develop answers, however mixed up, to fundamental questions: What's wrong with the world? Who can be trusted? What do we need to survive and thrive? One day we realize that we have developed a whole set of commitments and priorities.

The English word *religion* comes from the Latin *religio*, meaning "to bind." It speaks to our human need to bind disparate things together into a meaningful whole. We long to bind our experiences, values, and commitments, and through those bindings make meaning. Connecting one's complex life with some sort of narrative thread is a universal human activity.

Beyond this process of binding, three other words are important to understanding humanity's religious inclination. They are *trust*, *promise*, and *submission*. We will take each in turn.

Trust is something that humans develop as they begin to rely on particular people, places, or things. Humans come to trust that these particular objects, ideas, or institutions will provide them with meaning and security. For theists, trust is placed in a deity. For nontheists, trust might be placed in practices like hard work or education, meditation or mindfulness. A nontheist might also place their trust in a political party, cause, or ideology. They might place their trust in their spouse, their family, their race, or their tribe. Or, if all else fails, they might simply place their trust in themselves—their intelligence, common sense, or sheer will. Here we return to the idea of binding. As our trust develops, we begin to bind ourselves to our objects of trust—whatever they might be.

This brings us to our second word, *promise*. Humans are promise makers who aspire to be promise keepers. We bind ourselves to others through a series of vows. We make vows of solidarity to spouses, children, friends, coworkers, and fellow citizens. We promise fidelity to families, sports teams, companies, and nations. By and large, these promises are beyond all science or logic. They are products of belief and connection. There is no rational reason to bind ourselves to this particular friend, this company, or that nation. And yet, each and every day, we go on making promises and declaring our solidarity to all sorts of individuals and institutions.

This brings us to our third and final term, *submission*. In trusting and promising, we begin a process of submission. We offer and even surrender our individual selves to whatever our objects of trust demand. A hierarchy begins to develop. Those objects that have a lower priority may be subsumed or even sacrificed on the altar of a greater commitment. The term *submission* rightly evokes a shudder in the modern psyche. It connotes a hierarchal relationship of unequal value and power. It is here that these seemingly benign practices of trusting and binding turn into something unexpected and perhaps unwelcome. It is here that the personal becomes political.

When entire groups of people start elevating certain priorities over others, politics has officially entered the conversation. Broadly construed, politics is the construction of binding commitments and the hierarchies those commitments require.

Here, someone might protest: "But I'm different. I don't believe in or submit to anything!" Yet this statement reveals that the underlying object of belief is the self. There isn't really another option. If you refuse to submit yourself to an outside object, you are, a la George W. Bush, "the decider." If there is no external source of reference, then the ultimate power will be found within.

This, too, is an act of faith.

This is the tragedy of the secular or neutral public square. When secular people put up their yard signs, they struggle to own that they too have a creed. According to their creed, while other citizens are religious, they simply "are." Secular citizens who claim to have transcended religion fail to recognize that when they enter the public square, they too carry a whole raft of unfounded beliefs and commitments along with them.

The term *organized religion* is one of the reasons many secularists struggle to recognize their own religious impulses. In their mind, to be religious is to submit to a formal religious institution. Captive to the late modern definition of religion, the secular person believes religion involves a large building made of stone, with priests, governing structures, written laws, sacred texts, holy days, and formal traditions. Since secularism lacks these things, the secularist concludes that they have no religion.

Having liberated themselves from organized religion, the secular person imagines that they have escaped religiosity entirely. In ceasing to attend a local church, the new nonbeliever may imagine that they have ceased binding, trusting, and submitting. But they haven't. The secular belief that human beings can be spiritually neutral, indifferent, or completely unbound is exactly that, a belief. And—as beliefs go—it's a pretty shaky one.

German philosopher Friedrich Nietzsche himself admitted that, having killed God, an atheistic Europe would need to invent a new god.

Without Christianity, Europe would need a new set of rituals and rites. In one of his more famous passages, Nietzsche states,

> God is dead. God remains dead. And we have killed him. . . . How shall we comfort ourselves, the murderers of all murderers? What was holiest and mightiest of all that the world has yet owned has bled to death under our knives: who will wipe this blood off us? What water is there for us to clean ourselves? What festivals of atonement, what sacred games shall we have to invent? Is not the greatness of this deed too great for us? Must we ourselves not become gods simply to appear worthy of it?[8]

Abraham Kuyper, despite being a Christian, agreed with Nietzsche on this point. He argued that the throne of God couldn't remain empty. A secular Europe had to fill that throne with something. No nation, he argued, could "rest content with such a bare negation."[9] If people had dethroned God, something else inevitably had to be "placed on the vacant seat."[10]

Secular individuals bind themselves to ideas, movements, and charismatic leaders every day. They make promises, vows of solidarity, and profound and even heroic sacrifices. Over time, secularists develop beliefs about the good life, what's wrong with the world, what governments are for, and what their legacy should be. However mixed and muddled it might be, they each have a philosophy, a worldview. They too believe.

A Blind Spot with Political Consequences

This blind spot at the heart of secularism has real consequences for our political future. Having transcended religion, secular citizens start to imagine they've also transcended their religious neighbors. This assumption gets political very quickly.

An example from France illustrates the point. In 2004, the French parliament passed a law that banned Muslim girls from wearing headscarves in public schools. According to opinion polls, a large majority of French citizens believed this law was good, right, and justified.[11]

Moreover, they believed they were doing these Muslim girls a favor. Clearly, the thinking went, Islam had forced the girls into wearing headscarves. The law would liberate them. After all, a century earlier, the French had transcended the oppressive backwardness of Catholicism and had since achieved secular enlightenment. The 2004 legislation was their way of paying it forward to another group of benighted religious people who had not yet achieved enlightenment.

Secular people can easily imagine that they are responsible for overseeing the religious marketplace—which is now beneath them. After all, who better to referee a religious contest than those precious few citizens who have transcended the contest altogether?

This is one of the fundamental reasons why secular elites in the West disproportionately struggle to engage their religious neighbors with a spirit of curiosity, generosity, and humility. They fail to recognize that they themselves aren't neutral. Like their religious neighbors, secularists carry their particular and contested commitments into the public square. They too live by a sort of faith—one their neighbors do not share. This is why religious citizens often walk away frustrated when they try to engage their secular neighbors. How can a productive interfaith dialogue take place when one of the participants refuses to admit that they even have a faith?

Drawing on abundant quantitative and qualitative data, Aala Abdelgadir and Vasiliki Fouka found that the secular French policies prohibiting headscarves in public schools actually hindered Muslim girls from finishing school.[12] If secular interlocutors aren't willing to acknowledge that secularism itself can disenfranchise religious citizens, is there really much room for dialogue?

The belief that human beings can be divided into two neat categories—the religious and the secular—can easily turn into a hierarchal power play. Under this hierarchy, those who have transcended religion can provide solutions from above to the problem of public religion, while those who remain mired in religious belief down below are, quite simply, the problem.

Whenever someone outgrows religion, they may be tempted to turn around and ask their religious neighbors to follow their same path.

Muslims living in the West feel this pressure when they are told that Islam needs to go through a reformation or an enlightenment. Muslims must, in other words, follow the same path of historical maturation that Europeans did. The cultural imperialism here is not subtle.

Often described as backward or medieval, conservative Muslims are viewed as a historical anomaly in secular spaces. Muslims are students to be taught, immigrants to be assimilated, or terrorists to be defeated. Once again, a hierarchy of the religious and the secular makes Muslims into objects of Western salvation. Once again, Muslims are a problem to be solved.

When they do enter the secular public square, religious people of various traditions are regularly expected to speak and act secularly. For the sake of their neighbors, they must hide outward signs of religiosity. Religious people are asked to dress, speak, reason, think, and sometimes even *feel* in distinctly secular ways.

Once again, the headscarf illustrates this. Consider the words a Muslim woman will often use in a courtroom setting when, for example, she is asked why she wears the hijab. Rather than saying something like "I wear this hijab in faithful submission to Allah," she instead might say, "I'm expressing myself," "This is my personal belief," or "I find the hijab personally empowering." When put this way, Muslim women sound more modern and enlightened.

Moreover, many Muslim women quickly learn that their secular interlocutors have little interest in learning about Islamic teachings, history, or ethics. Questions about the hijab rarely arise from genuine curiosity. And so, in time, Muslim women learn to edit themselves. While this sort of code-switching might seem reasonable, religious citizens of all stripes will likely know (and feel) the pain of this example on a deeper level.

Asking religious people to suppress who they truly are in order to belong is increasingly a feature of an America without God.

Know Thyself: The Gift of Strange Religion

More than twenty-five hundred years ago, the ancient Greeks inscribed a foundational creed into the temple at Delphi. Their iconic admonition to passersby was "Know thyself." This dictum has been a hallmark proclamation of freshmen philosophy professors across generations. The Greeks believed that the first step into a life of wisdom involved self-reflection, self-critique, and self-discovery.

Along these same lines, we would suggest that the first step into a political life of pluralism is a sober self-evaluation of the things that one holds sacred. Every citizen in a democracy must go through an honest and vulnerable account of what they find both sacred and taboo. We must ask ourselves where we place our trust, what our priorities are, who we are in solidarity with, and why we believe what we believe. Democracy requires that hard work of self-examination. A yard sign alone won't do.

While we can't enforce this level of self-awareness in a secular democracy, there is something that religious citizens can do to help their secular neighbors in the process of self-discovery. We illustrate this by way of a story.

Two young mothers pass each other in the cereal aisle of a grocery store. They each have their young daughters at their side. One mother is wearing a hijab, the other Lululemon yoga pants. The mothers quickly glance at each other and continue shopping. After the brief encounter, the women begin to think about their own dress and their values surrounding their bodies, their commitments, and their lives. Recalling each other's clothes, the two women ponder their preconceived assumptions about gender, sexuality, and femininity. All these thoughts swirl about as they make their way home.

The woman in Lululemon soon goes off to a yoga studio where she is surrounded by other women who share her background and beliefs. And yet, while practicing her downward dog, she cannot shake the image of the woman in the hijab. She wonders why she wears it. Is it comfortable? Is it nice not to worry about the public display of one's hair? Does her husband force her to wear it? Will she make her daughters wear it?

Later that night, the two women are home with their daughters. The kids do what kids do. They ask questions. Why did that mom dress like that? Why don't we dress like that? Is her way of dressing bad?

Here, the democratic door opens. Both mothers can sit with their daughters and honestly examine the particularity of their respective lifestyles, beliefs, and commitments. Neither Lululemon nor the hijab is the one rational or universal choice for all women everywhere. Both forms of clothing represent a series of choices, commitments, and beliefs—beliefs that are different.

She may not know it, but in wearing her hijab to the grocery store, the Muslim woman has offered her secular neighbor a gift. The gift may have been unintentional, but a gift it remains. She has carried her religious "strangeness" into the public square. In doing so, she has invited a secular family to pause and reflect for a moment on their own unexamined beliefs and priorities. Through a simple headscarf, the Muslim woman has offered her neighbor a fresh opportunity to know herself.

And herein lies our first piece of advice for religious people living in a secular society. Don't be afraid to be religious in public. Be open about it. Do not edit yourself so much. When asked about your choices, go ahead and offer an unapologetically religious response. See what happens. Yes, doing so may be awkward, but that's the point. It's not only okay if nonreligious people trip for a moment over your religiosity; it's also good for them.

We aren't suggesting you be merely performative, but it is okay for people with different and even strange beliefs to offer those beliefs to others as they go about their lives. When we offer our strangeness to others, we offer them an opportunity to practice their own democratic curiosity. And more than that, we give secular citizens a chance to reflect on their commitments as well.

A Dose of Dutch Pragmatism

As we saw earlier, Abraham Kuyper believed that all people are religious and that all political movements are quasi-religious. He came to this conclusion because he saw it and lived it. Each of the four dominant ideological groups in the Netherlands—socialists, liberals, Catholics, and Protestants—wanted to take over the nation and reshape it in their own image. This division within the Dutch public square, while uncomfortable, inspired Kuyper to write some insightful Christian reflections on democratic pluralism and deep difference.

In Kuyper's day, public schools were a political flashpoint—as they often are. Each of the four main ideological tribes wanted to control the national school system. All four groups recognized the simple truth that if you control the nation's schools, you control the nation's future.

Predictably, the Dutch socialists, Catholics, and Protestants owned and named their ideological commitments; the liberals did not. They argued that they were neutral, unbiased, and above the fray. Because liberals had transcended ideology, they alone were qualified to run the nation's schools. For a time, the liberals successfully persuaded the voters that they alone could fairly govern the various ideological and religious minorities in the nation. But they overreached. The liberals imposed harsh school reforms that disenfranchised Protestants, Catholics, and socialists alike.

Into the fray came Kuyper. He sought to diagnose why the liberals had struggled to offer the diverse religious and ideological minorities of the nation just and equal treatment. In the end, Kuyper concluded that the liberals fundamentally misunderstood what faith is and how it works. According to Kuyper, they failed to recognize that faith is pervasive, public, and pluriform. We will explain each in turn.

Faith is pervasive, Kuyper argued, in that every human being has some form of faith. We all make commitments and promises, we all have priorities, and we all serve and submit to things. As Kuyper put it, "All knowledge proceeds from faith of whatever kind. You lean on God, you proceed from your own ego, or you hold fast to your ideal. The person who does not believe does not exist."[13] Honestly admitting that one's convictions rest on some kind of faith was, in Kuyper's eyes, simply a matter of intellectual honesty. Denying faith's role was a "culpable blindfolding" of the self.[14] Liberals who declared that they could transcend faith and base their thinking "exclusively upon the action of the senses" were "entirely mistaken and allow[ed] themselves a leap to which they have no right."[15] This was the liberals' mistake, and it ended up being a mistake with political consequences.

But faith is not only pervasive. For Kuyper, it is also public. Our private beliefs, Kuyper insisted, don't remain private for long. Our personal convictions will seep and spill into our public and political judgments. How can they not? Human beings aren't machines who can cordon off deeply held beliefs when they step out of the house.

For Kuyper, "every kind of faith has in itself an impulse to speak out."[16] A person of integrity can't have one faith in private and another in public. One can of course *try* to compartmentalize, but this would necessitate a conscious self-suppression and is unlikely to end well. Kuyper observed that you can't be a person of "character and intelligence, and still allow yourself to be tempted to split your conscience in two, professing your God in one half and in the other half bowing before laws that have nothing to do with him. That does not comport with reason."[17]

If there is no such thing as a neutral human heart, there is no such thing as neutral human politics. Every law written, every war waged, every budget balanced, every case resolved, and every tax levied is a spiritually influenced judgment. A nation's moral commitments affect its politics. Judges, politicians, and federal employees are not robots; they are spiritually charged individuals. The state, therefore, is shot through with faith commitments that are both public and pervasive.

Finally, Kuyper argued that faith is pluriform. By this, he meant that human faith comes in many forms—it is fractured, diverse, and divided. No matter how long nations search for total unity and uniformity, they will never find it. Humanity will never locate full and permanent consensus. There is no religion or political ideology that will gather together all the diverse peoples of the earth. A nation's faith is always and forever plural.

During Kuyper's time, Dutch liberals lamented the deep ideological divisions in the Netherlands. They longed to unite the divided nation around the modern values of liberalism. They believed diversity weakened the Dutch nation and held it back from modern progress. In the end, they tried to unify and assimilate the diverse faiths and ideologies of the Netherlands by imposing a centralized, secular school system.

Catholics, Protestants, and socialists alike protested. But Kuyper's objection to liberal dominance went deeper. A single national ideology wasn't simply unjust; it was unsustainable. The faiths of the nation were diverse and divided—and stubbornly so. No school system on earth, no political machine of propaganda, no mode of media influence could ever successfully unify the diverse faiths of the Dutch people into a secular whole. The liberal dream of ideological unity was nothing but a dream. And for those opposed to the imposition of unity, it increasingly felt like a nightmare.

Kuyper proposed an ingenious alternative to national uniformity. Today we call it "pluralism." While the Catholics, Protestants, socialists, and liberals each wanted to dominate the nation and remake it in their own image, he proposed a pluralistic democracy. He argued that the Netherlands should have a messy and noisy, diverse and competitive marketplace of ideas and beliefs, religions and ideologies. Each perspective should be allowed to openly advocate and organize for its understanding of the common good. He did not make this argument from a neutral or secular position. It came from his Christian conviction that Jesus had commanded him to treat all religions and ideologies with justice and equality, regardless of his disagreement with them.

Under this scheme, the national school system would not serve a single ideology. All the faiths and ideologies of the Netherlands would receive government support for their respective schools, provided they met certain basic educational standards. More than a hundred years later, Kuyper's approach to education remains. One can find a wide variety of Dutch schools built on a wide variety of philosophies, worldviews, and convictions, both secular and religious.

Kuyper's political response to deep difference offers us a way forward. The liberals of Kuyper's day, much like secular progressives in our own time, believed they could *and should* unify the nation under their enlightened umbrella. They thought they alone could referee the ideological marketplace from a position of neutrality. But, of course, they were wrong—not just morally but empirically.

The myth of neutrality isn't merely incorrect; it's dangerous. It actively undermines democratic health. When one group of citizens imagines they stand above the fray, pluralism becomes increasingly difficult, if not impossible. The secular citizen who displays a yard sign declaring "Science is real" while criticizing the neighbor who defends a belief in Scripture doesn't recognize that both actions stem from the same human impulse, the need to proclaim what we hold sacred.

As Americans drift away from traditional religious institutions, they carry their sincerest longings with them into the political arena. The mutual incomprehension between conservatives and progressives, between religious and secular citizens, stems not from one side being rational and the other irrational but from competing sacred commitments that cannot easily be reconciled.

Yet this recognition should not lead to despair. Understanding our common status as believers in something might actually foster the humility necessary for genuine democratic dialogue. Once we accept that faith is pervasive, public, and pluriform, we can begin the exciting work of discussing how diverse faiths can both contest and coexist with one another.

2

Conflict Is Inevitable

KEY TAKEAWAY

The dream of resolving human difference—through reason, education, or state power—has failed every time it's been tried. Both Christianity and Islam teach that conflict is part of the divine plan, not a problem to be solved.

It's a late night in the college dormitory, and two roommates are locked in an uncomfortable debate. One, an atheist, has been peppering his Muslim roommate all night long. They've discussed religion, alcohol, and sex, and now they've landed on politics. Try as he might, the atheist can't seem to break through the religious divide. The Muslim's convictions simply won't give way. In a moment of exasperation, the atheist throws up his hands and exclaims, "Can't you see that you're on the wrong side of history? How can you *still* believe these things?"

The young Muslim takes a breath and—one final time—tries his best to explain the teachings of the Quran and the example of the Prophet Muhammad. In a fit of disbelief, the atheist exclaims, "But it's 2026!"

The Muslim, unsure what is happening, asks his roommate, "Why are you telling me the date?"

While the young Muslim might feel confused, seasoned believers will know exactly what's going on. The dialogue is over. An announcement has been made—we now know the date.

At the heart of the modern West sits a fervent belief in, well, the modern West. It's the belief that history is marching toward a single and unified end. The modern West represents the end of history, the ultimate goal for all cultures, religions, and ways of life.

According to this view of history, human cultures might appear to be on many diverse religious and cultural paths, but this is merely temporary. Through the mystical power of modern progress—and with enough Western education, science, and reason—all people will find their true home atop the same secular Western mountain. Soon enough, with enough education, all people will sit together in the warm glow of the European Enlightenment.

British historian J. B. Bury notes that the modern belief in historical progress is akin to a spiritual truth, comparable to fate, providence, and immortality. Progress, he writes, necessitates an "act of faith."[1]

The declaration "It's 2026!" betrays the atheist roommate's confidence in the historical inevitability of modernity. In a fit of desperation, the roommate is, in essence, asking his Muslim friend, "If it is indeed 2026, why are we *still* different? Why has the power of modern education and reason not yet done its work on you? Shouldn't you and I be on the same path by now? Why are you still holding on to these ancient beliefs, given all we now know?"

These three final words, "we now know," are doing a lot of work. *We* assumes a universal humanity. The atheist roommate believes that humanity has (or should have) a universal consensus—a collective sense of human knowing—that this particular Muslim needs to join. The second word, *now*, assumes that the debate is over and that a conclusion has been reached. The Muslim's task at this point is to accept the conclusions of secular enlightenment. Finally, the word *know* assumes a modern distinction between reason and religion, facts and values, knowledge and belief. The atheist assumes there are certain facts that secular people know (which are objective, uncontested, and science-based), and there are values that religious people believe (which are subjective, contestable, and faith-based).

The two roommates, no doubt, experience the conversation in two very different ways. One is in the light, the other shrouded in darkness.

The atheist imagines he is bringing good tidings of great joy. The young Muslim receives this secular gospel quite differently.

Avoiding Conflict

As a species, we humans try to avoid conflict. We are social creatures, the sort who will go to great lengths to avoid dissension and disruption. When conflict becomes unavoidable, our bodies respond with ancient programming: teeth clench, heads cower, shoulders tense, and open hands turn to fists. As we prepare for either fight or flight, the bitter taste of adrenaline rolls over our tongue. As if on instinct—like a defensive fortress raising its gate—body, mind, and soul begin to turn in on themselves and harden.

Athletes prepare themselves for a match by getting both excited and loose. They stretch their muscles, hop up and down, and visualize success. Tense muscles are both disadvantageous and dangerous. Tense muscles can become pulled muscles. The best athletes don't avoid the contest; they relish it. They don't walk into the arena; they run.

But athletes are strange. We regular people dread the contest and the conflict that it brings. Far from loose and limber, our muscles are tense and tight. Far from visualizing success, we imagine disaster. As the moment of conflict draws near, our eyes dart about for the exit.

Closely related to our fear of conflict is our fear of difference. Whatever that difference might be—racial, cultural, religious, sexual, or political—the simple presence of difference signals to us that some sort of dreaded conflict might be on the way. Because of the fear that difference equals conflict, humans have long sought a variety of strategies to mitigate both. Fight and flight are, of course, the most popular methods for dealing with this fear: Either destroy the difference through a preemptive strike or run away from it.

But there are other ways humans cope with difference. Some try to use state power to assimilate uncomfortable differences into a national whole. Some—hoping the differences will go away on their own—ignore or dismiss them; hopefully they are not as real or as stark as they seem. Still others try to resolve conflict by abandoning their own convictions and adopting the behaviors of the majority for the sake of peace.

A part of us longs for sameness over difference. Every presidential speech calling for national unity speaks to this deep human desire for communal harmony.

This longing for harmony might sound pleasant at first, but these seemingly benign dreams of unity have in fact fueled the rise of many of the most aggressive and expansionist empires in history—both religious and secular. The medieval emperors of Christendom longed to unite Jewish and Muslim citizens under the imperial power of the crusader's cross. The Almohad dynasty broke away from the greater Islamic community during this same period, their revolt likewise characterized by military expansion and imposing their agenda on religious minorities through forced conversions, exile, and even violence.

Secular revolutionaries in France, despite the best of intentions, presided over a reign of terror and soon established an unyielding form of national secularism called *laïcité*. Through the power of his armies, Napoleon sought to impose his empire of secular reason on Christian Europe. Likewise, in the twentieth century, communists sought to unite the workers of the world through the violent and global power of the Communist Party. Religious communities under communist rule needed to be stamped out in the name of worker solidarity. Religion, Karl Marx famously said, was the opiate of the masses, and the masses couldn't be trusted to know what was best for them.

Today, Buddhist extremists in Sri Lanka long to unite their national community through Buddhist nationalism. Hindu nationalists harass Muslim and Christian minorities in India. They long for a pure and united Hindu nation. Zionist extremists in Israel long to establish a purely Jewish nation-state.

In light of these various campaigns for unity at any and all costs, we can say two things. First, this human longing for unity, when politically enforced, often leads—ironically—to *more* conflict. Second, our longing for sameness and our willingness to use political power to enforce it are not uniquely religious; they're human.

Every cultural and religious group on earth is vulnerable to the fear of difference and is tempted to impose artificial unity. This is why, throughout history, human beings have seen conflict and competition as a threat to be neutralized, a communal problem in need of political resolution. Longing for unity, humans have often asked their kings, presidents, clerics, priests, and czars to offer solutions to their cultural differences. Some leaders resist their people's longing for unity; others take the people's fears and enflame them. Be it socialism, liberalism, Islamism, or Christian nationalism, all man-made ideologies—brutal or mild—are tempted to artificially create sameness and crush political differences.

Your authors aren't immune to this reality. We acknowledge that Muslims and Christians have at times given in to these temptations and fears, to devastating effect. Muslims and Christians are not otherworldly; they are deeply human. When confronted with difference, Muslims and Christians alike have fallen—and will continue to fall—into the fight-or-flight mentality. In our human longing to avoid difference and enforce uniformity, Muslims and Christians, like anyone else, elevate themselves and their fears over God's commands for hospitality, justice, and peace.

And yet, while the political sins of both Muslims and Christians are well attested in history and in current events, this is not the case for one of the most powerful and fastest-growing faiths in the world—secularism. It turns out that secular people—like Muslims and Christians—are human beings as well. They too fear conflict. They also seek to avoid difference. They also ask, and even plead, with their political leaders to enforce a secular consensus.

Yet, as we will see, there is something unique going on today with the secular heirs of the European Enlightenment. Unlike traditional religions, secularism posits that human conflict can be resolved not in heaven but in the here and now.

The Modern Longing for Unity

The secular belief that human unity is achievable on earth has real political consequences. Religious minorities who refuse to climb aboard the secular train of progress find themselves tied, all too often, to the tracks.

As discussed earlier, conflict has haunted humankind throughout history. But modern secularists are alone in believing that they might be uniquely capable of solving the problem of tribal difference and conflict. Through the tools of science and reason, education and enlightenment, technology and capital, secularists are convinced that humanity might just be able to overcome its divides.

Secularists often see the modern state as a critical partner in their mission to overcome difference. Through government services, systems, schools, and social service agencies, leaders can use the modern state apparatus to effectively assimilate diverse citizens into a secular consensus. If difference and conflict are the problem, the unifying power of the modern state is the solution.

This is precisely what makes secular governance so paradoxical. Secularism presents itself as a neutral space of ideological mediation even though it is just one more ideology. As we established in the previous chapter, it's not neutral. The secular state may claim to represent all citizens equally, but it reconfigures and redefines religion on its own terms.[2] It decides which religious expressions are reasonable and which are dangerous, which belong in public and which must be relegated to private life.

Scholar Saba Mahmood states that secular forms of governance can actually deepen religious tensions by "hardening interfaith boundaries and polarizing religious differences."[3] In other words, the very governance that promises to secure peaceful coexistence often intensifies religious tensions. Under secular rule, religious minorities face an impossible bind: They can join the secular liberal order only by conceding that their faith is a private affair.

The secular project asks religious citizens to be docile—to accept that their beliefs are essentially matters of individual choice rather than public commitments with implications for the entire community. Religious communities that refuse to stay within the private sphere—those who insist that their faith has something to say about how we should organize society—are labeled irrational, ignorant, or dangerous.

At the close of the nineteenth century, Europe's colonial dominance of the Middle East, Africa, and Asia was animated by the belief that the reason, science, and markets of the West would enlighten the rest of the world. This sense of both confidence and finality empowered colonial powers to run roughshod over diverse cultures, faiths, and ways of life across the global South. By the mid-twentieth century, communism and capitalism had replaced colonialism. They too ran roughshod over diverse cultures and religions, attempting to flatten human difference in the process.

Accepting the Agony of Conflict

In almost every major democracy today, groups dislike one another. This is normal enough. You should like your friends and family; liking strangers you disagree with is more challenging. What's different today, though, is that dislike is giving way to contempt and hatred.

An unprecedented number of Americans see their fellow citizens as enemies from within, deplorables, threats to be monitored, and enemies to be defeated. In one 2022 poll, roughly 80 percent of Democrats and Republicans said the other party "poses a threat that if not stopped will destroy America as we know it."[4] Another study found that 77 percent of Trump voters and 80 percent of Biden voters believed their differences were about fundamental disagreements over core American values.[5] These sentiments make democracy much more difficult. If you believe your adversaries threaten everything you hold dear, you are less likely to accept election outcomes when your candidate loses. And, at some point, your candidate *will* lose.

If this existential tenor reflects real foundational divides over ultimate questions, then it can't—and probably shouldn't—be wished away or papered over. After all, how can you rise above seemingly insoluble differences if they are so deep that they can't be bridged? Too often, we assume that with the right knowledge and intentions, reasonable people acting reasonably can reach agreement.

This is an illusion. Such agreements are possible only in homogeneous societies with a strong, shared national identity, something most Western democracies can no longer claim. And because Western democracies are free and open societies, there's no plausible path back to cultural sameness, real or imagined. In other words, it's too late for consensus. It is generally difficult for modern democracies to engage in large-scale projects of cultural assimilation—if they hope to remain both democratic and liberal. Campaigns of national sameness normally involve body counts.

The question, then, is how can democracies function productively amid those enduring differences that make everyone uncomfortable. A somewhat obscure political philosophy called "agonism" offers some important insights.

Agonism comes from the word *agon*. The agon was the arena in which the ancient Greeks sparred with one another in a variety of athletic pursuits. The agon wasn't about winning; it was about the contest. As one scholar of ancient Greece explains it, the ritual produced "movement through struggle."[6] By bringing contrasting styles to their athletic contests, athletes created something new and superior. In other words, the contest was good. Or at least it could be.

While writing this book, we debated each other repeatedly on a podcast we host called *Zealots at the Gate*. Both of us try to model forms of religious difference and even conflict that can actually be productive. We try, in other words, to model "friendly conflict."

Scholars of agonism argue that democratic societies should allow—and even encourage—open, honest, and friendly conflict. Citizens with differing ideas and ways of life should stretch, loosen up, and run into the democratic arena. Cultural and political competition makes citizens and governments uncomfortable, but agonists argue that ideological wrestling is far preferable to an enforced unity.

Chantal Mouffe is perhaps the world's most prominent agonist. Born during World War II, she has been writing about and developing her political account of ideological struggle for decades. Despite her acclaim as a Belgian political theorist, she remains relatively unknown in the United States. Her writing has that European tinge of darkness, borne out of centuries of conflict and the devastation of two world wars. Optimistic Americans, with their bent toward finding pragmatic solutions, may find her pessimism difficult to digest. (But stick with us!)

Mouffe herself is not religious, but her work has had a strong influence on both of us and has helped us better understand what our own faith traditions teach about conflict and politics. Agonism, we've discovered, is not a new or novel modern idea. Our very own Christian and Islamic traditions have been wrestling with the same insights for centuries. But before we get to that, we need to grasp what exactly agonism points us toward.

For Mouffe and the agonists, some problems don't have easy solutions. As she puts it, "There are conflicts for which no rational solution could ever exist, hence the dimension of antagonism that characterizes human societies."[7] In this reading, political conflict can't be eliminated, and trying to force a consensus where none exists can only produce more conflict. Consensus is possible only when there is already a consensus, and there rarely is. For Mouffe, "All forms of consensus are by necessity based on acts of exclusion."[8]

Consensus is in fact illusory. Beneath the surface, there are always fissures. This is what makes consensus so dangerous and destabilizing. Because it is illusory, it needs to be enforced through state power. This places ideological minorities in a vulnerable position. The insistence on national consensus can also be destabilizing because when minorities are marginalized, they are more likely to respond in nondemocratic, aggressive, and even violent ways. This is why agonists pull back when politicians point to things like a common good or common ground.

An Enlightenment account of politics presumes that human beings either are rational or can be made rational with enough education. Under these circumstances, the thinking goes, "rational" politics will eventually satisfy everyone to some degree. Through careful deliberation and the wisdom of experts and elites, win-win solutions can be achieved. In a world where history has ended, there may still be ideological conflict, but there is no *need* for ideological conflict. To think of history as having an end is to think of political competition as having a satisfying conclusion for all involved.

For Mouffe, history has no end; it is just a long string of conflicts and competition. This thing we call politics is a long series of public confrontations "with no possibility of final reconciliation."[9] In a diverse political community, there is never a single or unified "we"; there are only varied and divided collections of plural "we(s)."[10]

But this lack of consensus is not something to lament. To recognize group conflict as inherent to politics is to accept that no victories or defeats are truly final, as long as democratic competition leaves open the possibility that diverse ideas and ideologies have the space to compete. Politics, then, is never stagnant. It is always moving—always wrestling. There is no end to history, no "we" to which we are striving. Democracy is—and ought to be—a permanent state of managed conflict. The athletes must be allowed to spar. For the agonist, the very human experience of moral and political disagreement is at the heart of what makes us human.

We humans can't help disagreeing on the biggest questions, because the biggest questions are difficult to resolve. What is the nature of justice? What does it mean to live a good life? Who gets to decide the common good? None of these questions are simple or straightforward. Debating them causes conflict.

But Mouffe and others prescribe a way to handle this conflict. First, do your best to accurately and fairly name the differences and conflicts at play. Honor your opponent by telling the truth about the chasm that lies between you. Second, attempt to channel your ideological passion through a nonviolent and democratic process. Once you accept that conflict is inevitable, then—and only then—can you begin to focus on channeling that conflict in a more peaceful direction.

A few key ideas can help us further understand the agonistic approach. First, agonists distinguish between having a political adversary and having a political enemy. An adversary is an opponent you wish to defeat, while an enemy is one you wish to destroy. In a healthy democracy, citizens want to win. There's nothing wrong with that. They want their own ideas and policy prescriptions to be victorious, but they do not, as Mouffe notes, "question the legitimacy of their opponent's right to fight for the victory of their position."[11]

Second, agonism is not antagonism. There is a difference between destructive and constructive conflict. We all feel the urge to make enemies out of those who disagree with us. At our worst, we might want to silence opposing voices or expel them from public life together. We must channel these aggressive impulses into something more productive. In essence, we must move from a death match in the Roman Colosseum to a wrestling match in the Greek agon. Swords will still be drawn, but they will be made of wood rather than iron. The athletes will emerge with some real wounds, but none of them will be fatal.

The third idea combines two seemingly opposite concepts: hospitality and hostility. Here agonists advocate for something called "hostipitality."[12] A healthy democracy is welcoming. It makes generous space for many different voices and perspectives. But it's also challenging—others will question, criticize, and even ridicule your most cherished and sacred beliefs. These contradictory experiences happen simultaneously in a healthy democracy.

The true agonist understands and accepts both realities. The agonist will resist all the naive and romantic dreams of a peaceful and loving multicultural society filled with nothing but warm feelings and cooperation. But the agonist will also resist a Darwinian nightmare of struggle for total political dominance and annihilation. The contest cannot be finished; the political wrestling match must continue.

Through these three important ideas, agonists seek to find a way for people in democratic states to effectively vent their potentially explosive passions. Venting is better than destroying.

Conflict in Our Faith Traditions

Agonism may seem like a relatively new, ingenious way of dealing with deep difference. In fact, many of its insights are thousands of years old *and quite religious*. Both Christianity and Islam contain the seeds of agonism's genius.

Both the Bible and the Quran contain rich accounts of difference and enduring conflict. And while the respective approaches of Islam and Christianity differ on some important points, we will begin by examining how these two faiths actually agree on the necessity of disagreement and the inevitability of conflict.

Unlike Western modernity, neither Islam nor Christianity tells a story of human progress toward unity and consensus. Neither faith expects to convert the whole of humanity. Neither religion imagines it can end division and conflict in the here and now. For both of our religious traditions, deep difference and conflict between individuals and groups are to be expected in this world and in this life.

According to both Muslims and Christians, God grants human beings the freedom to choose other gods and seek other paths. Both faiths hold that human beings exist in a sort of middle space, an interim time of God's patience in which religious and ideological diversity is divinely permitted. While divine judgment is coming, this interim age is a time when humans can differ and disagree with both God and one another.

This state of human division and disagreement, competition and contestation is not a surprise to God. Nor is it an accident. This struggle is part and parcel of a divine plan and order. God is not clutching any pearls while we humans wrestle. For Muslims, this conviction is captured in a famous verse from the Quran: "We have assigned a law and a path to each of you. If God had so willed, He would have made you one community, but He wanted to test you through that which He has given you, so race to do good: you will all return to God and He will make clear to you the matters you differed about" (Q 5:48).

The phrase "race to do good" deserves some reflection. According to Islam, in this present age God has created space for what we might call "ethical competition." The Quran states explicitly, "For every one there is a direction toward which he turns; *so compete with one another in good works*" (Q 2:148, emphasis added). As the ancient Greeks would say, humans are refined and improved through battling it out (peacefully).

Similarly, the book of Proverbs reminds us that one person's goodness can actually sharpen another's, just as "iron sharpens iron" (27:17). To be sure, two pieces of iron rubbing together is not a comfortable image—and rightly so. Iron sharpens iron via real force and real friction. But in the end, both sides emerge sharper.

In 1 Corinthians, the apostle Paul compares the Christian life to a competitive race for a prize (9:24–27). In his letter to the Romans, he exhorts Christians to participate in a sort of spiritual competition. He says they should seek to "outdo one another in showing honor" (12:10

ESV). For Paul, competition is not to be confused with militaristic violence or dominance. The goal is not to crush one's opponent. Rather, Paul is arguing that Christ followers should pursue virtue through a sort of friendly contest. Your neighbor is not an enemy to vanquish. Rather, they are your competitive partner in pursuing something greater. Like the Greek athletes in the agon, you will become better in and through this friendly competition.

The New Testament poignantly names the pain of moral growth through conflict. It describes God as a gardener subjecting people to a necessary but painful pruning (John 15:1–11). Followers of Jesus must be willing to accept that the pain they feel when sparring may very well be their divine gardener pruning them for growth. This brilliant metaphor manages to reconcile two realities about life in our polarized society: The pain from conflict is real and really can hurt, and yet that pain can produce real growth. We can be grateful for the growth our political opponents help us achieve; we can also weep over the bruises they inflict.

Adam Smith, an eighteenth-century economist, famously argued that economic competition is not a zero-sum game with one winner and one loser. Rather, through competition both sides can learn, gain, and grow. Later economists even speak of something they call "creative destruction," wherein competition actually breaks things but, in doing so, breaks open new opportunities for innovation and discovery.[13]

More than a millennium before Adam Smith, both the Quran and the Bible anticipated his insights for the spiritual and moral marketplace, where diverse religions and ways of life are free to compete. Here, encounters between neighbors are opportunities for moral growth on both sides. Sociologist Robert Wuthnow puts it this way: "Religious practices' influence in a democracy lies not in coercion but in articulating claims and counterclaims about what is right and good. Democracy benefits when these claims are voiced from diverse quarters, sometimes in harmony and sometimes in sharp disagreement. . . . We are protected from a religious establishment not only by the First Amendment but also by the disunity of religion itself."[14] Wuthnow understands what we often forget: Religious and ideological disagreement—though uncomfortable—can be good for our faith *and our politics*. This insight can have important consequences for the religious and nonreligious alike.

Let us return to our two college students. Rather than trying to vanquish his opponent in a zero-sum battle, what if the atheist had taken the chance to wrestle with and grow alongside a fellow athlete in good faith? A verbal sparring session might have allowed both the atheist and the Muslim to reconsider and reevaluate their own first principles. In this friendly wrestling match, the atheist might have realized that he too was a particular athlete representing a particular team. He too had a particular view from somewhere rather than a neutral position. In a contest of ideas, no one is above the fray. No one is truly neutral. The atheist might have left the sparring session with a spirit of gratitude (rather than exasperation). He could have left thankful for his Muslim opponent and for the struggle of ideas. The friction would not have been particularly comfortable, but both students could have become all the sharper for it.

Most of us participate in competitions, whether academic, athletic, or artistic, so we have an intuitive sense of how this works. What makes an athletic competition so delightful and engrossing is that neither the players nor the spectators know who is going to win. The possibilities are open. Because of this, both players and spectators must remain completely in the moment, in the interim age.

Like great soccer players who exchange jerseys after a grueling match on the pitch, the best athletes demonstrate a spirit of respect and even gratitude for their opponents. After an ideological sparring match, the proper response is to give thanks, to name the ways in which the struggle and your opponent pressed you to sharpen your arguments, deepen your faith, increase your learning, and develop your virtue.

Islam and Christianity are not simply belief systems about what happens when a person dies (when the wrestling match is over). Instead, they are two ways of being alive, two ways of participating in humanity's wrestling match.

The wrestling match is inevitable. All human groups and ideologies are participating in some way. What's important is how you will enter the arena. Will you be tense and tight, ready for fight or flight? Or will you enter loose and limber, ready to be contested, stretched, and grown?

Christianity and Islam offer ancient wisdom on a variety of productive ways in which to enter the fray. It's no accident, of course, that two thousand years ago the first name given to Christianity was simply "the Way" (Acts 9:1–2). The point was not simply to know Jesus but to walk in his way. Jesus did not come to rescue Christians from the fray but to show them a way to engage it.

In a similar vein, "Islam" means "submission," which is, of course, a Muslim's path or way. For Muslims, submission is the path to a good life and salvation, and it is pursued most commonly through the way of *sharia*. While "sharia" roughly means "Islamic law," it's more precise meaning is "the path." Understood in this light, sharia signifies not the ultimate destination but the way of Islam amid the wrestling matches of this world.

For some religions and ideologies, perceived human differences are either temporary or illusory. "All paths lead up the same mountain," people might say. Sure, it might *seem* like humanity is divided, but we are all actually on the same path. It might *seem* like human beings long for different things, but deep down we all basically want the same things.

Not so for Christianity and Islam.

Muslims and Christians believe that human differences are real and consequential. Muslims and Christians believe that distinct paths can lead to distinct destinations. Moreover, the paths we choose have real consequences. They don't all produce the same results.

We might say the following about how Islam and Christianity agree on the subject of disagreement. First, human disagreement isn't going anywhere. As long as human beings have free will and moral agency, they will continue to disagree. Sometimes that disagreement will bleed into conflict and even open violence. Second, while human conflict can lead to destruction, it also presents powerful opportunities for personal growth and gratitude. Growth comes through struggle and sometimes even suffering. Third, no mortal regime is equipped to end human conflict and enforce ideological or religious unity. Asking the state to eliminate human difference is not just foolhardy; it also dangerously places the state in a transcendent or quasi-divine position.

Having named the ways in which our two faiths agree on disagreement, we will close by naming a few of their particularities. Some of the following points will illustrate clear disagreements, while others will simply highlight a difference in emphasis.

Christianity and the Weight of Conflict

According to Christian theology, human beings were originally designed to have a peaceful relationship with God, the land, and one another. These relationships were to be just, loving, and joyful. The ancient Hebrew term *shalom* captures this state of complete peace and harmony.

In the Christian view, the Creator God delights in a diversity of human gifts, cultures, languages, races, and ethnicities. Directed toward God's love, all these diversities are good and wonderful things. In loving communion with God, all these human diversities could coexist in peace, harmony, and community.

But something went terribly wrong.

Christians will often use words like *evil* and *sin* to narrate the tragic origins of human conflict. Humans rebelled against God and severed their ties with him. This vertical rupture with God initiated a horizontal rupture between humans. Separated from God, they began to oppress, attack, and abuse one another. Without God as their center, humans began to "play God."

Breaking communion with God, humans sought a variety of diverse gods, truths, and purposes for their lives. Rather than walking toward God together, they took different paths that often conflicted. They began to fight. Rather than worshiping one God, they kneeled before a variety of man-made objects and objectives. Some sought wealth, others power, still others fame. This variety of conflicting goals and gods would have serious consequences.

For Christians, this present age of human conflict cannot be ended by any mortal force. No military, no king, no technology can ever bring about a lasting or just peace. Human beings can't synthetically create a state of perfect peace on their own. Perfect human unity is beyond our reach.

Ideally, this Christian doctrine should make Christians humble realists when they engage in politics. After all, if neither the state nor the church is capable of uniting humanity, then Christians should really chill out. Put simply, Christian citizens should accept that neither the church nor the state is God. Earthly institutions might be able to mitigate conflict and produce little bits of peace here and there, but neither the church nor the state can fix humanity. That is God's job, not ours.

While a Christian can appreciate an agonist's acceptance of the current state of play, a Christian differs from the agonist in important respects. First, for Christians, conflict is not the way of the world. This present age of struggle is not the way things are supposed to be. The pain we feel in a polarized society is real, and it is terrible. It is right to weep. We were made for peace, for shalom. And according to the Bible, a new age of peace is coming. This present age of political struggle feels inhumane *because it is*.

Second, in light of this, Christians don't need to endure conflict like an agonist with mere Stoicism. Conflict breaks our hearts, our relationships, and our communities. It is right and good for citizens to cry out at the pain of disagreement and conflict. This is why Christians repeatedly ask God, "How long, O Lord?" and cry out, "Come quickly, Lord!" These Christians actively yearn for God to bring peace.

Throughout human history, ambitious conquerors, emperors, theocrats, nationalists, and religious extremists have fought horrible wars to force an artificial unity on the world. Christianity condemns their hubris and bloodshed. But in an odd sort of way, Christianity sympathizes with their longing. Although these people caused great terror, they carried with them something deeply human: a longing for all the tongues and tribes of the world to come together in unity.

Their fatal mistake, among many, was that they got way ahead of themselves. They took it upon themselves to end human conflict, which was beyond their mortal control. These despots sought a throne that was not theirs to take. As we have seen repeatedly across time and place, authoritarian dreams of religious and political unity are doomed to end in violence and destruction.

This is why mainstream Christianity has historically resisted authoritarianism, be it secular or religious. Neither the church nor the state is God. Theocracy—the rule of the religious elite—is blasphemous because the throne belongs to Christ, not Christians.

It goes without saying that Christians have not always lived up to these convictions. Being sinful human beings—like everyone else—Christians are tempted to seize power, fame, and glory. In their longing for unity, Christians have regularly supported theocratic governments. They have also capitulated to secular projects of human unity like fascism and nationalism.

These have been tragic errors. Human beings are both finite and fallen. Not being perfect—and not being God—disqualifies them from a throne that is not theirs to take.

A Christian Critique of Theocracy

Here we return once again to Abraham Kuyper. Throughout his career, Kuyper was adamantly opposed to aspirations of theocracy. We should heed his warnings against trying to resolve human difference by forcing consensus under the banner of God's kingdom on earth.

Kuyper argued that the purpose of the Christian church is not to dominate or absorb the disparate faiths of the world. Rather, it is to preach a strange gospel that will both unite and divide humanity. He called the Christian church "antithetical."[15] By this, he meant that Christianity is fundamentally out of place and out of step in the world. Given its strangeness, the church can never be absorbed into any other faith or ideology. Kuyper believed that Jesus of Nazareth started a movement that is, in one sense, quite divisive.[16] The movement's purpose on earth is not to make everyone agree. It is to offer the world a specific choice, a unique path, and a very particular object of belief. Human beings can either receive or reject this choice, but there is no in between, no synthesis. Being antithetical, the church is called to preserve its strangeness. It will not fit in, and it should not force others to fit in either.

Theocracy is bad, Kuyper argued, not simply because it is unjust and unsustainable. It is bad because you end up filling your churches with people who don't really want to be there, who don't understand or even desire Jesus. In this way, theocracy destroys the integrity of the church. In the strongest possible terms, Kuyper argued that theocracy saps the church of its freedom and power, castrates its preaching, debases its integrity, and perverts its mission.[17]

Kuyper lamented that different churches throughout history became enraptured by the theocratic dream. In doing so, these churches attempted to span divisions that only Christ can bridge. Kuyper identified two destructive ways in which churches had attempted to bridge unbridgeable divides. The first was through the forceful assimilation of religious and ideological minorities into the church. The second was through allowing the church to be assimilated into a synthetic, secular national community.[18]

Kuyper argued that these efforts to solve conflict and manufacture political sameness harmed both the church and the state. Both strategies ignored the deep differences between church and state. Furthermore, both strategies undermined the responsibility of the church to remain strangely committed to Christ alone. The church could not dedicate itself to both following Jesus and making nations great again. It had to choose. As Jesus said, "No one can serve two masters" (Matt. 6:24).

For Kuyper, when the church seeks political power, cozies up to political leaders, and attempts to unite nations under one religious banner, bad things happen to the church. Winning the title of "national church" was, in Kuyper's estimation, the greatest loss the church could endure. Such a victory would "only lead to the spiritual death of the church. . . . [It] deprives the church of Christ of its freedom of movement, which is one of its vital conditions. It turns its pastors and teachers as if by magic into vapid and haughty magistrates. . . . This weakens the church, causes it to pine away, and numbs its spirit."[19]

After all, according to Kuyper, Jesus was not born in a Roman palace. He was a poor boy born on the margins of the empire. There was no room for him in the inn. He was banished to the stable. In the same way, the Christian church must accept the politics of the stable and stop trying to capture and control Rome, for the "church never sank away more deeply than when she went back to the inn and sought to become a national or state church; neither did she revive again in spiritual vigor, except when the Lord drove her out of the inn and pointed her back to the stable."[20] When the church tries to rule and forcibly unite a nation, it has only bad options before it. It can abandon Christ's call to peace and persuasion as it attempts to violently impose its faith, or in an attempt to gently unite the nation it can thin out its beliefs so that everyone can accept them. Lamenting the banal and boring sermons in national churches, Kuyper complained, "We want to be inspired, not put to sleep. We seek God's glorious ordinances, not hollow words or empty phrases."[21]

Is Difference God's Will? An Islamic Account

In one sense or another, religions are founded in conflict. People lose their way, so God sends new prophets to warn them and to challenge humanity to follow the way of justice. Islam was radical in its monotheism in a land of idols, its egalitarianism in a highly stratified society, and its basic demands of justice that tribal elites in Mecca had denied. The very existence of Islam challenged the existing power structures in Arabia. The Prophet Muhammad and the early Muslims were threatened with annihilation, as the tribes in the surrounding area gathered their forces to defeat or expel the Muslims over the course of several battles.

Islam teaches that evil exists. The potential for evil lies within each of us. Evil must be opposed and resisted internally and externally. Sometimes there is no way to do this without some conflict.

It's a profoundly human thing to be conflicted, to face different paths with a sense of uncertainty and moral dilemma. No human being is free from error and sin. And it's not just the bad or unworthy who are tempted. The best among us are too. After Muhammad's death in AD 632, some of his closest companions and followers engaged in thorny debates about who should rule and how, which threatened to spill over into outright civil war. The Prophet had not clearly designated a successor, and any successor would have been far less than he was. Others were not, nor could they be, prophets. And so from Islam's earliest moments, there was a question mark. There was no consensus.

Sometimes these disagreements festered, breaking out into violence between factions who believed that the future of the *ummah* (community) was at stake. In the Battle of the Camel, Islam's first *fitna*, or civil conflict, two of the most righteous figures in Islamic history, Ali, the Prophet's son-in-law and cousin, and the Prophet's beloved wife Aisha, fought against each other. The Prophet's wife was shot by an arrow but survived. Two of the Prophet's companions fighting alongside her, Talha and Zubayr, were killed.

Even in its most successful periods, Islam constantly veered between harmony and discord. Conflict was always there. It was only a question of what form that conflict would take and whether and how it might be contained. From the beginning of Islam, deep difference and disagreement were a given. If God had willed, he could have made it so that the line of succession after the Prophet's passing was clear and unmistakable. But he did not do so.

Various other tensions were evident in the early development of Islam, pushing and pulling in contrary directions. First, there was the Prophet's undeniable worldly success. The founding of Islam here serves as a contrast to early Christianity. Jesus was a marginal dissident against the reigning state. He never had the opportunity to rule. He never led an army. Early Christians lived as minorities subject to the whims of princes and despots. That early Christian theologians came to see politics as fallen was no accident. Muhammad, on the other hand, was not just a prophet and a preacher but also a politician and the head of a proto-state in Medina. This meant that politics and governance, not just preaching or proselytization, would fuel the rise of this new faith.[22] As scholar Andrew March notes, "The biography of the Prophet does away with the myth of the political as an inherently fallen sphere of human activity."[23]

The divisions that emerged between the Prophet's companions were regrettable and tragic, of course, but they were not an indictment of politics as such. Islam's early political leaders were remarkably successful in a remarkably short span of time, extending their geographical reach across North Africa, into the Indian subcontinent, and deep into Europe in just a matter of decades.

Lacking a conception of original sin, Islam didn't lend itself to political despair. Inequality, corruption, and oppression were very much real (and could be found in abundance under various rulers), but Muslims had only to correct or resist these political excesses. For most of Islamic history, perhaps until the modern period, there was, as John Voll remarks, a "link between faith and worldly success."[24] Islam did not respond to political injustice and conflict with hopelessness or passivity; it responded with political pragmatism and action.

Islamic history was, in a sense, an ongoing project to pragmatically manage human diversity and difference and to do so with as little resort to violence as possible. What resulted was a sort of cacophony of currents and countercurrents within Islam, fashioning a rich, expansive, and diverse body of Islamic interpretation and legal reasoning on how to manage difference. Ultimately, though, the Quran was the first and last word on how Muslims, irrespective of time and place, should think about human conflict and disagreement.

The Quran, rather than encouraging readers to accept its passages without question, continually encourages them to reflect on and contemplate its words using their minds and intellect. Indeed, the theme of *tadabbur*, or contemplation, is recurrent throughout the Quran. God asks, for instance, "Do they not contemplate the Qur'an? Or do hearts have their locks upon them?" (Q 47:24). While Islam recognizes that truth exists and that everything revealed in the Quran is directly from God, it also acknowledges the possibility of conflict over how the Quran's words will be interpreted.

As if to underline this sentiment, the Islamic tradition is shot through with something called *ikhtilaf*—the etiquette of disagreement. Islam recognizes diverse interpretations on contentious issues while upholding respectful discussion and mutual understanding. This approach welcomes opposing viewpoints as chances to further investigate and develop Islamic thought. The struggle of ideas is meant to be formative. Even failure and falling short can be clarifying. A prophetic saying is instructive here: "If you were not to commit sin, Allah would sweep you out of existence and He would replace (you by) those people who would commit sin and seek forgiveness from Allah, and He would have pardoned them."[25] This hadith, or saying of the Prophet Muhammad, underscores that conflict—including conflict within one's own self—is simply part of being human.

The Roommates Return

The roommates we met at the beginning of this chapter need not remain locked in their standoff. Both the atheist's frustrated cry of "But it's 2026!" and the Muslim's bewildered response reveal something profound about our political moment.

We live in an age when the dream of rational unity and secular consensus collides daily with the stubborn reality of human difference and conflict. Yet, as we have seen, this collision may itself be the point. What Christianity and Islam offer is not a resolution to the conflict but rather a reframing of the conflict itself. Both traditions suggest that the diversity and differences we find so troubling are not a problem for us to solve. When necessary, we can wrestle and compete with our opponents. We can contest their claims in open competition. But we fight with swords of wood, not iron. We seek victory, but we do not wish to vanquish. The Quranic vision of humans "racing to do good" and the Christian understanding of this age as a time of divine patience both point toward a politics that neither despairs of difference nor attempts to eliminate it. We don't give in to our opponents, nor do we seek to destroy them.

This is where agonism, drawing on analogies of wrestling matches and sparring sessions, finds resonance with religious thought. Athletes who thank their opponent after a bruising contest understand something that both our frustrated atheist and our modern prophets of progress have forgotten: We become who we are not in spite of resistance but through it. Iron sharpens iron, the Bible reminds us, but only through friction, force, and, yes, even some destruction. The question is not whether we will have opponents in this life—we will. The question is whether we will see them as enemies to be destroyed or adversaries whose right to compete we defend even as we seek to defeat them.

The secular project promised us the end of history. Instead, it gave us an endless state of political anxiety as it tries to keep a promise that simply can't be kept. Christianity and Islam, for all their failures, offer something different: the patience to endure a world where the contest continues, where the wrestling match is not yet finished, and where the final victory belongs not to any wrestler but to a judge who has yet to step out on to the mat. In a polarized age, these two traditions suggest a third way: not the false peace of forced consensus but the true peace of knowing our small place in a larger story whose ending we do not get to write.

3

God Only Knows

KEY TAKEAWAY

Democracy doesn't need fewer convictions; it needs fewer certainties. You can hold your beliefs with real confidence while still reserving the last word for God.

The Beach Boys song "God Only Knows" is a classic within the modern rock canon. Reminiscing on the writing process, Brian Wilson recounted how he prayed with his brother Carl during the recording sessions, turning them into a sort of religious ceremony.[1]

Wilson and lyricist Tony Asher had long discussions about whether to keep the word *God* in the song, given God's alleged un-coolness in the 1960s. They needn't have worried. The song spoke to the universal teenage yearning to fall in love and the universal teenage dread of what would happen "if you should ever leave me."[2]

Little did Brian Wilson know that a simple phrase like "God only knows" meant so much more.

The idea that God only knows has a long and storied history in the three Abrahamic faiths. The phrases "Lord knows," "God willing," and "Inshallah" are part of the modern secular lexicon—even if we don't fully appreciate their religious origins. These phrases carry significant spiritual meaning and, as we will see, powerful political consequences.

Each statement tacitly admits a state of human ignorance, weakness, and uncertainty. The speaker is confessing, "I do not fully know. I'm not in total control." To say "God willing" is to acknowledge a fundamental difference between the almighty Creator and the not-so-mighty creature. While God is all-knowing, our knowledge is inherently limited. We are defined by finitude, limits, and doubt. We, after all, are mere mortals, who pale in comparison.

Wilson sings, "God only knows what I'd be without you," and he is right. He can try to imagine what his life would be like if the girl ever left him, as he fears she might, but he can never know for sure. God alone—here a stand-in for the great beyond, a higher power, or some spiritual life force that we can't grasp—can know. We can't. Not knowing, it seems, is at the heart of what it means to be human. And it's at the heart of what it means to love and be loved.

God Knows, I Don't

Contrary to popular wisdom, "following your truth" is not always the best idea. *Not* believing in yourself can actually be the right thing to do. In fact, total certainty is bad for us, and it can be deadly for democracy.

Think about it: If you have all of life's questions completely settled, what is there left to debate? If you know perfectly what justice demands, what is there to discuss? If one political tribe has full and complete access to the truth, why should they include other tribes in the democratic process? Once one group possesses "the truth," the give-and-take of democracy becomes a nauseating waste of time. We don't worry about citizens who have doubts. We worry about the ones who believe in themselves all the way down to their feet. Run, don't walk, in the other direction if you encounter them.

Citizens who believe that they, and they alone, have found the truth will scream at their opponents on cable news, talk radio, and social media. They will dox their opponents, seeking to get them canceled and fired. They will sever ties with classmates, neighbors, coworkers, and even family members who have the "wrong" opinions. If opponents can't see the light, there is little point in discussion, much less friendship.

It's pointless to engage in dialogue with those who are asleep. Best to wait until they're woke.

A healthy democracy requires citizens who possess some level of intellectual humility, who can shrug their shoulders from time to time and say, "God only knows." Intellectual humility is a trait and a practice that allows citizens to accept their limitations. Is it "evil" to prefer a marginal tax rate of 42 percent over one that is 36 percent? If two citizens are fighting over whether a particular intersection should have a stop sign or a traffic light, there may not be one right answer. It may just be a matter of preference, with each side having a legitimate argument. Even if we suspect that we are right, we must accept that we might be wrong. The truth is larger and more complex than a single human can comprehend.

With intellectual humility come the gifts of curiosity and hospitality toward other opinions. Even if other ways of thinking make you uncomfortable, intellectual humility enables you to open yourself up to persuasion and compromise.

This might all sound banal and obvious, but we're not sure that it is. Quickly rejecting "bad" opinions—and rushing to label certain political beliefs as reflecting deep moral flaws—is not ideal in a democracy in which bad ideas will always be plentiful. When someone disagrees with you, that doesn't by default mean they are a bad person. It most likely just means that they're different. Citizens must reject the notion that, as philosopher Kevin Vallier puts it, "others disagree with our moral, religious, and political viewpoints solely because of some cognitive or moral vice."[3]

This is where simple phrases like "God only knows" become more than just an offhand phrase or a lyric in a Beach Boys song. They represent an essential starting point for a healthy democracy.

Certainty Versus Confidence

More than a millennium ago, Muslim clerics began a practice that nicely illustrates our point. Whenever these jurists would write a *fatwa* (a religious declaration), they would end it with the phrase *Allahu a'lam*, which roughly translates to "God only knows." To be sure, these jurists were not moral relativists. They believed that their particular edicts were correct. They had real confidence in their rulings. However, at the very end of each declaration, the jurists would always reserve the last word for God. It was as if they needed to remind both the reader and themselves of their own shortcomings.

Here we can begin to distinguish between human confidence and human certainty. The difference is absolutely critical for democratic life. Confidence in one's beliefs is critically important for any democracy. Absolute certainty in one's beliefs, on the other hand, is dangerous for any democracy. Chances are it won't remain democratic for very long.

Christians have their own version of *Allahu a'lam*. Christians believe that the Bible is divinely inspired—"God-breathed," as Paul puts it (2 Tim. 3:16)—even though it was written by flawed human beings. But Paul doesn't pretend that every word he writes carries the same divine weight.

When Paul discusses marriage ethics, he's remarkably transparent about his sources. "For those who are married," he writes, "I have a command that comes not from me, but from the Lord"—essentially, don't get divorced (1 Cor. 7:10 NLT). Fair enough. But then Paul encounters a thornier question, one that Jesus never directly addressed: What happens when a new Christian is married to someone who wants nothing to do with the faith? Should they divorce? Paul has an opinion—he thinks they should stay married. But listen to how he frames it: "I do not have a direct command from the Lord" (7:12 NLT). In other words, "This is my best judgment, but I'm flying a bit blind here."

Think about what Paul is doing. The apostle himself is willing to say, "Look, Jesus didn't specifically cover this scenario, so I'm doing my best to figure out what God would want." It's a remarkable moment of intellectual honesty. Paul isn't abandoning his authority, his confidence, or his convictions. He's simply acknowledging that even apostles have to make judgment calls when facing new situations that lack clear divine instructions.

The lesson is unmistakable: If Paul—writing under divine inspiration—could admit the limits of his certainty, then maybe the rest of us should too. Sometimes wisdom means saying "God only knows" even when we're pretty sure we know what God would want.

Philosopher Slavoj Žižek argues that *all* citizens—religious and secular alike—long for total certainty. Žižek rejects the claim that only religious people fall prey to the temptation of fundamentalist certainty. He asks, rhetorically, "Who, in fact, *are* fundamentalists? To put it simply, a fundamentalist does not *believe* in something, but rather *knows* it directly. In other words, both liberal-skeptical cynicism and [religious] fundamentalism share a basic underlying feature: the loss of the ability to *believe* in the proper sense of the term."[4]

Think about how we learn anything—from quantum physics to a toddler's first steps. It doesn't happen in isolation. We learn within communities that share certain assumptions about what counts as true and valuable. Even scientists operate within communities of trust. They adopt theories not just because the data demands it but because those theories seem elegant, rational, and comprehensive to their scientific community. A child learns to speak by trusting that her parents know which sounds convey which meanings. She does not critically examine each and every sound.

Religious communities work the same way. They hold knowledge together, debate it openly, and remain willing to refine their understanding over time. What emerges from these communities is what we might call "confident knowledge"—beliefs held firmly enough to act on but humbly enough to keep questioning.

British theologian Lesslie Newbigin captures this beautifully when he says that "there is no knowing without believing."[5] Even our most rigorous scientific knowledge starts with a leap of faith in scientific discoveries of the past. Scientists don't start from zero. They build, by faith, on the discoveries of the past. This is why religious traditions have always insisted that they can know things with confidence (literally "with faith" in Latin) without claiming to know them with absolute certainty.

Democracy requires that citizens hold tight to this difficult distinction between having confident convictions and having total certainty about those convictions. The former is great; the latter is dangerous. A democracy thrives when citizens bring their convictions into the debate.

But when citizens bring godlike certainties, democratic institutions and norms begin to crack and crumble. Once again, this distinction between confidence and certainty is a difficult one to maintain. But it's critical to our democratic way of life.

A sincere faith does not depend on absolute certainty, and it's unfortunate that our broader religious and political culture continues to equate the two. Feeling comfortable and confident in our convictions can actually engender greater intellectual humility, not hubris. After all, if we know where we stand, we may find ourselves less threatened by others' convictions.

Let's return for a moment to the Muslim jurists and the *fatwa*. Here, the distinction between faith and fundamentalism is clear. In his ruling, a Muslim jurist is holding two critical things together at the same time. First, he is saying that he believes with real confidence that what he has proclaimed is indeed the path that God is commanding. And yet the jurist also understands that God alone knows best in the end. The jurist knows that he and his readers always need to remember the fundamental difference between his judgment and God's.

Trusting God rather than themselves enabled these jurists to approach their legal opponents with generosity. If truth belongs to God alone, that changes the fundamental purpose of debate. As the great jurist Imam Shafi'i (d. 820), one of Islam's most influential scholars, put it, "I never once argued with anyone hoping to win the debate; rather I always wished that the truth would come from their side."[6] The search for truth, rather than victory, is the goal.

In the broader sweep of time, we can see this more clearly. The great Muslim scholars, like thinkers in any tradition, changed their opinions on key questions over the course of their lifetimes. Being wrong when we thought we were right is part of the human condition, one that we might recognize if we looked inward.

We, your authors, would like to uphold this standard. Each of us understands that our opinions over, say, a ten-year period are going to change. With new information and insight—and by engaging in political combat with worthy challengers—our views evolve. As they should. If we are products of our context, then our ideas will change as our context changes.

In one of our Christian-Muslim dialogues at the University of Minnesota, a student asked me (Shadi) how I felt about the fact that many evangelicals—including Matthew—want me to know Christ, embrace him as my savior, and anchor my life in his grace. I feel no such need to see Matthew convert to Islam, so I can't entirely relate to the impulse. I was a bit stumped about how to respond, since I was well aware of the imbalance in our perspectives.

Frankly, I'm still uncomfortable with the idea that a dear friend might wish for me to replace one set of foundational beliefs with another—to, in effect, become something other than what I am. But I understand better now. My friendship with Matthew is premised on trying our best to understand each other. And if this is what Matthew believes, then I can't expect him to suppress his own commitments as an evangelical who, by definition, has an interest in evangelizing. He wants me to convert to Christianity, and that's okay.

Matthew and I wrestle with moral and political uncertainty every day. We have found that our respective religious traditions do not forbid this wrestling. In fact, they enable us to wrestle more productively with our questions and our doubts.

So how can citizens hold political confidence while at the same time avoiding the destructive temptations of political certainty? Much will be said on this matter throughout the book. In the end, however, it comes down to this: To be a person of political confidence is to place your confidence in something beyond yourself, something you cannot fully comprehend or control. To be a person of political certainty is to place your confidence in yourself and your ability to fully comprehend and control the truth. Confidence and certainty are fundamentally different things, and our religious traditions help explain why. Writer Anne Lamott says, "The opposite of faith is not doubt. The opposite of faith is certainty."[7] This is not just another clever aphorism. It speaks to something deep and, dare we say it, true about what it means to be human.

Give Us an Answer

Ali is one of the most beloved figures in the history of Islam. He was the son-in-law and cousin of the Prophet Muhammad and the last of the four "rightly guided" caliphs. He was assassinated in AD 661, provoking a civil war that haunts Muslims to this day. The unique circumstances surrounding Ali's murder provide a cautionary tale of the dangers of making premature political judgments.

Before he was killed, the issues facing Ali were the perennial questions of political life. Who knows, who decides, and who rules? Who can issue a final decree with utter certainty, closing off all alternative paths in the process? In a word, who is sovereign?

Ali was embroiled in an ongoing dispute with a chieftain who wished to seize power from him. To settle the matter, Ali submitted himself to a formal process of arbitration in which an ostensibly neutral party would adjudicate each man's claims. Many of Ali's followers were outraged that their beloved leader would humble himself in this way. How could he—the leader of the holy faith, blessed by the one true and immortal God—subject himself to the ruling of a mere mortal?

Upon hearing their grumbling, Ali did something startling and strange. He brought forward a copy of the Quran and touched it. Ali then declared in front of the crowd, "Oh Qur'an, speak to the people!" His followers were confused. "Oh Ali, why do you mock us?" they asked. The Quran, Ali explained, does not speak by itself.

It was a brilliant religious demonstration with profound political consequences. For Muslims, the Quran is indeed the word of God, every letter and word divine. As such, the book *is* ultimate certainty—Truth with a capital *T*. But the Quran's precise meaning and application are anything but.

The Quran requires a human interpreter. It was "written in straight lines between two covers," as Ali said, so it cannot speak for itself.[8] Human beings, with all their flaws and foibles, have to read, interpret, and apply it themselves. When they read the holy text, they bring their own biases. Like any book, the Quran requires readers. And readers can always find what they are looking for—if they look hard enough.

There, lying before the crowd, were God's exact and precise words of truth, unmediated by human authorship. And yet, even here, Ali's word of caution was clear: Try as you might, you cannot directly access God's true and perfect intent. The Quran will not speak exactly to this or that situation. Readers need to discuss, debate, and come to their own imperfect decisions. You can judge your fellow humans, but do so with care because your judgments will necessarily be limited. Not only that, but ultimate judgment will never be yours, and it will not happen in the here and now. Ultimate judgment will be delayed until another world and another life. Only at the very end of time will God clarify who was right and who was wrong.

Ali's exhortations failed to satisfy his angry supporters—who soon became his betrayers. They wanted absolute certainty. They wanted answers. So they killed him.

The story of the Quran that would not speak—and Ali's refusal to answer on its behalf—might be surprising to those who associate the early days of Islam with fundamentalism, fanaticism, and the often misunderstood term *sharia*. Ali's pluralistic ethic was baked into the sharia itself. Sharia is Islam's sacred law, but its origins come from a word that means "way to the watering-hole."

According to a saying of the Prophet Muhammad, if a person strives to faithfully interpret God's path and is successful, they will receive two rewards. If they try but get it wrong, they will still receive one reward for their good-faith attempt. If two interpreters of the Quran disagree with each other, only God knows which one of them is correct. As the Quran says, "No one knows the soldiers of God but God" (Q 74:31).

According to some scholars of the Quran, there may not be a single "correct" answer to begin with. What truly matters is the humble and pious search.

Christians as well have a long history of cautioning readers of the Bible against believing that they fully possess the Word and will of God.[9] Paul speaks to the partial and incomplete nature of human knowledge in a letter to Christians in Corinth. He admonishes them that one day they will know God with absolute certainty, but that day is not today. For today, "we know in part and we prophesy in part, but when completeness comes, what is in part disappears. . . . For now we see only a reflection as in a mirror; then we shall see face to face. Now I know in part; then I shall know fully, even as I am fully known" (1 Cor. 13:9–10, 12).

Paul here invites Christians to live with mystery and tension. Christianity is full of difficult questions. Consider the following: How is it that Jesus is both fully God and fully man? How is it that God is both one and three? How can God be both just and merciful? The Bible invites fundamentalists to wrestle with questions and problems they can't possibly solve. And this is a good thing. As God declares to the prophet Isaiah, "My thoughts are not your thoughts, neither are your ways my ways. . . . As the heavens are higher than the earth, so are my ways higher than your ways and my thoughts than your thoughts" (Isa. 55:8–9). Paul invites his readers to both accept and marvel at the incomprehensible mysteries of God. He writes, "How unsearchable are his judgments and how inscrutable his ways! 'For who has known the mind of the Lord, or who has been his counselor?'" (Rom. 11:33–34 ESV).

The earliest Christians ran with this idea. For centuries after Jesus died, church leaders from Alexandria to Jerusalem to North Africa hammered home the same point: We can know God only in part. Figures like Clement, Tertullian, and Augustine—men whose names still echo through seminary halls today—all insisted that human beings can never fully grasp the divine. It isn't that God is hiding from us or playing games. It's that our finite minds simply can't contain the infinite. Even our best theological thinking gets us only so far.

Navigating a deeply polarized political environment of chaos and confusion, citizens naturally look for someone who will offer them clarity. We want answers. In a world of undulating moral and political forces, strident ideologies offer us something seemingly strong and stable to hold on to. But certainties are illusions, and as we will see, they are dangerous.

Islam and the Illusion of Certainty

The Islamic concept of *tawhid*, or the oneness of God, is the foundation of Islamic theology and the animating conviction undergirding the religion as a whole. Muslims utter the following phrase countless times in the form of the *shahada*: "There is no god but God, and Muhammad is his prophet." In the original Arabic, *ilah* means "god" or "deity," whereas *Allah* means "God"; hence, Muslims are effectively saying, "I don't believe in any deity or divinity except the one true God." The negation powerfully declares that no one or no thing is like God. The lesson is simple but critical: Prayer, at its base, is the recognition of a simple but powerful reality that "I am not God."

Five times a day, a Muslim's body, mind, and soul are placed into a posture of humility and dependence. As they wash, kneel, and prostrate their entire bodies to the ground, Muslims are reminded—through the repetitive acts of ritual—that they are less than and profoundly dependent on something beyond themselves. Putting one's head on the floor in prostration represents submission. One of the great sins, pride, is illustrated in the Quran by Satan's refusal to bow his head before God. Prostration, the greatest form of humility, is a reminder that every created being is rightly placed in a posture of submission.

The rejection of certainty in favor of a variety of opinions represents a healthy dynamic in Islamic law and emphasizes the inherent complexity of human knowledge. Rather than perceiving differences as indicators of strife, Islam, as we saw in the previous chapter, sees them as an expression of God's will.

According to a well-known Muslim proverb, "The disagreement of the scholars is a mercy." In the spirit of healthy debate, it should be noted that not all Islamic scholars accepted this adage. However, a great many of them did, such as notable figures like Umar ibn Abd al-Aziz, the fifth caliph in Islam, and Ibn al-Qayyim, a fourteenth-century jurist and theologian. They held that good faith differences in opinion can be praiseworthy. Ibn al-Qayyim writes, "Whoever issues [a] fatwa to people based only on what is transmitted from books despite the differences in their customs, norms, eras, localities, situations, and circumstances, then he is misguided and misguides others. His crime against the religion is greater than the crime of the physician who treats all people with what he finds in a single medical book while neglecting the differences in their lands, norms, times, and physical natures."[10]

In effect, Muslims can fully believe that God's words in the Quran are true and immutable and also hold that no single person has exclusive claim to God's intended meaning. Jurists distinguish between the sharia as God's law in the abstract—his true divine will—and their human understanding of it. From this evolved an entire discourse as well as maxims such as "laws will invariably change with the change of circumstances," conveying again that sharia as an ideal is unchangeable, while human understanding and implementation entail change and evolution.[11]

Against Certainty

Exactly how close can a Christian get to grasping God's truth and justice?

In the two-thousand-year history of Christian philosophy and theology, there is, of course, a wide variety of perspectives on the matter. Some Christian theologians have been more confident in the human capacity to know God's will and apply it than others. Debates between the optimists and the pessimists continue to this day.

Optimistic theologians—looking to inspire confidence in Christian knowledge—point to human beings being created in the image of God. They argue that human beings were created to be intelligent, wise, and rational. God has given human beings the gifts of perception and reason. The optimist further argues that God created an orderly and knowable world. Given all this, human beings can clearly advance in science, technology, and study of the natural world. In addition, God gave us the Bible, which Christians can confidently read and discern. Because we have access to all these sources of information and means of reason and revelation, Christians should be relatively optimistic about their ability to grasp God's truth and apply it to the world.

Pessimistic theologians point to the other side of the story (and there are always, of course, at least two sides). They posit that, compared to God, humans are both finite and fallen and that human knowledge emerges from a limited and circumscribed human vantage point. No human being has a God's-eye view of the world or its truth.

By "fallen," theologians mean that all human knowledge is twisted, clouded, and distorted by human selfishness and sin. When humans decided to rebel against God, their senses, reason, and cognitive abilities became muddied and darkened. With eyes and minds clouded by self-deceit, human beings began to argue with one another about the nature of truth and the precise meaning of Scripture. In their darkened confusion, humans began to fight.

Obviously, both the optimists and the pessimists make excellent points. It's clear that human beings are both rational and irrational, both incredibly wise and terribly foolish. A wise Christian will, no doubt, hold both of these realities at once.

If Christians are indeed willing to learn from both the optimists and the pessimists, they will be equipped to do two things at the same time:

1. With the optimists, Christians will confidently declare, "There is such a thing as real truth and real justice, and I have a responsibility to do my best to wisely discern what those things are and confidently advocate for them in political life."
2. With the pessimists, Christians will humbly confess, "My political mind is both finite and fallen, clouded by selfishness and sin. Because of this, my politics will always fall short of a perfect understanding of truth and justice. As a result, I will do my best to carry myself with humility and a willingness to learn and grow."

Holding these two truths together, Christians will be citizens of conviction but not certainty.

Three thousand years ago, the ancient Israelites managed to hold this twofold conviction in a single worship song. Singing together, they declared, "The decrees of the Lord are firm. . . . But who can discern their own errors?" (Ps. 19:9, 12).

Once again, Christian citizens in a pluralistic world should be able to say these two things together. The demands of justice are urgent and real, but we will also continue to twist them toward our own ends. We should be confident, not certain.

Muslims and Christians disagree on many things but come together on one critical point: A mortal's claim to fully comprehend the infinite truth of an immortal God is something close to blasphemy. In claiming intellectual certainty and mastery, blasphemers put themselves in the place of God. In Islam, one of God's ninety-nine names—the names that make God God—is the All-Knowing. By definition, humans cannot aspire to anything comparable.

Here we begin to see why claims of absolute certainty and the political fundamentalism that often follows are not simply bad manners or undemocratic; they're something worse. Political fundamentalism is, at its heart, a rejection of human finitude and frailty. In this sense, it is a rejection of the most important distinction in Islam and Christianity—the distinction between the created and the Creator.

While there are some particularities and disagreements between Islam and Christianity on these matters, we must remember the crucial agreement that connects these two global faiths. Rightly understood, political certainty is out of bounds for Muslims and Christians alike.

4

Make Politics Mundane Again

KEY TAKEAWAY

Healthy democracies take themselves seriously, but not too seriously. Political debate should not be an apocalyptic battle between the forces of good and evil. Democracies need a way to lower the stakes of conflict.

Ritual sacrifice is still a thing. In 2020, Reuters reported a tragic new phenomenon in American public life: families were being sacrificed on the altar of politics. There were cases of children disowning parents, as when Mayra Gomez's son told her, "You are no longer my mother because you are voting for Trump." Married couple Gail and William McCormick separated over competing political allegiances. Two of Gail's grandchildren stopped speaking to her over her support for Hillary Clinton. Rosanna Guadagno was cut off from her family over politics in 2016; when her mother died six months later, Rosanna was informed in an email from her sister-in-law.[1] These stories will be familiar to anyone who lived through the rancorous 2016 election and the even more contentious 2020 and 2024 elections. The Capitol insurrection grabbed all the headlines on January 6, 2021. On January 7, family dinner tables across the country erupted with their own insurrections.

We both came of age in the relative political calm of the 1990s. Political discussions on C-SPAN were rather dull and family dinners rather mundane. The '90s were not perfect by any means, but if we're honest, we long for a time when political discussions were not so explosive and existential. How do we make politics mundane again?

Filled with political zeal, American citizens today are sacrificing their time, their money, their emotional health, and even their most intimate relationships for the sake of their political loyalties. Americans spend hours every week developing and reinforcing their political identities and enmities. Through quasi-ritualistic participation in social media, podcasts, and cable news, they solidify their devotion to their tribal identities. They offer their emotional lives to social media feeds that will cause their souls to rise and fall dramatically with each new controversy or conflict. Political mantras, memes, and movements take on ultimate significance, leading to more disruption in their public and personal lives. Political conflicts become cosmic. Elections become eternal.

Ancient religious teachers had a word for this sort of devotion, when human beings take something ordinary and mundane and make it ultimate: idolatry. Our working definition of an idol is a person, place, or thing that's inappropriately elevated or made central in a person's life. An idol is a finite thing that has been granted an infinite, supernatural, or godlike status. When we practice idolatry, we humans make two critical movements: We *elevate* things that should be lower, and we *center* things that should be peripheral. If you don't want to sacrifice your family, time, money, or emotional health on the altar of your political loyalties, both Islam and Christianity offer important practices that can help you resist the temptation to do so. Muslims and Christians disagree on a lot, but when it comes to idols, they speak with one voice: "Smash them." They call this process "iconoclasm." It can liberate you from a destructive downward spiral in which you are sacrificing good things (money, time, relationships, health) on the altar of something that does not deserve it.

The ancient practice of iconoclasm—rightly understood—carries within it crucially important political wisdom. Political loyalties are, and ought to be, mundane. Barring extreme circumstances, we must never sacrifice our friendships and family relationships for something temporary and passing. Politics does not deserve this type of sacrifice.

Our political loyalties need to be humbled, to be cut down to size. Iconoclasm can greatly enrich our lives by lowering the stakes of our politics and nipping our political polarization in the bud. Iconoclasm offers a way to make our politics (and our family dinners) mundane again.

To begin, we must first consider the psychological—and spiritual—power of political tribalism. In short, Americans have turned the political into the eternal. In a political environment in which every election is "the most important of our lifetimes," politics starts to feel like a holy war—a clash of good and evil, heaven and hell. As we saw earlier, when politics becomes eternal and existential in this way, our democratic life together is damaged. We should resist making political ideologies into little saviors and satans.

Of course, that's easier said than done.

The Psychology of Political Tribalism

Political tribalism is intense loyalty to one's political group that often creates an us versus them mentality. Support of one's group can override objective principles, foster deep division, and lead to hostility. The psychology at work in political tribalism is more primal than we care to admit. As Jonathan Haidt has demonstrated, our political allegiances are not the product of calm and reasoned analysis. Our tribal attachments and emotional reactions come first, with reasoning following behind to justify them. Human beings are "political animals," Haidt argues; they are 90 percent chimps pursuing their own self-interest and 10 percent hive-minded bees craving the transcendence of belonging to something larger.[2] This explains why our moral postures on political issues feel so obviously correct to us and the opposing side's views feel so obviously wrong. We quickly rationalize and fiercely justify our deeply held desires, fears, and interests.

Haidt offers a compelling metaphor for how our intuitions steer our conscious reasoning—the elephant and the rider—that helps explain why appeals to facts and evidence so rarely change minds in political arguments. In this metaphor, the elephant represents our fast, intuitive tribal judgments, while the rider is our slower, reasoning mind, often tasked with justifying decisions the elephant has already made. The rider may believe he is in control, but more often than not, he's simply rationalizing the elephant's instincts.[3]

The evidence for political tribalism is overwhelming. According to a Pew Research Center survey, more than half of both Republicans and Democrats report having just a few or no friends from the opposite party, with 14 percent of Republicans and 21 percent of Democrats admitting they have no friends at all from the opposing party.[4] The percentage of politically mixed marriages plummeted from 30 percent in 2016 to 21 percent in 2020, with marriages between Democrats and Republicans falling from 9 percent to just under 4 percent.[5]

Even more troubling is how rapidly these boundaries are solidifying. In one study, political scientist Lynn Vavreck found that in 1958, 18 percent of a random sample of Americans said they would prefer their daughter marry a Democrat and 10 percent a Republican. By 2016, those numbers had risen dramatically to 28 percent and 27 percent respectively, suggesting that more people believe their children shouldn't marry across party lines. Among strong partisans, the shift is even more pronounced—from 33 percent of Democrats and 25 percent of Republicans wanting same-party marriages in 1958 to 60 percent of Democrats and 63 percent of Republicans in 2016.[6]

Our geographic sorting has followed suit. The percentage of "super landslide counties"—where a presidential candidate won at least 80 percent of the vote—jumped from just 6 percent of all counties in 2004 to 22 percent in 2020.[7] Americans are no longer simply voting at the ballot box; they're voting with their moving vans.

When political affiliation determines our choice of romantic partners and neighborhoods, we lose our capacity for democratic deliberation. America has gone beyond mere disagreement and fallen into existential fear. And a recent Johns Hopkins University poll found that nearly half of Americans now think members of the opposing political party aren't just wrong—they're "downright evil."[8]

The stakes are obviously high. The personal increasingly becomes political, and the political increasingly becomes personal. When citizens elevate their political identities, mantras, and movements and put them on a (quasi-divine) pedestal, they put themselves on a dangerous path. Following this path, citizens come to a singular throne, one that will demand a profound and costly sacrifice.

How can politics become a more mundane and peripheral aspect of our lives? To put it another way, how can we make politics delightfully boring?

The Politics of a Cartoon

Someone drew the Prophet.

From time to time, a public controversy will erupt in the Western media over Islam. The storm usually lasts a week or two. Someone drew the Prophet, and a group of Muslims on TV are angry. Confounded by their religious outrage, secular media outlets dredge up a group of pundits to answer questions about why Muslims are so angry and what is the threat from a simple cartoon.

Secular Westerners often struggle to understand Islamic prohibitions against drawings of the Prophet. Why, they ask, is so much energy spent protesting a simple cartoon? It's just an image. In Islam, there is a long-standing legal debate surrounding the depiction of animate beings, but scholars have generally agreed that portraying the Prophet in any artistic form is impermissible. The Prophet is considered the most noble and perfected of humanity, deserving of the highest reverence after God himself. (Note that for Muslims the prohibition against depicting Muhammad extends equally to Jesus, Moses, and any other prophet.) Any human attempt to depict Muhammad diminishes his exalted status and infringes upon his sacred dignity. Even the most well-intentioned representations cannot capture the honor and respect owed to him.

The prohibition against divine images is, of course, much older than Islam, finding its origins in ancient Israel and the Ten Commandments. Moses, revered in all three Abrahamic faiths, led the Israelites out of slavery in Egypt. The Ten Commandments arrived as the Israelites were in the desert, trying to form a new spiritual and political community.

This new nation would not be founded on a human leader or a human manifesto. It would center and elevate a deity who could not be handled or controlled by human hands. The Hebrew representation of God's name, YHWH, was widely considered too sacred to be written by human hands or spoken by human mouths. God offers no human explanation of his name's meaning beyond the circular insistence "I am." His divine name cannot—will not—be pulled down to a human level.

The ancient Israelites were not the first human beings to pray, worship, or offer sacrifices. This is not what made them special or novel. What was remarkable about the Israelites was their refusal to offer worship to anything other than the one almighty God.

People tend to define "monotheists" as people who believe in one God. This, however, is only half of the equation. Monotheism is also a negation. It's an ardent refusal to place one's faith in other gods and other powers. The first line of the Muslim testimony of faith is one of negation: "There is no god but God, and Muhammad is his Prophet." Islam begins with a refusal to ascribe divine status to any power on earth. Christians have their own version of this negation. In the first century, the early Christians were often labeled "atheists" and "unbelievers" by the Roman Empire. The Romans accused them of being irreligious because they refused to bow and make sacrifices to the Greek and Roman gods.[9] Thus, while the worship of God is certainly valued by Christians, Muslims, and Jews, their refusal to worship anything but God is also a critically important marker.

For the Israelites, no other being could ever be elevated or centered in public life. God alone is worthy of ultimate allegiance. This is why the very first political law in the new nation of Israel was a deeply religious one: "You must not have any other god but me." This first commandment was upheld by a second: "You must not make for yourself an idol of any kind" (Exod. 20:3–4).

For Christians, Muslims, and Jews, it has historically been vitally important to uphold the boundary between mundane things that were created and the one and only Creator, who was not. Idolatry transgresses that boundary.

Anything can be turned into an idol: physical objects (the sun and stars, statues and drawings, wealth and possessions), people (political leaders, celebrities, entrepreneurs, athletes), or ideas (various political and spiritual philosophies, ways of life and culture). These idols share one thing in common: They are all constructs. At one point in time, each of them was made. God, on the other hand, has no maker. He has no beginning and no end.

Following in the tradition of Moses, the Islamic faith is particularly strident and uncompromising regarding the dangers of divine images. The Quran is perfectly clear on this matter: God has no physical or human form. God is utterly transcendent and completely other from humanity.

Islam's rejection of divine imagery is not merely a historical quirk or cultural sensitivity; it is a theological insistence on the complete otherness of God—what Muslim scholars call *tanzih*, or the assertion that nothing is like God. The Quran speaks unequivocally: "There is nothing like unto Him, and He is the Hearing, the Seeing" (Q 42:11). This is not metaphor. It is a metaphysical claim. God has no form, no face, no figure that can be conjured. To depict God is to violate God.

No Kings

Monotheism in ancient Israel was a religious doctrine with political consequences. The Israelites were not simply prohibited from bowing to other gods; they were prohibited from bowing to other kings as well. God alone was king.

This was a radical shift in religious and political consciousness. In the ancient world, it was quite common for nations to have a variety of gods and kings whom they worshiped. But for Israel, God alone was God and God alone was king. In other words, *no kings*.

The Israelites would eventually have a human king, just like all the other nations, but the story is a sad one. The Israelites' request for a human king was a rejection of God's kingship (1 Sam. 8:7). Taking a human king was an affront to the one, true King. While the other nations told grand stories of their human kings' births, childhoods, and crownings, the story of Israel's kings was one of decline and destruction.

In Islam, the religious act of surrender to God alone carries with it very real political implications. If God alone is deserving of total submission, then no human king can demand such a thing. There is no divine right of kings in Islam. The caliph is not a god but a *khalifa*—a deputy, a steward. He is fallible, replaceable, and accountable. God alone is sovereign.

If a king possessed a statue of God or a box that contained God, he could pick it up, carry it around, and claim a divine right to do anything he chose. In this way, religious prohibitions against divine drawings and statues can actually have a political benefit. Political leaders are not permitted to claim possession of God. In a very important sense, God's divine power and will are always and forever beyond their grasp.

The Politics of Idolatry

Islam's prohibition against divine images is meant to protect the honor, mystery, and transcendence of God. The God of the universe is not a "thing" you can hang on your wall or put in your living room. God is beyond human comprehension and control. God is too large, too wild, too free to be controlled by human hands.

In this way, Islam offers one of the most strident safeguards against political idolatry. Not only is God unseen, but no one—no tribe, party, movement, or man—may presume to speak for God with finality. The Quran issues a warning against this: "Do not falsely declare with your tongues, 'This is lawful, and that is unlawful,' only fabricating lies against Allah. Indeed, those who fabricate lies against Allah will never succeed" (Q 16:116). Even the attempt to legislate divine authority, if done presumptuously, is a kind of idolatry.

What we see in Islamic theology, then, is not just a refusal to depict God visually. It is a refusal to collapse the infinite into the finite, the sacred into the profane, the eternal into the temporal. This refusal, at its best, keeps politics in its place. We may not draw God, nor may we claim him for our political tribe.

It's no accident, therefore, that Islam has little patience for nationalism. Giving one's nation divine status is idolatry of the most seductive kind. In his *Risalat al-Tawḥid*, the nineteenth-century Egyptian reformer Muhammad Abduh argues for a rational, liberating monotheism—one that distances the divine from all attempts at political appropriation. The essence of his warning is that political tyranny often begins with the theological error of imagining that God can be placed in human hands.[10]

The Islamic doctrine of divine transcendence is not simply abstract theology. It is the first and final line of defense against the sacralization of political power. It reminds us that no matter how inspiring a leader's rhetoric, how urgent the cause, or how desperate the moment, the throne belongs to God alone.

While Christians and Jews might not be quite as stringent as Muslims in their prohibitions against divine images, they retain this central concern: God's unique name, image, and status must be honored and protected. Christians, Muslims, and Jews all agree that God cannot be fully captured in paintings and statues fashioned by human hands. After all, who can draw a hurricane, much less the one who created the universe.

But this is a book about politics, not art. And the truth is that idolatry concerns more than mere drawings; it's political.

Empathizing with Idolaters

The word *idolatry* grinds in the ears of moderns. It sounds archaic, superstitious, and—worst of all—judgmental. Labeling someone an "idolater" feels like an insult straight out of a Shakespearean play—a worthy pretext for a medieval duel. What can modern people possibly gain from the use of such a backward epithet? In an important sense, your authors agree: "Idolater" is a potentially destructive label. For this reason, we need to make a careful and rather counterintuitive argument. We need to defend and even empathize with the practice of idolatry.

Imagine, if you will, that you are an ancient Bedouin shepherd and you've fallen on hard times. The local drought is in its third year. You have a hungry family, and your small flock of sheep is dwindling. Grassy fields for grazing are increasingly few and far between. You're in debt. If the rains do not return soon, you will not be able to repay your debts.

You will lose your flock and then your freedom and your family. Things are desperate.

And then, in your hour of need, a stranger walks over the hill. He carries with him a small statue and a message of hope. The stranger comes from a country of green grass and thriving flocks. He promises that if you buy this statue, if you pray this prayer, if you make this sacrifice, your fortunes will change. Rain, grass, new lambs, and—soon enough—healthy children and even grandchildren will be on the way.

And so in desperation you give the idol a try. You give the stranger your last bit of money and follow his instructions. First, you elevate the statue to a prominent and cherished place within your home. It sits above every other mundane tool and possession. Second, you center the statue and its sacrifices within the communal life of your household. Your family's daily routines, meals, and work are reordered around this idol.

Driven by desperation, you imagine that if you sacrifice enough, maybe your life will be great again. When it doesn't work, you double down. You find more ways to elevate and centralize the idol. You look around for more things to offer it.

The shepherd's story offers an important insight for modern political life: We need to feel empathy for those who have fallen into political idolatry. It shouldn't be too difficult for readers to empathize with the desperate shepherd's choice. He's out of options. Thirsty for hope and—quite literally—for rain, the shepherd is being offered both rain and hope in abundance.

Ancient Bedouins wanted what all of us moderns still want: food and safety, peace and security, growth and fertility. In this sense, the ancient practices of idolatry were deeply rational. If someone is promising a better life (an ancient stranger with a statue or a modern politician with a smile), desperate people will think that a sacrifice is worth a shot.

Turn now to America's political culture and its democratic crisis. Consider the silly and often tragic ways in which Americans sacrifice their friends and families on the altars of their political loyalties and mantras. Consider their willingness to reorder their dating lives and marriages around these identities. Think of what they are willing to sacrifice for the political identities they hold dear. This is idolatry: the reordering of one's home around an object that does not deserve sacrifice, elevation, or centering.

In 2008, Barack Obama came over the hill with promises of hope, change, and national healing after President Bush's ill-fated venture into Iraq and his violations of public trust. Obama promised to bring political unity but left our politics more divided than ever. Why were people disappointed at the end of Obama's term? As Barbara Walters put it, "He made so many promises. We thought that he was going to be—I shouldn't say this at Christmastime, but—the next messiah. . . . People feel very disappointed because they expected more."[11] Speaking of his election, Obama declared, "This was the moment when the rise of the oceans began to slow and our planet began to heal."[12] It's no surprise that people were disappointed.

Similarly, in 2015, Trump rode down an escalator, promising to bring rain to the desiccated Rust Belt. Desperate crowds rallied around Trump's promises of growth, security, and a new golden age of American industry. Conservative evangelicals put Trump on T-shirts next to Jesus Christ, imagining that the New York real estate developer was the second son of God.

Whether we are an American voter or a Bedouin shepherd, we're all vulnerable to leaders who promise rain.

It is easy to scoff at political "sheep" who cry at Obama rallies or drape themselves head to toe in MAGA gear. But scoffing at political idolatry should not be our first response. Instead, we would like to suggest responding with empathy and understanding. *People are thirsty.*

If you allow yourself—in a moment of honesty—to admit that there is a sort of logic to political idolatry, and if you allow yourself to go so far as to empathize with the "sheep" at these rallies, you might just be willing to consider an even more disturbing possibility: that you too have the capacity to believe politicians who claim to control the weather.

While the ancient term *idolatry* might grind in our modern ears, it is exactly what these ears need to hear.

Idolatry and Diversity: A Parable

A benevolent queen reigns over a small kingdom. Walking the city streets surrounding her castle, the queen sees walkers and runners, scooters and bikes, cars and buses. She delights in the beautiful and historic subway stations, she admires the newly polished hot rods, she smiles at the ways little girls decorate their bikes, and she is awed by the discipline and dedication of the runners. Under the queen's reign, citizens are free to move about the city in different ways. As she strolls the bustling and diverse city streets, the queen takes some measure of pride and delight in the variety of transportation available within her realm.

Then something goes wrong.

The biking club has a new leader. He is charismatic and filled with tremendous zeal for the goodness of biking. He convinces his fellow bikers that biking is the key to the good life and that cars and buses, scooters and subways are the source of all the kingdom's problems. The bikers enthusiastically agree; the activity of biking has filled their lives with joy and beauty, health and friendship. Gripped by the joys of biking, the biking club becomes convinced that bicycles should be elevated and centered throughout the kingdom.

(Our sincere apologies to bicyclists everywhere. Every ideology is vulnerable to the sad story we're about to tell.)

The cyclists go out into the streets to passionately share the good news of bikes throughout the queen's peaceful kingdom. Runners and walkers are soon captured by the beauty and internal logic of biking as a lifestyle. As the bicyclists grow in number and influence, they begin to demand that the queen herself use a bike. They demand that she elevate and center bicycles throughout her kingdom. She must instruct the mosques and schools, the bakeries and newspapers to center and value the bike.

The queen refuses.

She loves freedom and diversity. She likes that some people choose to walk, run, scooter, and drive. She loves the colorful buses, the old cars, and the charm of the historic subway stations. She finds that the messy complexity has actually grown on her.

The bicyclists conclude that the queen has to go. For the good of the kingdom, the bicycle must be elevated throughout the kingdom. A coup is planned, and the queen is killed. The next morning the flag of the bicyclists is hoisted on her castle mount.

Newly enthroned, the cyclists destroy all the buses and cars, the subways are closed, and the running shoes are thrown away. The streets become simple and uniform. The vibrant, messy cacophony of runners and walkers, buses and scooters is now organized and coordinated into a monolith.

The point of our parable is both simple and critical: Idols destroy diversity.

When a single idea is vertically elevated, it has horizontal consequences for human diversity. The worship of an object has social consequences for diversity. When a nation bends its knee to an idol, its diverse ways of life are transformed into the idol's singular image. Idols cannot—will not—permit diversity.

This explains why the cities of communist Russia were so famously gray, drab, and uniform. Economic uniformity was centered and elevated as the ultimate value, while other human considerations like aesthetics, architecture, religion, and culture were flattened or destroyed. The only community permitted was the community of workers. Communities of study, play, worship, and artistic creation were all forced to serve the one flag that was centered and elevated—the workers' flag.

Idols cannot bear diversity.

How to Spot an Idol

Monotheists have warned about the civic and social consequences of idols for millennia.

St. Augustine argued that cities will always organize themselves around the objects they worship.[13] Ancient Sparta loved warfare and military strength. It organized its families and schools around the raising of young warriors for battle.

In the same way, a city might choose to center and elevate wealth, racial superiority, religious purity, individual choice, or worker solidarity.

Whatever a city chooses to love will dictate how the city organizes itself. If a city decides that wealth creation is its central value, then its schools and universities will need to be redesigned and reordered to ensure young people grow up to be wealthy. Parents, teachers, and professors will be evaluated on that singular standard—their ability to make young people rich. A complex and diverse society will need to become uniform to pursue its deepest love.

Christians, Muslims, Buddhists, and a variety of Indigenous spiritualties have—at one time or another—attempted to build their cities around a singular religious value to the exclusion of all others. Buddhist extremists in Sri Lanka, Islamic theocrats in Iran, and Christian nationalists in the United States want to forcibly assimilate diverse religions and philosophies into their own vision of a unified whole.

But this is not only a "religious" problem; it is a universal human temptation. The modern world offers a number of secular movements in which the same dynamics were at play. Communism, fascism, colonialism, liberalism, nationalism, and capitalism come to mind. In certain societies, life was reordered around a secular object of affection—be it national power, economic redistribution, racial superiority, or colonial empire. Entire societies were violently reordered to serve these singular ends.

Religious or secular, all citizens are vulnerable to the temptations of political uniformity and idolatry.

The Bible and the Quran offer helpful insights on how to identify an idol. We can't discuss each of these at length, but we've provided a list of the common attributes of an idol.[14] As always, there are important differences between Islam and Christianity. However, when it comes to idolatry, the family resemblance is quite profound.

1. Idols tend to exalt the strong and crush the weak. Political movements that prey on the weak and identify them as "the problem" are worthy of critical investigation. (See Isa. 1; Amos 2; Q 83:1–3.)
2. Idols tend to manipulate human fears and base desires. They speak to the id. Rather than bringing calm, they tend

to increase anxiety, fear, and a sense of chaos. (See Jer. 10; Q 38:26.)

3. Idols often flatter. They affirm. They play on human longings for significance and self-righteousness. Idols rarely inspire vulnerable personal reflection, confession, and humble reconciliation. (See Isa. 44:9–11; Hab. 2:18–19; Rom. 1:25; Q 25:43.)
4. Idols encourage governments to capture independent houses of worship. They have no patience for rivals. (See 1 Kings 12:28–33; Q 53:19–23.)
5. Idols warp the conscience of a nation. Lies, bribery, moral compromise, and sexual promiscuity flourish beneath an idol. (See Jer. 2; Hosea; Q 29:17.)
6. Idols warp economic relationships. God's law forbids economic greed and demands economic generosity and care for the poor. When these commands are being ignored, another god is most likely at play. (See 1 Kings 21; Q 106:1–3; 107:1–3.)
7. Idols collect power; they never give it away. Power is drawn up and into the palace mount. Power is never sent down and out to the city streets. (See 1 Kings 12; Hosea 8; Q 28:4, 38.)
8. Idols are quid pro quo. They promise flourishing in exchange for sacrifices. They have a contractual relationship with their followers, as opposed to a covenantal one. (See Isa. 44; Matt. 4; Q 26:69–82; 36:74–75.)

As you read this list, you might have been thinking of your political opponents and all the ways they fall victim to idolatry. As Jesus said, it is easy to spot the speck of dust in our neighbor's eye but much harder to spot the log in our own (Matt. 7:3).

How to Avoid Political Idolatry

Perhaps some readers still don't like the religious language of idolatry. That's okay. Our primary hope is not to convince you of our religious language. Our hope is to convince you that something like idolatry exists and that it's pretty bad for human communities. It is tearing apart our families and friendships. It's wreaking havoc on our mental health and dissolving the democratic foundations of our republic.

Whatever you call it, idolatry is destructive. You might not believe in Islam or Christianity, but these two religions have been wrestling with the challenges of idolatry for millennia. Best to give them a listen.

A Christian Response

How can we avoid the temptation of idolatry? Two thousand years of Christian wisdom reveal far more than we can recount here. We will limit ourselves to two pieces of advice. The first concerns ordered love, the second the emptying of power. We expect that most readers will easily accept the first piece of advice; we expect more resistance with the second.

According to Christianity, human loves and desires are beautifully complex. We love spouses and children, we desire beauty and nature, we long for play and sex, we devote ourselves to our cities and nations. Christianity does not denigrate this complex array of human loves and desires. It believes that these things are all worthy of human affection and desire.

The question is how we *order* these loves. Some of these loves and desires belong near the top, while others belong near the bottom. We must place our loves and desires in their proper order. St. Augustine called this framework *ordo amoris*—the right ordering of love.[15] If we love our career more than our children, if we love our political tribe more than our neighbors, and if we love our country more than justice, we have disordered loves.

Augustine argued in *The City of God* that human communities inevitably organize themselves around their ultimate loves. "Two cities have been formed by two loves," he wrote. One city loves God, and the other city loves itself.[16] As we said above, a community that loves warfare will organize its families and schools around the raising of warriors; a community that loves wealth will structure its institutions to accumulate wealth. The question is not whether we have ultimate loves but what those loves will be and how they will shape our common life.

Here we arrive at politics and the power of political idolatry.

Augustine taught that political communities become dangerous when they elevate penultimate goods—military strength, economic prosperity, national pride—to ultimate status. This is precisely the dynamic we explored in our parable of the queen and the bicyclists. When a particular object (the bike) is elevated and centered in a political community, it inevitably destroys diversity.

Christianity, for its part, does not advise citizens to extinguish their political passions and longings. It does not argue that we should repress our political dreams or desires. Christianity actually encourages citizens to have a long list of complex loves. This list can include politics but should not be exhausted by politics.

The key insight is this: Political loyalties and longings should be properly ordered within a larger complex of loves—for family and neighbor, art and culture, work and play. Political commitments must always remain penultimate—never ultimate.

Most Americans will understand and accept this advice. It has a ring of common sense to it. Political passion has its place, but political obsessions aren't healthy. Most of us intuitively understand this.

Now we come to the second and more challenging piece of advice. This is where many non-Christians will likely respond with a polite "Thanks, but no thanks." In fact, as we consider the actual words of Jesus, it is likely that many Christians will become uncomfortable as well.

For Jesus, the solution to political idolatry is not simply a matter of common sense or willpower. Jesus demands something much more radical than just "chilling out" about politics. Jesus demands that citizens take all their political commitments, their political dreams and hopes, their political traumas and loyalties, their political beliefs and manifestos and sacrifice each and every one of them to God. A true follower of Jesus has to be willing to approach the throne of Jesus and hand over all their political loyalties, power, and plans.

This is where the Christian story leaves common sense behind and becomes truly strange. While the political movements of the world seek to accumulate influence, control outcomes, and collect power for themselves, Jesus goes in the opposite direction. He gives power away.

Christian theologians use the word *kenosis* to describe this upside-down relationship with power. *Kenosis* describes the strange way that Jesus literally empties himself of power for the sake of others. Jesus binds himself so that others can be liberated. He becomes weak so that others might be strong. He goes down so that others can rise up. Strange though it may be to hear, Jesus says that when he is finally king, "the last will be first, and the first will be last" (Matt. 20:16).

Philippians 2:5–11, which early Christians recognized as a hymn about Christ's *kenosis*, describes how Jesus, "though he was in the form of God, did not count equality with God a thing to be grasped, but emptied himself, by taking the form of a servant" (vv. 6–7 ESV). This kenotic pattern—power exercised through self-emptying service rather than domination—provides a fundamentally different political model for how authority should function. Kenotic rulers will always be looking to lift others up, even those who differ from and even oppose them.

Christ's upside-down relationship with power was truly offensive to the political logic of secularist philosophers such as Friedrich Nietzsche. Nietzsche famously argued that modern man needs to shrug off religious humility, courageously seize divine power for himself, and forcibly impose his will on the world. Jesus demands the opposite: Lay down your claim to power for the sake of your neighbor. This sort of Christian humility was disgusting to Nietzsche. He called it a "slave morality,"[17] a backward view of power—something the West needed to liberate itself from.

Idolatrous political movements promise a great political future for all who bow to them. Once again, Jesus promises the opposite. He promises his followers a political future of suffering, sacrifice, and service. While idols promise a future in which you will get to watch your political enemies suffer and pay, Jesus promises that if you bow to him, *you* will be the one to suffer and sacrifice—sometimes for the sake of your political enemies.

The political implications of Jesus's upside-down relationship with power are as obvious as they are striking. Followers of Jesus should be deeply suspicious of political movements that aim to dominate their opponents. They should instead be drawn to politics that prioritize service, sacrifice for others, and the distribution of power to all.

The Christian tradition can offer what no political movement can: a unique form of political desire that does not depend on political power or success. In Jesus, we can find a source of political hope that transcends electoral outcomes. This is how Jesus makes politics mundane again. We will never have "the most important election of our lifetimes." That was two thousand years ago when Jesus elected to save us. We can chill out about politics because the real election is already over and won.

A Muslim Response

As we saw earlier, for Muslims, the antidote to political idolatry begins with a simple but profound declaration: *La ilaha ill Allah*—there is no god but God. This statement, which hundreds of millions of Muslims recite daily, is both theological and political. When Muslims declare that there is no god but God, they are making a radical claim: Ultimate allegiance belongs to God alone. No earthly leader, no political movement, no nation-state can claim God's power for itself.

This is why the early Muslim community was so threatening to the established rulers of seventh-century Arabia. Muslims weren't just challenging religious beliefs; they were undermining the entire political order by claiming that something mattered more than raw power and realpolitik.

The word *Islam* itself means "submission," but submission to what? To whom? Not to kings or presidents or political parties but to God alone. This creates what we might call a sovereignty problem for any political system that demands absolute loyalty. How can you give your complete devotion to a political cause when you've already surrendered yourself to something else?

Consider how this plays out in practice. In Islamic thought, the concept of *tawhid*—God's absolute unity and uniqueness—serves as a permanent check on human pretensions to divine authority. No matter how charismatic the leader, how urgent the cause, or how noble the ideals, *tawhid* reminds us that these are all human constructs, flawed and finite. This theological insight has deep political implications that go far beyond what many people understand about Islamic political thought. The Islamic tradition is rich with resources for keeping politics in its proper place—resources that have been overshadowed by extremist interpretations and Western misunderstandings alike.

Take, for example, the classical concept of *shura*—the Islamic principle of communal decision-making and consultation. This isn't just a nice idea about getting input from others. It's a foundational principle of Islamic governance, derived from the Quranic mandate that believers are those "who conduct their affairs by mutual consultation" (Q 42:38). Even Muhammad—whom Muslims consider infallible in the form of divine protection from sin but whose infallibility did not extend to foreknowledge of all things—commonly discussed political and other strategic issues with his most trusted followers, influencing Islamic political theory for centuries to come.

When you know that you don't know, you're more willing to listen to others, more humble about your own certainty, more open to compromise and negotiation. Politics becomes less about imposing your will and more about seeking wisdom within the community.

Second, consider the concept of *bay'ah*—meaning allegiance. It functioned historically as something like a constitutional contract between leaders and their people. This allegiance could always be withdrawn if rulers violated Islamic precepts. Ultimate authority rested with the community, not any individual ruler.

These concepts, while strong in theory, weren't always respected in practice, so checks and balances were added to protect against the caliph becoming a political idol or seeing himself as one. Scholars of Islam have documented how the clerical class provided a crucial constraint on the caliph's executive power and authority. As keepers of God-given law, the clerics ensured that the caliph was bound by something beyond himself. The sharia—which bound ruler and ruled alike (at least in theory)—provided something resembling what we would today call "rule of law." The caliph could not claim unlimited sovereignty. That belonged to God and God alone.

Building on these Islamic protections against political idolatry, contemporary Muslim scholars have developed sophisticated frameworks for resisting political absolutism. Through democratic processes, the people and their elected representatives give collective shape and meaning to the sharia according to their particular context. In a sense, as the Tunisian Islamic thinker Rached Ghannouchi has argued, the sharia is whatever the people discern it to be through good faith consultation.

Along these lines, Iranian philosopher Abdolkarim Soroush has championed a distinctive form of religious democracy that separates religious and political authority while allowing Islam's moral influence in democratic societies.[18] The Egyptian-American legal scholar Khaled Abou El Fadl distinguishes between *sharia* (divine guidance) and *fiqh* (human interpretation), preventing political authoritarianism by acknowledging the fallibility of human understanding.[19]

Even hardline figures like Egyptian political theorist Sayyid Qutb, though often associated with extremist movements, grappled genuinely with problems of political tyranny and oppression. While his solutions may have been radical, his critique of leader-worship remains relevant. Writing from an Egyptian prison in the 1960s, Qutb dwells on the Islamic concepts of freedom and liberation repeatedly: "Islam is a declaration of the freedom of man from servitude to other men."[20] Elsewhere, he writes, "Any system in which the final decisions are referred to human beings, and in which the sources of all authority are human, deifies human beings by designating others than God as lords over men."[21] This is an explicit condemnation of political idolatry. A mere mortal who exercises control or domination over another is usurping a role that is God's alone. True freedom comes only from the breaking of political idols.

Qutb, as evidenced by his political execution, was responding to the experience of living under the authoritarian regime of President Gamal Abdel Nasser. It is easy to see how Qutb's ideas were misused for extremist purposes after his death. But his diagnosis of the problem—that humans have a dangerous tendency to worship political power—remains compelling and relevant.

Moreover, a growing body of scholarship suggests that thinkers like Qutb have been fundamentally misunderstood. Political scientist Muqtedar Khan has argued provocatively that Qutb should be understood primarily as the "Muslim John Locke" rather than a theorist of religious extremism. As Khan puts it, "Anyone who takes time to read the works of Qutb would make a perplexing discovery. His formative writings are not too far from those that adorn Christian thinking during the period of the Enlightenment. That is how I came to see him as the John Locke of the Muslim World, who advocated freedom—and supported rebellion against tyrannical rulers."[22]

Khan reminds us that both Locke and Qutb believed in the importance of freedom and the ultimate sovereignty of God. He argues that "both Locke and Qutb imagined freedom in the same absolutist terms. The human individual was, by virtue of his divine creation, subordinate to God—and God alone—and therefore was a free agent."[23] Both Locke and Qutb justified human resistance to tyrannical governments that violated their social contracts with their people and with God.

The key difference is that Locke was writing in the context of emerging liberal democracy, while Qutb was writing under Nasser's brutal dictatorship. When Qutb wrote about *hakimiyyah*—divine sovereignty—he wasn't advocating for theocracy so much as he was arguing that no earthly ruler should be able to claim absolute authority over human beings.

This doesn't excuse the ways Qutb's ideas have been weaponized for the sake of religious zealotry, nor does it resolve all the contradictions in his political theory. But it does suggest that the Islamic intellectual tradition contains more resources for opposing political absolutism than is often recognized. Even thinkers who are often dismissed as extremists grappled with questions that are as vital today as they were then: How do we prevent the concentration of power? How do we hold leaders accountable? How can religion help resist tyranny?

At its best, Islamic political thought does indeed provide citizens with a framework for resisting political tyranny and idolatry. If God alone is sovereign, then no earthly ruler can claim total authority. But if God has established principles of justice and consultation, then we cannot retreat into political nihilism either. We must engage with politics, but always with the knowledge that our political commitments are provisional and subject to a higher judgment.

This is why the Islamic tradition places such emphasis on concepts like *adl* (justice) and *maslaha* (public interest). These provide criteria for criticizing idolatrous political systems and policies that offer an all-consuming interpretation of worldly power. A government that systematically oppresses its people or ignores their welfare has lost its legitimacy, regardless of its religious rhetoric.

What does this mean for American politics? It means that Muslims—and hopefully non-Muslims who appreciate this wisdom—have the resources they need for resisting the totalizing demands of contemporary political movements.

When your ultimate loyalty belongs to God, you simply cannot give yourself completely to any earthly cause, no matter how righteous it appears. This doesn't make you politically apathetic or disengaged. If anything, it should make you more engaged, because you're freed from the desperate need for political victories to validate your existence. You can work for justice without needing your side to win every battle. You can advocate for your beliefs without demonizing those who disagree. You can care deeply about political outcomes without despairing when they don't go your way.

The Islamic principle of *tawhid* offers something that secular politics cannot: a way to be both engaged in politics and chill about it. When you remember that God is God and you are not, politics becomes what it should be—important but not ultimate, serious but not sacred.

When Muslims submit themselves to God in prayer five times a day, it becomes harder for them to also submit themselves completely to political idols. The daily practices of Islam—prayer, fasting, the remembrance of God—serve as a constant reminder that there are more important things than political combat. Spiritual combat is more urgent. When you orient your spiritual life toward the eternal, the temporal demands of political movements begin to lose their grip on your imagination. You can work for practical change without needing to be the agent of salvation. You can oppose injustice without needing to destroy your enemies. You can engage in the messy, frustrating work of democracy without losing your soul.

These are Islam's and Christianity's gifts to American political life. Islam and Christianity offer not a set of policy prescriptions but a framework for keeping politics in its proper place. In a culture that has made idols of political movements and tribal identities, perhaps what we need most is the simple reminder that there is no god but God—and politics isn't him.

5

The Case for Hell

KEY TAKEAWAY

You don't have to believe in hell to appreciate its political utility. If divine justice is coming later, you can afford to be a little more patient and forgiving with your neighbors in the here and now.

"Go to hell!" The phrase slips out naturally in traffic jams and online fights, a reflexive response to life's daily frustrations. But do we *really* wish eternal fire and damnation on the guy who cut us off? Probably not. (Hopefully not!)

Although we differ on the specifics, both of us believe in hell. This makes us part of a shrinking majority. Only 59 percent of Americans today believe in hell. That's down from 71 percent in 2001.[1] But these figures, while striking, fail to capture the remarkable shift currently underway in the United States. No one talks about hell much anymore, at least not publicly—not even religious people. We've both attended weekly religious services for most of our adult lives, and there's just no other way to put it: Hell comes up less.

Simply defined, hell is a place of final judgment and punishment for the wicked. There are allusions to postmortem punishment in the Hebrew Scriptures, but they are relatively few compared to later discussions of hell in the New Testament or the Quran. This is one of the reasons why fewer Jews believe in hell than Christians and Muslims.[2]

In elite, educated circles today, believing in hell—or at least openly admitting it—is rare. In recent years, we've discussed "the politics of hell" in academic talks and lectures, and audiences have responded with confused looks and hostile glances. When I (Shadi) brought up the problem of hell in a conversation with one of our greatest living philosophers, Martha Nussbaum, she found it odd. And it *was* odd. She seemed to think that we moderns have moved past hell, that "religions today think of the afterlife as a source of hope rather than fear." Nussbaum remarked that "if you look at the requiem mass for Queen Elizabeth, for example, it's all about love and the afterlife."[3]

Nussbaum is not alone. We can't count the number of times the afterlife has come up with modern friends and liberal colleagues and the response has been something along the lines of "But you're so intelligent. You don't *really* believe in hell, do you?" In much of the United States, particularly in progressive urban centers, hell—at least as it's described in the New Testament and the Quran—makes its presence known by its increasing absence.

Hannah Arendt was one of the few modern philosophers who grasped the political consequences of losing belief in hell, writing, "The most significant consequence of the secularization of the modern age may well be the elimination from public life, along with religion, of the only political element in traditional religion, the fear of hell."[4] The contemporary retreat from hell has any number of causes, many of them understandable. As pastor Robert Golding notes, modern people find the concept of hell "illogical, unnecessary, and cruel."[5] Innovations in criminal justice now emphasize rehabilitation over mere punishment and bristle at the thought that anyone—even hardened criminals—deserves endless punishment or, worse, death. In this reading, criminals are not born criminals; they are products of difficult circumstances who are often motivated to harm others because of poverty and desperation.

Talk of hell can indeed be dour and depressing. It's no laughing matter. A hadith of the Prophet Muhammad observes that, after hell was created, the angel Michael never laughed again.[6] But as hard as it might be for modern people to imagine, we intend to argue that this ancient doctrine of hell can be an unexpected resource for modern democracies for both believers and nonbelievers alike.

Many readers will, no doubt, scoff at this idea. They might protest, "I could never believe in hell!" That's okay. We're not going to try to convince you to believe in it. One need not believe in hell to grasp its importance or its utility.

In this chapter, we hope to demonstrate two things. First, for the good of our democracy, you should want your religious neighbors to take their belief in hell more seriously—not less. Second, even if you don't believe in hell, you should take some time to ponder its political utility and ask yourself how you intend to make up for its absence in your own life. Hell, in a sense, is a bit like God. If it didn't exist, we would need to invent it. In the next section, we will explore the new "hells" that the modern world is creating in its absence.

Hell Hasn't Gone Away

There are dangers with the doctrine of hell. Both of us have been put off by pastors or imams who turned our rich faith traditions into simplistic morality plays of heaven and hell with their fire-and-brimstone preaching. We take modern criticisms of hell seriously. Neither religion nor politics is healthy when it is driven by fear.

In addition, hell can easily be used for religious and political manipulation. If leaders claim to hold the keys to heaven and hell, their judgment of who is damned and who is not can quickly stifle dialogue and debate. After all, what is the purpose of consultation or compromise if one person wields the powers of damnation and salvation?

Despite the religious and political dangers of hell, its retreat from the public square hasn't fixed modern politics. In fact, political life appears to have become even *more* hellish in the absence of hell. This might not be an accident.

The casual way modern people still shout "Go to hell!" points to a paradox: While a belief in literal hell is declining in the United States, the idea of or even longing for hell continues to flourish. For all our disgust, hell retains a grip on our moral and political imaginations.[7] As author Vinson Cunningham puts it, hell is right here on earth—and always has been. He argues that "our ancestors developed their ideas of Hell by drawing on the pains and the deprivations that they knew on earth. Those imaginings shaped our understanding of life before death, too. They still do."[8]

We spend a lot of time in hell—or what feels like it. Politics is hell. Social media is hell. The modern workplace is hell. Dating apps are hell. Climate change is hell (sometimes literally, if we take hell to be a consuming fire). In an America without God, we haven't destroyed damnation; we've secularized it. We don't believe in hell, and yet it feels like it's everywhere.

Take contemporary American politics. Many of us feel politically isolated and homeless, like no one sees or cares for us. Some of us are afraid that our political tribe might be crushed by another. Some of us are terrified of saying the wrong thing in the wrong circle out of a fear of being ostracized or canceled. Religious people believe that hell is a place of constant fear and dread, anger and alienation, wrath and judgment. Sound familiar?

The new, secular forms of hell seem to differ, however, from their religious counterparts in one important way: There's no clear path out. Religious people believe they can avoid eternal hell by living righteously or receiving divine mercy; secular hell, on the other hand, feels inescapable. We don't so much fear going to hell someday. We wake up to find ourselves already there.

The irony, of course, is that by any objective measure, we're living in what previous generations would have considered heaven. Global poverty has plummeted. Medical advances have conquered diseases that once decimated populations. The working class in developed nations, and even the poor, often have access to luxuries and technologies that medieval kings could have only dreamed of.

Yet the more comfortable we become, the more fixated we become on our own impending destruction. Media critic Derek Thompson argues that "negativity bias" is journalism's greatest bias, worse than any perceived ideological slant.[9] We doom scroll through news feeds, consuming one apocalyptic prediction after another. Sea levels rising. Global warming. The end of democracy. The return of fascism. Artificial intelligence running amok. The end is always nigh, even as our actual lives grow longer, more prosperous, and—as hard as it is to believe—more peaceful.[10]

The rise of secular hell reveals something fundamental about human nature: As a species, human beings need to make sense of the persistence of human evil and suffering. We need a story to tell, a villain to blame, a jail cell to slam shut. It turns out that the ancient belief in hell serves as more than just a deterrent to sin. It is also an explanation for why the world feels so hopelessly wrong.[11] Today, people still have this haunting sense that something is deeply wrong with the world. This is because we haven't abolished hell; we've just relocated it. And this relocation has profound implications for how we understand politics, democracy, and one another. To understand how this happened, we need to go back to one of the architects of modern statecraft, Thomas Hobbes. The famed seventeenth-century philosopher saw Christian belief in demons, evil spirits, and hellfire as a dangerous political problem—one that he was committed to solving.

The Modern Reinvention of Hell

England was being torn apart, and Hobbes wanted peace—at any cost. If you think polarization in the United States is bad, you've clearly not studied the civil war in England. Hobbes struggled with a question that sounds too familiar in a culture of constant religious and political quarreling: How can a nation hold together?

Hobbes believed that the natural condition of human beings was violence and domination—a war of all against all. In this natural state of lawlessness and fear, the only way citizens could end religious and political strife was to empower a single sovereign, whom Hobbes called "Leviathan."[12]

With a monopoly on power and violence, Leviathan could put a forceful end to all the fighting. Leviathan would not make peace; he would enforce it. In order for Leviathan to enforce a lasting peace, he would need to wield the most potent political weapon of all: fear.[13]

According to Hobbes, fear is the primary political motivator for human beings. The first humans established a government, Hobbes argued, because they were afraid of one another. All politics, in his reading, are quite literally built on fear. This is why Hobbes argued that England's religious and political conflicts would come to an end only when the Leviathan state invented a way to control people's fear. The lasting peace of England would come not from the nation's hope but from its dread.

If the English were afraid of a particular tribe, religion, race, or political faction, Hobbes would make sure that they were even more afraid of Leviathan. The only way English citizens would put down their arms and leave other factions alone was if their primary fear was the wrath of Leviathan. Soon enough people would keep their religious and political squabbles to themselves because Leviathan patrolled the streets.

While having a monopoly on material violence is rather straightforward—simply control all the soldiers, weapons, and police—a monopoly on a nation's fear is something else entirely. Leviathan had a formidable competitor when it came to scaring the English people—the church. While Leviathan could condemn English subjects to prison, the church could condemn them to hell. Leviathan could make them suffer and even die, but, unfortunately, it could kill them only once. By damning them to hell, the church could make them suffer for eternity. In a contest between the fear of prison and the fear of eternal damnation, hell tends to win out.

This was precisely Hobbes's discovery. Hell is not simply a religious belief; it's a political power.

Hobbes had discovered a political problem at the heart of hell: If you are a political leader, it is difficult to control a population that is more afraid of God than it is of you. You might demand that your citizens follow your instructions, you might demand their attention, but their eyes will be constantly darting over to God. This lack of fearful focus on the state troubled Hobbes. Leviathan needed the people's focus; it needed their fear.

Ultimately, Hobbes concluded that if the state was going to establish peace, it needed to undermine the citizens' belief in hell: "The maintenance of civil society depending on justice, and justice on the power of life and death (and other less rewards and punishments) residing in them that have the sovereignty of the commonwealth, it is impossible a commonwealth should stand where any other than the sovereign hath a power of giving greater rewards than life, and of inflicting greater punishments than death."[14]

Hobbes tried to undermine the belief in hell in a variety of creative ways.[15] His primary strategy was to mythologize and psychologize hell. Denying that hell is a real place, he treated it as a mere state of mind or condition. He argued that human beings are superstitious by nature and that their beliefs in demons and eternal judgments are the irrational manifestations of psychological confusion. In a particularly cynical turn, Hobbes wryly suggested that human beings invented religion because they were afraid of ghosts.[16] Both the church and the state were invented by humans as a way to deal with their fears.[17]

If human fear is inevitable and fear inevitably leads to fighting, then, Hobbes suggested, it was best to unify and collect that fear in the hands of the state, not the church. Allowing any sort of division or competition of fears was dangerous and combustible. It could lead to conflict. As Christopher McClure remarks, Hobbes was trying to make "|the fear of violent death," which man can always be sure is a real possibility, "the most reliable passion on which to found political society."[18]

If English subjects became rebellious, they would now fear the damnation of the state, not the church. This was the secularization of hell. Hobbes did not abolish the power of hell. He took it from God and gave it to the state.

Hobbes began a pattern that has been repeated throughout the modern, post-religious West. First, modern citizens reject hell—a distant place of wrath, judgment, and alienation—in the hopes of creating peace. Second, they discover that contemporary society has become a place where citizens visit wrath, judgment, and alienation on one another.

Once again, the modern world does not abolish hell; it reimagines it.

The Spectacle of Secular Hell

An American college student is on her first trip to Paris. She decides to visit the Louvre. She walks amid the grand and majestic works of the

Greeks, the Romans, and the Renaissance. She is satisfied and serene. But then she turns the corner and finds herself in the medieval wing. Here, to her horror, she finds outsized and gruesome paintings of the punishments of hell. Demons and devils bounce about with great delight, finding all sorts of creative ways to torture their human subjects. As the student leaves the Louvre, the images of suffering haunt her. She wonders how a society could make punishment such a spectacle.

Returning to her hotel room, she opens her laptop and begins to scroll through social media. She watches a viral video of a black man being chased down by police officers and dragged off to prison. She reads detailed stories about male celebrities being sued for sexual harassment. She watches as her favorite commentators give these men their due justice. She watches a video of ICE agents raiding a factory and deporting a group of immigrants. Finally, in an effort to wind down before bed, she catches up on her favorite courtroom television show, in which a man who might be innocent (but also might not be) is given a long jail sentence. Closing her laptop, she lays her head on the pillow and wonders to herself again how those strange medieval artists could turn punishment into such a spectacle.

Human beings not only thirst for justice; they want to see it happen. There is something in us that wants to take in the spectacle of bad guys "getting theirs." There is something about watching the hunt and the chase. Our television sets are filled with true-crime shows, celebrity scandals, and legal dramas. We scroll through social media with a sort of delighted horror as bad guys are caught and punishment is served.

On an international scale, things are not so different. We want armies to send a message. We want more than victory; we want shock and awe. It is not enough to bring force. We have to *make* a show of force. This is what it means to secularize the spectacle of hell. We no longer believe that evildoers go to hell, so we're forced to bring it to them.

But Hobbes had a problem, and so do we. Fear and spectacle work, but only to an extent. No matter how spectacular the disciplinary action, modern forms of punishment fail to bring unity and peace. Despite the incredible power of the modern world to surveil and cancel, incarcerate and bomb, the whole system is still ultimately fragile and fallible.

While those medieval paintings in the Louvre might have been horrifying to our traveling student, the medieval idea of hell contained within it a number of surprising and rather unexpected advantages compared to its modern heirs.

Hell: Medieval Versus Modern

As we've seen, the modern citizen demands a form of public punishment and wrath that is both spectacular and swift. Justice delayed is justice denied. What do we want? Justice! When do we want it? Now! Lock her up! Drain the swamp!

As we scan the current political discourse on the right and the left, it is clear that our patience for political dialogue, negotiation, and due process is waning. There is a spirit growing within the West that demands a solution to human evil that is immediate and final. A distant deity does not hold the keys to hell; we do.

Medieval hell is different. It might be gruesome, but it's both delayed and distant. Medieval hell affords both the offender and the offended a measure of time and space—a critical opportunity for confession, transformation, and reconciliation. As long as the offender has breath, they still have a chance to be transformed and redeemed. The door to hell is left open a crack. Hell is not here. It is not now. There is still time for persuasion. This belief allowed early Christian theologians like Origen (ca. AD 185–253) to openly wonder if God might one day persuade Satan himself to change his path and be redeemed.[19]

But there's an even more profound difference at work here—something that emerges when we look closely at the ancient words that Jesus uses when he talks about hell. Jesus never uses hell as a weapon to judge outsiders. He never says, "Here is why those people—the ones you don't like—are going to hell." Instead, Jesus uses hell as a mirror. When he talks about hell, he's talking about you. Where might you go when you die? What eternal destiny do you deserve? What path are you on? For Jesus, hell is not a weapon we throw at others. It is not a tool of social or political control. It is a humbling and sobering mirror that each individual must hold up to themselves. Jesus wants his audience to think primarily about their own sin, not the sins of others. He wants them to ask hard questions like "Is my heart in the right place?" and "Do I deserve punishment?" If we actually read the words of Jesus, they do not inspire us to hope for hell for other people. They cause us to look for the signs of hell within ourselves.

This approach to hell creates an entirely different political dynamic.

A college student may be scrolling through social media looking for hell in the lives of criminals, broken politicians, scandalous celebrities, and sexual harassers. She never pauses to look for the power of hell within herself. Her social media feed is specifically designed to feed her what she wants: swift and spectacular forms of punishment and judgment. Through these feeds, she becomes addicted to the hellish ritual of public shaming, relishing the satisfying moment when someone gets what they deserve.

From Demons to Demonization

Beyond hell, Hobbes was also critical of religious belief in demons and devils. The real demons, he argued, are flesh and blood humans who threaten the unity and peace of the nation.

Here again is a tragic consequence of the secularization of hell. In Hobbes's attempt to abolish *spiritual* demons, he inadvertently encouraged the secular belief in *human* demons. In this brave new world, demons are the people you don't like.

It's common for modern politicians to speculate on the nefarious workings of some unwanted group of outsiders. These deplorables are lurking about, threatening the well-being of the nation. To be sure, these politicians don't believe in real demons, but they will happily demonize outsiders. With the passion of a religious zealot, these politicians will argue that the outsiders must be canceled, defeated, or deported. Voters don't call upon a priest to exorcise national demons. That is the politician's job.

There is another critical difference between the modern practice of demonization and the medieval belief in demons. People back then believed that human beings were porous; their bodies and souls were susceptible to demonic attack. To be human was to be constantly vulnerable to corruption. This is why Europeans would always say "God bless you" when someone sneezed. They were not simply wishing someone good physical health; they believed that the human soul was particularly vulnerable to spiritual attack during a sneeze. It was at this moment that demons and devils saw an opening to get in.

What do ancient sneezing rituals have to do with modern politics? The medieval sneeze would elicit a brief moment of spiritual and social concern: Your fellow citizen is not a demon, but they are vulnerable to the power of demons—just as we all are.

This represents a fundamentally different way of thinking about our fellow citizens and political opponents. They are porous and vulnerable, just like we are. They can be infected by evil political forces, just like we can. All of us are politically porous. All of us are prone to self-deception. Contrary to the modern misconception, we are not the masters of our own fate. Each one of us is vulnerable to catching a political disease. Our porous souls are vulnerable to political demons.

The Bible never names a single real person who goes to hell—not Judas, not Jezebel, not Pharaoh, not Caesar. We see these villains in all their wickedness, but we never witness their final destination. Though things look grim for these villains, the Bible leaves their final resting place a mystery. On this side of eternity, the door to redemption is always open. In fact, Jesus forgives the penitent criminal at the very last moment before he dies (Luke 23:39–43). This theological mystery has profound political consequences. When you think about your own political villains—perhaps Donald Trump or Kamala Harris, Sean Hannity or Rachel Maddow—you don't know the end of their stories either. As Christians, we are commanded to pray for them. Jesus says in Matthew 5:44, "Love your enemies and pray for those who persecute you." The final destination of their souls is not something you can control or predict. This lack of knowledge leaves the door open a crack—for connection, conversation, and freedom.

While we might laugh at our medieval counterparts for being afraid of demons, we are afraid of one another. In the world of modern politics, we pray for protection not from demons but from those who are different from us.

Our medieval forebearers could never be quite sure where the demons were, what their names were, or what they were up to. There was an element of mystery to their haunting. In modern politics, there is no mystery. We know with certainty who the evildoers are, and we can point out all their evil deeds. We have the receipts, and they will feel our wrath.

An Invitation to Hell

In the face of evil, democracy appears to require two conflicting things of its citizens. On the one hand, citizens must identify and confront social and political evil. On the other hand, citizens have to accept that democracy cannot rid the world of evil—because that same evil also lives within them. We're all capable of being led astray, even if we think we're right. Citizens must make judgments, but those judgments are never ultimate.

The persistence of hell in our modern vocabulary reflects a fundamental human intuition that actions must have consequences—that somewhere, somehow, accounts must be settled. As a constant stream of political sins goes seemingly unpunished, our moral intuition transforms into political outrage. We cry out against the countless villains who appear to get away with it, from war criminals to corrupt oligarchs, from genocidal leaders to corporate executives who knowingly harm millions for profit. In this context, hell serves a vital democratic function. It represents a firm guarantee that justice will one day be served. Criminals won't get away with it. Ultimate accountability will come regardless of the failures of our earthly structures to bring it about.

In this vein, the Quranic conception of hell operates on a principle of reciprocity: Every soul receives precisely what it has earned. This isn't mere punishment—it's also divine accounting. The metaphor of wages and earning appears repeatedly in the Quran: Actions are weighed, measured, and requited in perfect balance. More striking still is the notion that hell itself possesses a kind of intelligence, able to distinguish between degrees of wickedness and adjust punishments accordingly. Islam unequivocally views hell as a real place. Minority positions within Islamic traditions speak of hell as being metaphorical and non-corporeal,[20] but the orthodox position is that hell is real and that people will feel physical suffering and mental anguish if they are condemned to hell as their final abode.

Christianity's doctrine of grace does not mirror Islam's vision of precise reciprocity. According to Christianity, Christ has—rather unfairly—borne the consequences of sin in the place of sinners. We will explore in greater detail Christian notions of grace and mercy later on.

Hell in both Islam and Christianity is profoundly egalitarian. Simply said, anybody can go there. It doesn't matter if you are rich or poor, black or white—all people will receive a judgment. There is no way to buy, manipulate, or threaten your way out. All stand before the throne vulnerable. In this way, the doctrine of hell creates a level playing field based on an individual's character rather than their wealth or power.

Modern forms of wrath and punishment can be escaped with a good PR firm, lawyer, private island, or army. Here on earth, the wealthy can buy their way out of consequences; the powerful can shield themselves from justice. Consider how this plays out in contemporary society. When powerful figures escape justice—whether dictators dying peacefully in exile or corporate criminals receiving minor fines for major crimes—it corrodes public faith in democratic institutions. The apparent lack of just deserts for the powerful has political consequences. It feeds populist rage and democratic cynicism. In this context, the concept of ultimate justice, of a future hell, serves as a crucial safety valve.

But hell's democratic function goes beyond mere deterrence or consolation. Traditional religious conceptions of hell actually embody principles that modern democracies strive to implement: proportional punishment, equal treatment for equal crimes, consideration of both actions and intentions. The Islamic tradition, in particular, emphasizes that divine justice operates with perfect fairness, treating similar actions alike while accounting for individual circumstances and intentions.

Christianity and Hell

Christianity and Islam have several important differences when it comes to hell. But one of the most important is Christianity's strange and scandalous view of divine grace. According to the Bible, heaven is filled with people who don't deserve to be there. Christians believe that they themselves do not deserve to go to heaven—no one does. So how are all these "illegal immigrants" getting past the walls of heaven?

Repentance.

Recall the story of Jesus hanging on a cross next to a dying criminal. Approaching death, he confesses that Jesus is Lord. Seeing his honest confession, Jesus famously declares, "Today you will be with me in paradise" (Luke 23:43). If a wicked person repents, even at the last moment, they are immediately released from the threat of hell regardless of their immoral behavior on earth.

This is scandalous. Where is the justice? Non-Christians reading this are likely confused and perhaps even angry. The purpose of this section is not to convince you that this Christian belief in radical divine mercy is true, just, or rational. Instead, our goal is to offer you an invitation to consider the potential political consequences of this strange Christian belief in grace.

Think for a moment about your worst political opponents and enemies, how you want to see them lose and be brought to justice. This instinct to write off your opponents and enemies is worthy of serious democratic reflection. When a political tribe is written off, members are deemed no longer worthy of dialogue or debate. You determine that it is impossible to persuade them. Soon enough you decide that since this political tribe cannot be reasoned with, it must be defeated.

Writing off your opponents as beyond the pale is an act of democratic despair. It is here that we begin to see that democracy, at its core, requires something mysterious and ineffable—something religious communities call hope. Democracy lives and dies on the hope of debate and the hope of persuasion. Democracy depends on a mysterious and stubborn conviction that it is never too late and that no one can be written off entirely. There is always a chance to change someone's mind, always a chance for redemption.

Heaven on Earth?

Martin Luther King Jr. famously proclaimed that "the arc of the moral universe bends toward justice,"[21] a phrase that Barack Obama further popularized when he told his followers they were "on the right side of history."[22]

While King and Obama both subscribe to the Christian belief in a distant and transcendent heaven, their rhetoric in these particular moments points to the modern aspiration to work toward a more present and immanent heaven on earth. It is no accident that secular leaders have comfortably appropriated King's progressive vision of history. The promise of the modern world—particularly in the advanced democracies of the United States and Europe—is to progressively work toward the perfection of society.

Shadi's family is from what remains the world's most authoritarian region: the Middle East. What were the two most promising Arab Spring countries, Tunisia and Egypt, soon reverted to full-blown dictatorship. Injustice in the Middle East is the norm, something experienced daily by tens of millions of Arabs. And of course there are wars that seem to have no end. The dramatic decline in interstate warfare and battlefield deaths ended with Russia's invasion of Ukraine in 2022. Then Israel's brutal wars in Gaza and Lebanon followed. In times like these, King's and Obama's promise that the universe is bending toward justice feels like a cruel joke.

Some people see tragedies such as these and wonder how a higher power could ever let such things happen. This is known as "theodicy," or the puzzle of why a good God doesn't intercede to prevent suffering. In other words, this is a problem of evil. What we know of God, at least in the monotheistic faiths, is that he *could* intercede but sometimes doesn't. Despite the suffering, God sometimes allows human beings the freedom to continue on their path to destruction. God doesn't always bend history toward justice. For the sake of human freedom, God allows history to bend in multiple directions—some of them quite terrible. For example, if God had somehow acted to prevent Vladimir Putin from invading Ukraine, he would have negated Putin's freedom to decide. So, we are left with situations of profound and persistent injustice. There is a reasonable chance that, in this life, Putin will get away with it. Perhaps, then, the only prospect of true and ultimate justice for Putin and those like him is that they will face their reckoning in the next.

But Putin is only an extreme example of something that plays out in our everyday political lives. Bad people get away with things. The wrong political party wins. The righteous political referendum is defeated. Politics—because it is human—can't help but fall short of our hopes for a more just and moral universe.

There is a real cost to losing hell.

Contemplating death—and, dare we say it, punishment—has a way of focusing the mind. As Marsilius of Padua, a predecessor of Machiavelli, once noted, "The function of the priest, in fact, is to supplement the action of the police and judge by the fear of hell."[23]

The premodern state didn't have bureaucratized prison systems. Police forces were relatively small. Surveillance capabilities were obviously limited. Mass incarceration didn't yet exist. You couldn't rely on surveillance to monitor and impart justice. The medieval justice system was finite and sparse. In far-flung rural areas, police and prisons were largely unheard of.

The modern criminal justice system, on the other hand, boasts a wealth of resources for dispensing justice. Yet despite its incredible technological and financial scope, it can't perfectly dispense justice—not even close. And so in the absence of justice, what are we left with?

To put it bluntly, in a world of persistent cruelty and injustice, hell appears to be a necessary part of being human. This is why the question of hell has political consequences.

Of course, there have been ideological movements like communism that were unwilling to accept the imperfect nature of political arrangements in the here and now. If heaven wasn't possible in another world, it would have to be made possible in this world. Or so the thinking went. This gave rise to various utopian schemes.

If a political movement promises heaven on earth, most of us know, instinctually, that it's time to run for the hills. Historically speaking, such movements are willing to crush the things of earth for the sake of their heavenly vision. Communists sought to create a heavenly state of sharing and the perfect distribution of goods. They made the lives of millions a living hell as a result. This wasn't exactly surprising.

There are other, less obvious turns of phrase that we take for granted, like the notion that we can "overcome evil" through politics. Have we ever really taken a moment to think of the implications of such a phrase? It's messianic. It is a way of superimposing the vastness of God onto the smallness of politics. In reality, the domain of temporal politics is simply not equipped for a goal as ultimate and transcendent as ending evil. Perfection—at least in this life—isn't possible.

The late Jesuit priest and philosopher James Schall had a wonderful, albeit frightening, way of capturing the paradox of secularism's desire to overcome evil: "The belief that evil can be removed by political action, thus, turns out to be the cause for the secularization of hell as a political instrument to justify the good life."[24] This is why hell is so important. If you take hell seriously, it can lift a critical burden from your politics. Suddenly, the next election does not need to fulfill all your hopes and dreams. It does not need to make your country great again. It does not need to bring all evildoers to account. It does not need to dispense perfect justice, because that justice is coming from elsewhere. It is not yours, and it is not today. But it will come soon enough.

6

From Cancel Culture to Covenant Culture

KEY TAKEAWAY

Cancel culture is a form of mob justice that offers no room for redemption. The ancient concept of covenant offers something our politics desperately lacks: the conviction that we're bound to one another even when we can't stand each other.

Halloween was coming, and Yale was spooked. It was 2015, and a group of deans worried that some students might wear racially insensitive Halloween costumes. Doing what deans do, they wrote a strongly worded letter instructing students to select culturally appropriate costumes.

In response, Nicholas and Erika Christakis, who served as co-masters of a Yale residential college, sent an email to their students gently suggesting that they could make these judgment calls for themselves. Their gentle pushback against a top-down approach to cultural policing unleashed an extraordinary level of outrage from some of the students. The controversy did not go viral until a video was released of Nicholas attempting to engage angry students in a thoughtful and respectful dialogue. They would have none of it. Enraged, they surrounded Nicholas, yelled obscenities, and called him disgusting.

By the end of the academic year, both Nicholas and Erika had resigned their positions. Erika—a scholar in early childhood education—never taught at Yale again.[1]

This incident perfectly captures what is known as "cancel culture"—a phenomenon in which perceived transgressors face overwhelming social punishment for a perceived error or offense. The university crowd's visceral reaction to a mild email about Halloween costumes shows how today's moral conflicts rapidly escalate into confrontations that allow no room for proportionality or forgiveness.

One of our main arguments throughout this book has been that as religion recedes from American public life, political disagreements take on a quasi-religious fervor. The Yale incident exemplifies what we might call "religion without religion." What's missing in this new age is not the religious intensity of moral conviction but rather the ancient religious frameworks for humility and reconciliation when violations inevitably occur.

Both Islam and Christianity teach us that strong moral convictions don't necessarily require excommunicating those who disagree with us. As we will demonstrate, we can believe sincerely in our convictions without needing to expel others. Religious traditions actually provide resources for maintaining community despite deep disagreements. Far from constantly demanding exclusion, both Islam and Christianity contain rich traditions of inclusion, reconciliation, and maintaining community bonds even amid disagreement. This is the "covenantal" aspect of religion.

"Covenant" is a way of speaking about the fundamental fabric—the sacred bond—that connects individuals to one another and to God, embedding individuals in something deeper and more lasting than a mere contract. Rather than a passing relationship built on fleeting self-interest, covenant implies a commitment to one another that transcends temporary disagreements or political differences. Signing on to a covenant, whether literally or figuratively, means that while you may disagree with and even dislike your covenantal partner, at the end of the day you share a sacred bond that goes beyond self-interest and keeps you united.

American citizens today still have the remnants of a sort of covenantal bond. We pledge allegiance to this ineffable community we call America. We sing songs, offer oaths, raise flags, praise heroes, honor martyrs, and observe moments of silence. To be sure, the covenantal bonds of our national community are increasingly thin and tattered, but they're still there. If we think of the United States as its own kind of covenantal community whose sacred bonds run deeper than mere self-interest, the same logic applies: However much you might feel repelled by the political beliefs of some of your fellow Americans and however much you might wish they would just go away, *they're still your fellow Americans*.

That means something, or at least it used to.

Defining Cancel Culture

The term *cancel culture* refers to bad actors (real or perceived) being called out in a public forum. These individuals are surrounded, bullied, and ultimately excommunicated from public life and polite company. They may lose their jobs, platforms, relationships, or livelihoods. Pilar Blitvich defines cancel culture as "a modern form of ostracism in which someone (the *cancelee*) is thrust out of social or professional circles as a result of being fired, deplatformed or boycotted by others, the *canceler*s. The *cancelee* is also subjected to public shaming and censorship and often faces serious financial, and even legal, repercussions for having engaged in different types of behavior perceived as immoral."[2] There is always an element of mass hysteria in cancel culture, as if the desire to punish has its own mind and can't be stopped, no matter how silly or absurd the attempt might be.

We see the destructive effects of cancel culture in universities, newspaper staffs, political campaigns, corporate spaces, and social media. In their book *The Canceling of the American Mind*, Greg Lukianoff and Rikki Schlott note that cancellation attempts reached their peak in 2020. The result was a climate of fear and self-censorship. Seventy-two percent of conservative faculty members said they feared losing their job or reputation for expressing unpopular opinions, while 45 percent of liberal professors admitted they were willing to discriminate against conservatives in faculty searches.[3] Historian Paul Du Quenoy has observed that 48 percent of Democrats believe that cancel culture seriously threatens their personal freedoms, while an astonishing 88 percent of Americans believe that cancel culture is a problem. He notes that more than half of the US population fears losing their job if they express an unfavorable political opinion, while a shocking 80 percent of American college students have self-censored their speech for fear of negative repercussions.[4]

Victims of internet-based cancellation encounter a novel form of retributive justice, compared with traditional forms of tribal or religious excommunication. Tribal discipline often comes from a known authority figure, an elder or patriarch. It is limited by shared history, tradition, and custom—a communal covenant. Religious and tribal justice are always enacted face-to-face through an embodied and established relationship or institution. By contrast, people being canceled in recent years faced instantaneous, chaotic, and anonymous disciplinary action from a mob of online strangers. The stones are hurled with great force from everywhere, and yet seemingly nowhere.

Cancel culture is often viewed as a left-wing phenomenon, but it can just as easily come from the right, as we have increasingly witnessed with the attempts by the Trump administration and other Republicans to punish individuals for pro-Palestinian speech.[5] Increasingly longing for ideologically pure communities and organizations, those on both the right and the left regularly (and with great vigor) purge their own political parties of those who are ideologically impure. Cancel culture has popped up in right- and left-wing colleges, businesses, churches, clubs, organizations, and even families.

One point of clarification is important here: We are in no way concerned with negative press directed at criminals, predators, and abusers. Lawbreakers should be punished. This chapter concerns, rather, the trend in American public life wherein people are forcefully shamed and excluded simply for believing in, or appearing to believe in, the "wrong" thing. Moreover, sometimes a passionate "angry mob" is exactly what democracy requires. Sometimes quick shifts in public opinion are important. Sometimes people need to speak out and say enough is enough. In one prominent example, the #MeToo movement fostered an important cultural shift in which many victims of sexual violence and exploitation were emboldened to share their personal narratives on social media. As the movement gained prominence and as more and more victims spoke out, figures like Harvey Weinstein, who sexually exploited women for decades, were unmasked as predators, subjected to criminal prosecution, and eventually imprisoned. So-called angry mobs are, in this way, a vital and necessary element of the democratic process.

That said, angry mobs need to be paired with—and chastened by—things like due process and basic democratic institutions, norms and virtues, and checks and balances. Detached from reality, community, and basic decency, a mob cannot impact democratic life for the better; it can only contribute to its destruction. When we describe cancel culture, we are neither objecting to protest nor denying that the court of public opinion has a role to play. Rage against real evil matters. Rather, we are insisting that the mob must remain connected and committed to due process, democratic norms, and the deeper covenantal bonds that connect us as Americans. Without these things, our moral longing for justice endangers the very democratic culture it depends on.

Canceling Democracy

Democracy rests on a cultural and moral foundation. This includes the assumption of basic human dignity, the presumption of innocence, the possibility of compromise, the capacity for patience, and equality before the law. Cancel culture actively undermines them all. In the world of cancel culture, the law is selectively enforced, and justice is arbitrarily executed. When cancel culture wields the gavel, the punishment meted out will be determined by the momentary enthusiasm and attention of the crowd. If they get distracted, you're off the hook. If they fashion an effective meme, watch out.

Democratic institutions depend on compromise, patience, consensus building, and negotiation. Cancel culture, however, sees these actions as a sign of moral weakness and corruption.

Modern democratic states are massive and complicated bureaucratic machines. Discussing their reform requires careful attention to detail and comfort with complexity. Cancel culture is allergic to complexity.

Democratic cultures need citizens and leaders who practice patience, humility, and forbearance; cancel culture rewards and often encourages their opposite. On social media, a "cancel warrior" is rewarded with more followers if they are constantly engaged in righteous battles for ideological purity. Social media's cancel economy will never ask them to reflect on their own need for personal growth, patience, or humility.

Cancel culture does not have the patience or capacity for real political reform. In fact, it actively undermines it. Exhausted by constant fits of outrage, citizens lack the requisite energy to do the long, hard work of grassroots political organizing. Social media outrage saps voters of the persistent focus and strength they need for lasting action and sustainable change. In the end, cancel culture convinces citizens that slow political engagement in the system is pointless. The only viable option is mob justice.

Healthy democracies require what we might call a culture of risk-taking, a courageous willingness on the part of citizens to step into a noisy and competitive public square and share their political opinions, feelings, and convictions. Democracy requires that citizens be ready and willing to take chances and make mistakes. Bad ideas are not only welcome but also needed. To be sure, the public square will never be a safe space; ideas will be contested. That said, citizens need to believe that the public square is *safe enough* for them to voice their opinions without having their lives destroyed.

Cancel culture inhibits democratic risk-taking. Citizens are no longer willing to take chances. They begin to keep their moral and political opinions to themselves. They start to speak two languages—one in public and one in private. They edit themselves.

Unaired, their political and moral grievances begin to smolder beneath the surface. Soon enough citizens create small, secluded, and anonymous echo chambers where they air their grievances. They hang out in the dark corners of the internet where they receive no critique or correction. Their bad ideas are only affirmed and amplified. Grievances fester, then explode.

In a healthy democratic culture, bad ideas remain, but they are regularly vented. Openly voiced, bad ideas and grievances can be examined and challenged.

We've Always Canceled

"What he just said is completely beyond the pale." "Beyond the pale" is a tired phrase, but its origins offer important insight.

In the Middle Ages, England controlled a portion of the wild and "uncivilized" land in Ireland, which was blocked off by a series of wooden fence posts—or pales. "Within the pale" meant the realm of English law and order. "Beyond the pale" was a realm of Irish barbarism and violence. For the English, to be beyond the pale was to be lawless, uncivilized, unholy, almost subhuman. Once labeled "beyond the pale," the Irish barbarians could be subjected to English imperial violence and reeducation. Being subhuman, they were a problem to be solved.

While *cancel culture* is a new term, it reveals a universal social practice. Simply put, protect the herd. In the interests of social purity and security, members of a tribe gather to police the boundaries and expel all social sickness, real or perceived.

In a way, canceling people is a tribal necessity. Every human community has some sort of boundary—a limit to what the community will tolerate. You can't be a Red Sox fan and also cheer for the Yankees. If all the Red Sox fans cheered for the Yankees, their community would cease to exist. In this sense, canceling a Yankee fan helps Red Sox fans understand who they truly are. Moments of expulsion are a way of becoming a human community.[6] Members of the group come to know who they are by asserting what sorts of behavior are out of bounds.

That said, things can get out of hand quickly. If you've spent any time in the outfield bleachers, you know what we mean.

Hannah Arendt has observed that political ideologies create an "iron band of terror" that compresses people against one another, destroying the in-between space where genuine pluralism can exist.[7] You are either for us or against us.

Social scientists have found that a human being's capacity for cruelty tends to grow in and through their connection to a larger social group. In the infamous Stanford prison experiment, university students were arbitrarily divided into two groups of guards and prisoners to simulate the circumstances of life in prison. The guards were trained to think as a group rather than as individuals. After only six days, the experiment had to be shut down because of the guards' increasing cruelty. With little prompting, the group had transformed itself into a mob. The individuals found themselves behaving in ways they could not have imagined had they been on their own.[8]

Christian theologian Reinhold Niebuhr attests to this mob mentality in his famous book *Moral Man and Immoral Society*. Niebuhr's thesis is clear: Groups tend to magnify individuals' selfish impulses. Left on their own, individuals might be capable of controlling their anger and suppressing their selfishness. Incorporated into a tribe, these individuals might not be so selfless. Niebuhr argues that collective identities—whether social, economic, or national—can dampen our individual moral restraint and even encourage coercion.[9] The tribe has an interest in creating conflict because this is how it sustains its sense of unity, identity, and purpose. If we are not fighting, who are we?

Niebuhr's work can help us understand a vexing tragedy of public life. How can a young man's selfless love for his country—his desire to serve and even sacrifice himself on an individual level—so quickly be swept up in collective movements of violence, hatred, and evil? Niebuhr writes, "The paradox is that patriotism transmutes individual unselfishness into national egoism. . . . The unselfishness of individuals makes for the selfishness of nations."[10] For the sake of the tribe, the group is willing to do awful things no individual would imagine or consider.

Who Are You Calling "Tribal"?

Following the contentious presidential election of 2016, University of California Berkeley linguist Geoff Nunberg selected *tribalism* as 2017's word of the year.[11] In doing so, he drew attention to a fundamental shift in American public life. Politics was replacing religion as the most central form of American identity formation.[12] More than this, tribal acts of cancellation and expulsion were the primary ways in which political movements were developing their sense of identity and purpose.

Today, the term *tribal* is an epithet, a sort of shorthand for group behaviors that are selfish and cruel, distrusting and uncivilized. The term is also unfortunately a backhanded insult to ancient and Indigenous communities. The assumption here is that ancient tribes were violent, fearful, hateful, and irrational, while modern communities should be civilized, open, selfless, and forward-thinking. To be tribal is to be uncivilized.

But anthropologists have studied real tribal societies, and they have demonstrated that tribal acts of exclusion and excommunication were only one part of a much larger and more multifaceted process by which tribal identity was formed. These practices were ultimately the means by which individuals were restored to the community.

Devaka Premawardhana has drawn from participant observation of life among the Makhuwa people of Mozambique. He argues that Indigenous tribes have, for millennia, "put at least as much energy into forging alliances and seeking new terrain as they have into closing ranks and bearing arms."[13] They see themselves as flourishing best in community—their lives are bound up in one another's. The Makhuwa people form their identity primarily around acts of communal restoration and inclusion rather than exclusion.

Life among so-called tribal peoples such as the Makhuwa operates not according to the Western Darwinian law of survival of the fittest or the idea of the isolated individual ("I think therefore I am") but according to the trans-African notion of *ubuntu* ("I am because we are, and we are because I am").[14] An individual's process of becoming is not an individual journey; it is bound up in the group's process of becoming. The term captures a recognition of human dignity and interdependence. To be human is to grow in recognition and respect of others.

When South Africans needed to develop a modern response to the horrors of apartheid, they reached all the way back to this idea of *ubuntu*. The injustice and hatred of apartheid had left the social ties and bonds of modern South African society in tatters. They needed a way to repair those ties. If democracy was going to work, they needed to find a way to cultivate civic trust. Lacking modern resources for individual connectedness and interdependence, they found that they needed to look back in time, not forward. Black and white communities torn apart by violence and mistrust could never be stitched back together with a mere contract—they needed a covenant.

Designed for Covenant

As a species, we are obsessed with making promises. We make promises in friendship and business; we pledge ourselves to spouses and nations; we swear on the lives of our children and in the names of our gods. Politicians have never met a promise they didn't like. Wherever we go, we are constantly making commitments, vows, and oaths. As independent as we moderns pretend to be, we just keep binding ourselves with promises.

Why?

The answer can be found in the ancient Hebrew term *berith*. Translated as "covenant," the term connotes a form of solemn commitment between two parties that speaks to a deeper connection that cannot be fully defined—a divine bond of solidarity and fellowship. A covenant says, "We are committed. We are bound."

A covenant is much more than a legal contract or a spoken promise. It is grounded in a sacred understanding of a sort of divine webbing that binds individuals to one another and to God. This divine webbing demands our respect and honor.

In Judaism, Islam, and Christianity, covenantal bonds are both vertical and horizontal. Human beings have a vertical bond with God and a variety of horizontal bonds with their neighbors. In a nation bound by a covenant, individuals are not the captains of their fate. They are bound to one another in civic loyalty. In this way, the ancient concept of covenant humbles our individual claims to autonomy and self-interest.

Covenant invokes a strong preference for inclusion over exclusion, for restoration over excommunication. On a purely pragmatic level, if

Christians and Muslims were endlessly obsessed with religious purity, exclusion, and expulsion, they wouldn't have been able to grow their adherents to roughly four and a half billion people. Historical examples of religious excommunication attract considerable attention precisely because they are so rare and traumatizing for both the individual and the covenant community.

Muslims, Jews, and Christians believe that when God created human beings, he knit these individuals together into mutually reinforcing communities (marriages, families, tribes, and so on). God designed human beings to live in covenantal community. Human beings were created as social beings, woven into collective bodies larger than their individual selves. They were made to be both independent and dependent, free and bound.

Whenever modern people make a promise that includes "I swear to God"—to their friends, their business partners, their constituents, or even their nation—they're appealing to a deeper form of human connection and communion. When they name God, they're introducing a third party, a witness, someone to guarantee the oath (whether or not they believe in God or intend to keep the promise). Their vertical covenant with God demands they honor their horizontal covenants with others—honesty in trade, fidelity in marriage, allegiance in citizenship, and truth telling in speech.

Covenant in Ancient Israel: A Bloody Mess

Abraham is regarded as the spiritual forefather of Jews, Christians, and Muslims alike. The book of Genesis tells a particularly strange and gruesome story of a divine promise that involves something called a "bloodpath." Within this path, a bond between God and Abraham is sealed in actual blood. While the story seems rather ghastly and gory, this ancient ritual offers an important political insight for modern cancel culture.

Abraham is old and childless. And yet, despite this, God pledges that Abraham's descendants will outnumber the stars in the sky. God will bind God's very self to Abraham and his many descendants. He will be their God and they will be his people. This is God's solemn covenant, and this promise will be sealed in blood.

God instructs Abraham to take a heifer, a ram, and a goat and to cut each of the animals in half. The two halves of their bodies are then placed in symmetrical rows so that their blood flows into a center path between them.

In the ancient world, when two parties wished to make a covenant with each other, they would walk together through the bloodpath to viscerally convey the costly consequences of either party breaking the covenant. The gory nature of this ritual communicated the seriousness of the bond. Walking the bloodpath together communicated that both parties were equally responsible for fulfilling the covenant.

But that is not what happens with Abraham. Abraham does not walk with God through the bloodpath. God goes alone. According to the story, a smoking firepot and a flaming torch—symbols of God's presence—pass through the path (Gen. 15:17). In other words, God takes full responsibility for the covenantal bond by taking the consequences for its violation upon himself. God thus ensures that, regardless of Abraham's behavior and regardless of his failure, God will honor the bond and God will follow through on his promise to Abraham's descendants no matter what. This is not a contract that dissolves when one side makes a mistake. It's a covenant.

Even if you've never read the Bible, what God is doing in this story is clear: God is forging an eternal bond.

What seems like a private ritual between Abraham and his God has profound public and political consequences for Abraham's descendants, Christians and Muslims included. The nation of Israel is expected to form covenantal bonds with one another and with their tribes. Among the children of Abraham, the connections between husbands and wives, workers and employers, children and parents, priests and people are to be covenantal, not contractual. These relationships are not to be based on competition or consumption, persuasion or power. Rather, God wants the fundamental grounding for all human relationships to be that of covenant.

Reality, of course, is much messier. The children of Abraham constantly fail to honor their covenant commitments. But regardless of their failures, God not only remains faithful to his commitments but also continually restores their families, tribes, farms, and communities.

We still experience something like this today in the United States. Despite our political divisions, we continue to come together. Despite our fighting and our failures, we continue to long for community and connection. We continue to make promises. Why? Because we're made for it.

Judaism, Islam, and Christianity would argue that the reason Americans continue to connect and commune with one another is that God designed human beings to be communal and covenantal creatures. The ties that bind us are not mortal—they are divine. They originate in God, and it is God who sustains them.

Whenever we pledge ourselves—to our nation, our spouse, or our friend—our vow speaks to a deeper reality, to a human connection that comes from God. We were designed for dependence. We were designed for one another. It is a human thing to make a promise. It is a divine thing to keep it.

Why does it hurt so much to be canceled? Why is the threat of cancellation so powerful? It is not because a social contract is being nullified; it is because a sacred covenant is being destroyed.

Restoring the Canceled in Ancient Israel

If covenantal bonds were so important, the ancient Israelites would need a way to restore canceled individuals and welcome them back into the bonds of their community. The Israelites had five practices for restoration after the traumatic moment of exclusion and expulsion.

1. Confession: In the presence of their covenant community, individuals could publicly admit and confess their wrongdoing and ask for forgiveness (Lev. 5:5; Num. 5:5–7; Prov. 28:13).
2. Reparation: In the presence of their covenant community, individuals could pay an equitable reparation to the offended party (Exod. 22:1–4; Num. 5:6–8; Ezek. 33:14–16).

3. Atonement: In the presence of their covenant community, individuals could make a public sacrifice atoning for their sin. Once and for all the sin would be gone (Lev. 4:27–31; 6:1–7; 16:30).
4. Purification: In the presence of their covenant community, individuals could undergo a ritual purification by which they were permanently and completely cleansed of their sin (Lev. 13–14).
5. Declaration: In the presence of their covenant community, the priest could publicly declare the guilty individual to be fully cleansed and deserving of communal reintegration (Lev. 13–14; Num. 6:22–27).

One more ancient practice bears mentioning here. In the world of cancel culture, it is not uncommon for the *children* of the cancelee to suffer guilt by association. Despite their innocence, these children are shunned for something their parents did. We might call this the problem of "cross-generational cancellation." Consider a president's children and grandchildren who are forced to reckon with the sins of the father.

Ancient Israel had a practice that speaks directly to the generational aspect of cancellation. Imagine a particular Israelite farmer is a drunk, a gambler, a criminal, or just plain lazy. His debts pile up, and he loses his family farm. His personal mistakes (and debts) would be visited upon his children and grandchildren for generations to come with no end in sight.

The Israelites had an ingenious way to stop this kind of generational devastation. Every fifty years, God commanded the Israelites to observe a year of jubilee, when all debts were canceled and all family farms were returned to their original owners (Lev. 25). By right of jubilee, a family's dignity and livelihood could never be ruined by a single generation.

Cancellation, it seems, had an expiration date.

Jesus and Cancel Culture

Human groups have always understood the necessity of communal discipline and mercy. They are a creative combination of both hard truth and generous grace. One of the challenges of cancel culture is that it wrongly assumes that holding an individual accountable and offering them mercy are somehow mutually exclusive. It is admittedly difficult to hold these two elements together at the same time. But, as we will see, it's absolutely critical.

Christianity is not ultimately about a set of beliefs. It's about a person—Jesus. According to Christians, Jesus in his personhood perfectly embodies both accountability and mercy, both truth and grace.

A story from Jesus's life captures this critical connection. In John 8, a group of religious leaders drags a woman who has been caught in adultery before Jesus. They interrupt Jesus's teaching and demand to know if she should be stoned. While they shout for an answer, Jesus does a curious thing.

> Jesus bent down and started to write on the ground with his finger. When they kept on questioning him, he straightened up and said to them, "Let any one of you who is without sin be the first to throw a stone at her." Again he stooped down and wrote on the ground.
>
> At this, those who heard began to go away one at a time, the older ones first, until only Jesus was left, with the woman still standing there. Jesus straightened up and asked her, "Woman, where are they? Has no one condemned you?"
>
> "No one, sir," she said.
>
> "Then neither do I condemn you," Jesus declared. "Go now and leave your life of sin." (8:1–11)

Here we see Christ offering both accountability and mercy. Jesus speaks a word of accountability to the woman. She is indeed guilty of adultery, and Jesus says so. She must change her ways and leave her life of sin. But Jesus does not stop there. He also speaks a word of grace. She need not be canceled. She need not be killed. Instead, she is offered a path to communal restoration.

Offering both accountability and mercy at the same time, Jesus embodies a Jewish principle he learned as a child. The prophet Micah asks God, "What do you want from the Israelite people? How should we behave? What should we bring you?" Here is God's reply: "He has shown you, O mortal, what is good. And what does the Lord require of you? To act justly and to love mercy and to walk humbly with your God" (Mic. 6:8).

How can we modern citizens hold together our longing for public accountability and our own need for grace and forgiveness? The prophet Micah suggests it will require a third element: a more humble form of walking through the world.

The story of the adulterous woman contains two other critical lessons. The first concerns hypocrisy. Jesus demands that the cancelers do the hard work of introspection. They must take their eyes off the woman for a moment and consider their own lives. Jesus invites them to consider the fact that their lust for accountability resembles the lust of the woman. If they go forward with condemning this woman, they open themselves up to their own condemnation. If they take a hard look at themselves, they will have to admit that they are also worthy of cancellation. In a similar fashion, the apostle Paul cautions his fellow Christians:

> You, therefore, have no excuse, you who pass judgment on someone else, for at whatever point you judge another, you are condemning yourself, because you who pass judgment do the same things. Now we know that God's judgment against those who do such things is based on truth. So when you, a mere human being, pass judgment on them and yet do the same things, do you think you will escape God's judgment? Or do you show contempt for the riches of his kindness, forbearance and patience, not realizing that God's kindness is intended to lead you to repentance? (Rom. 2:1–4)

There is a second important lesson in Jesus's encounter with the woman. Cancel culture longs to bring swift justice to perpetrators, but Jesus chooses to slow things down. While the accusers are peppering him with questions, he stoops down and slowly draws in the dirt. Slowing things down, Jesus calmly invites the accusers to pause and reflect on what they are doing.

Jesus's disciples mimic this practice of slowing down. One of them, James, famously declares that the Christian community must be "quick to listen, slow to speak and slow to become angry, because human anger does not produce the righteousness that God desires" (James 1:19–20).

In the Gospel of Matthew, Jesus provides further instruction on dealing with offenders. Rather than dragging them into the city square for a public shaming, Jesus recommends an initial private conversation: "If your brother or sister sins, go and point out their fault, just between the two of you. If they listen to you, you have won them over. But if they will not listen, take one or two others along, so that 'every matter may be established by the testimony of two or three witnesses.' If they still refuse to listen, tell it to the church; and if they refuse to listen even to the church, treat them as you would a pagan or a tax collector" (18:15–17). The wisdom of this approach is that the offender is given multiple opportunities to repent. Once again, pace is a factor. The accuser and offender both are given a critical pause, a moment of reflection, in between each confrontation.

But Jesus is also a realist. He is fully aware that some offenders will refuse to confess and change no matter the evidence, no matter the scale of confrontation. Even Jesus has limits. And so he concludes that if the offenders refuse to listen even to the church, they have to be excluded. Jesus commands that his community show tremendous mercy to repentant sinners, pagans, and tax collectors, but the key is that they actually have to repent.

If one day the offender changes their mind and decides to return, repent, and change their ways, Paul says that the community has no choice in the matter. It must offer the offender restoration. He writes, "You ought to forgive and comfort him, so that he will not be overwhelmed by excessive sorrow. I urge you, therefore, to reaffirm your love for him" (2 Cor. 2:6–8). The covenantal connection must immediately be reestablished, the bonds restored.

Canceling Muslims

Muslim Americans have experienced cancel culture in two very different contexts: the American cancellation of Islam post-9/11 and the practice of individual Muslims canceling one another. Both phenomena are rooted in a failure of certain parties to engage critically and compassionately with differing perspectives, and both run counter to the principles of healthy democratic coexistence and the teachings of Islam itself.

Since September 11, 2001, American politicians and pundits across the ideological spectrum—though primarily on the right—have built careers on fearmongering about creeping sharia and Islam's supposed incompatibility with American values. These aren't just intellectually dishonest arguments; they're deeply harmful ones that reduce a global faith tradition and its approximately two billion adherents to a flat caricature of suspicion and hostility. In the post-9/11 era, prominent American Muslims have been routinely targeted for being unfaithful to the American Constitution, for being sympathetic to terrorism, and for speaking out about the Palestinian cause.

Consider the grotesque spectacle that unfolded when Keith Ellison became the first Muslim elected to Congress in 2006. Dennis Prager, writing in his widely circulated column, declared that Ellison should not be allowed to use the Quran for his ceremonial oath, arguing that "if you are incapable of taking an oath on [the Bible], don't serve in Congress."[15] More recently, we witnessed an even more stomach-turning display during Adeel Mangi's confirmation hearings for the Third Circuit Court of Appeals in 2023. Despite being an Oxford- and Harvard-educated corporate lawyer with sterling qualifications, Mangi—who would have been the first Muslim American federal appellate judge—was subjected to what can only be described as an inquisition. Senator Ted Cruz demanded, "Do you condemn the atrocities of the Hamas terrorists?" Senator Tom Cotton asked whether he believed "Zionist settler colonialism was a provocation that justified Hamas' atrocity." Most repulsively, Senator John Kennedy insinuated that Mangi "celebrate[s] 9/11."[16] These questions had nothing to do with Mangi's legal qualifications and everything to do with performative loyalty rituals. Needless to say, Mangi wasn't confirmed. When we cancel Muslims in this way, we're not just attacking a religion—we're attacking the dignity and humanity of millions of our fellow Americans.

This behavior closely mirrors a problem within Islam itself: the misuse of *takfir*—the practice of declaring someone a nonbeliever.

Like today's cancel culture, *takfir* has been weaponized by some Muslims to ostracize those who think differently, even though the practice is one of the harshest things a Muslim can do to a fellow believer.

Against the rush to judge others' faith, the Prophet Muhammad issued a stern warning: "When a person calls his brother (in Islam) a disbeliever, one of them will certainly deserve the title. If the addressee is so as he has asserted, the disbelief of the man is confirmed, but if it is untrue, then it will revert to him."[17] In other words, to call another Muslim an unbeliever is to make yourself into an unbeliever. Another tradition puts it more starkly: "Cursing a believer is like killing him, and whoever accuses a believer of unbelief, it is as if he killed him."[18] The Quran also cautions, "O believers, when you are journeying in the path of God, be discriminating, and do not say to him who offers you a greeting, 'Thou art not a believer,' seeking the chance goods of the present life" (Q 4:94).

God warns us of the pitfalls of judgment because God alone can truly judge the heart. Human beings, with our limited perspective and understanding, should be far more circumspect about rendering final verdicts on others. Once again we see the power and necessity of intellectual humility. We are not God. We are mere mortals, and however smart or well-intentioned we think we are, our knowledge and understanding are inherently limited.

Yet throughout Islamic history, just as in our own time, some Muslims chose to ignore this wisdom. The early Kharijites provide a cautionary tale. They were notorious for their rigid criteria of belief and their eagerness to excommunicate anyone who fell short of their standards.[19] Their legacy—and the destruction they wrought—reminds us that the impulse toward ideological purity and exclusion is nothing new.

What's fascinating is how Islamic scholars developed sophisticated frameworks to counter this very human tendency. The great fourteenth-century theologian Ibn Taymiyya, despite his hardline reputation, was remarkably careful about excommunication and escalating disagreements more generally. He wrote, "Many of the disagreements among people stem from general and ambiguous terms and from lack of understanding what the other person means. . . . If this were clarified, much of the disagreement would vanish."[20] His approach was to seek understanding first, exclusion last.

But perhaps no figure better exemplifies Islam's resistance to cancel culture than the eleventh-century scholar al-Ghazali. He essentially argues that *takfir* is a dangerous dead end—that extreme caution should be exercised before writing someone off as beyond the pale.[21] In his work *Faḍāʾiḥ al-Bāṭiniyya*, al-Ghazali differentiates between the leaders of deviant sects—those who knowingly promote erroneous doctrines—and their followers, who may have been misled into adopting such views. To these followers, whose theological understanding is limited, he attributes only heresy rather than outright apostasy.[22] Al-Ghazali understood something that our contemporary cancel culture seems too often to forget: Human beings are complex, capable of confusion but also of growth and change. Religious texts can yield multiple interpretations. What looks like apostasy to one person might be sincere searching to another.

Islamic scholars make another crucial distinction that modern cancel culture completely misses: the difference between exterior actions and interior intent. This is the distinction between what classical scholars called the *zahir* (apparent) and the *batin* (hidden).

When the great jurist Imam al-Shafi'i declared that the famous hadith "actions are judged by intentions" comprises "one-third of knowledge," he wasn't being hyperbolic.[23] As Ibn Rajab explains, motivations and intention transform everything—the same physical act can be worship or mere exercise, charity or showing off, depending on what moves the heart.[24] But—and this is where it gets fascinating—Islamic law insists that we can judge only the *zahir*, the outward manifestation. *Nahnu nahkum bil-zahir*, the principle goes: We judge by what's apparent. What we can't see, we can't judge. Allah alone knows the secrets of hearts.

This creates an almost impossible standard for *takfir*, for declaring someone an outsider. You need definitive proof of an invisible intention—something humans rarely possess. The tradition even encourages Muslims to make "seventy excuses" for their fellow believers.[25]

Before you rush to judgment, exhaust every charitable possibility or interpretation.

Consider how different this is from cancel culture. When someone appears to make a mistake or expresses an unpopular view, cancel culture reduces them entirely to that moment and that apparent choice. There's no space for context, no time for explanation, no room for growth, no possibility for redemption. The person becomes nothing more than their worst social media post or most poorly chosen words.

In the Islamic understanding, the door to redemption is never permanently closed. God remains infinitely receptive to sincere repentance, *tawba*, and this divine model is meant to shape human communities as well. We're supposed to create space and time for people to acknowledge their mistakes, learn from them, and find their way back into community.

Only God possesses perfect knowledge, which makes all our human judgments necessarily provisional. Maybe, just maybe, we might be wrong about someone. Maybe, just maybe, they deserve another chance. The Islamic tradition suggests a humble approach: Judge carefully, forgive readily, and always leave room for redemption.

Purity over Covenant

Cancel culture is committed to purity. And yet, in its zeal for purity, it destroys community.

Dietrich Bonhoeffer, a German Christian who resisted Nazism, wrote about the danger of communities that value purity above all else. He believed that the dream of a pure community was detrimental to building a real community with real people—who are, by all accounts, quite difficult to live with. In his landmark work on human community titled *Life Together*, Bonhoeffer warns, "The person who loves their dream of community will destroy community, but the person who loves those around them will create community."[26] True community, for Bonhoeffer, requires accepting rather than expelling the imperfect. Dreaming about a pure, ideal community as opposed to building a real community with members who are anything but perfect is dangerous.

Similarly, Martin Luther King Jr., when advocating for racial justice and reconciliation, found that he needed to draw on ancient Jewish and Christian metaphors to do so. Based on his understanding of the "beloved community," King insisted that communal restoration was always possible even though it would always be messy. He wrote, "There is some good in the worst of us and some evil in the best of us."[27] To believe this—and act accordingly—is easier said than done, but that doesn't make it any less necessary.

In the fourth century, Gregory of Nyssa was the first church father to formally speak out against the practice of slavery. And yet, while Gregory condemned the slave trade, he did not condemn the enslavers. Instead of canceling them, he engaged them directly in a process of patient yet strong persuasion. He did this in a unique and telling way. In a sermon, Gregory reminded the slave owners of their covenantal connectedness to both God and slave alike. The practice of slavery dishonored this covenantal bond. Gregory argued,

> If man is made in the likeness of God, and rules the whole earth, and has been granted authority over everything on earth from God, who is his buyer, tell me? who is his seller? To God alone belongs this power; or rather, not even to God himself. For [God's] *gracious gifts*, it says, *are irrevocable* (Rom. 11:29). God would not therefore reduce the human race to slavery, since he himself, when we had been enslaved to sin, spontaneously recalled us to freedom. But if God does not enslave what is free, who is he that sets his own power above God's?[28]

Gregory called enslavers into a closer covenantal relationship with both God and the enslaved. Within these covenantal bonds of sacred dignity, so the thinking went, slavery becomes unimaginable. After all, if Jesus established a covenantal relationship of freedom with the slave, shouldn't slave owners do the same?

Cancellation Is Cheap; Covenant Is Costly

Cancel culture is a universal temptation. Both religious and secular tribes fall prey to it. If healthy democratic cultures are going to flourish, all of us—religious and secular—are going to need resources to resist the temptation to excommunicate and expel.

This is especially important in a pluralistic democracy like the United States. Here, people of different faiths, cultures, and moralities need to not only coexist but also challenge one another with a spirit of civility and openness. For creatures who are naturally tempted to cancel, this is a tall task. Cancellation is cheap; covenant is costly.

Coauthors W. Christopher Stewart, Chris Seiple, and Dennis Hoover coined the term *covenantal pluralism*.[29] By this, they mean a commitment to a shared life across deep differences that doesn't demand agreement but does require relationship. The authors aren't advocating for moral relativism; rather, in their view, "a world of covenantal pluralism is characterized both by a constitutional order of equal rights and responsibilities and by a culture of reciprocal commitment to engaging, respecting, and protecting the other—albeit without necessarily conceding equal veracity or moral equivalence to the beliefs and behaviors of others."[30] This approach rejects both the cruelty of exclusion and the callousness of indifference.

As secular democracies continue the search for creative ways for people to live together amid difference, Christianity and Islam have important resources to offer. Our religious traditions teach us that failure is inevitable and that the temptation to cancel is universal. The important thing is that democratic societies provide pathways for restoration when citizens fall short. Sometimes we make mistakes, we sin, we break our covenants. But we always need a way back, and that way back is possible only when our fellow citizens recognize our inherent worth and the sacred worth of the ties that bind.

The covenantal model emphasizes our mutual obligations to relationship—that even when we disagree profoundly, we are still bound together. In Christianity, the practices of confession and forgiveness create a framework for reconciliation. In Islam, the emphasis on compassion (*rahma*) and community (*ummah*) similarly provides a pathway back to the fold. Both traditions recognize that human beings are fallible and that mistakes—even grave ones—shouldn't define a person for eternity. We are not the worst things we've said. What matters is the willingness to acknowledge wrongdoing, make amends, and commit to doing better in good faith.

When we forget how to forgive and restore, when we create permanent outcasts based on momentary failures, we undermine the very foundations of democracy. We become a society that can destroy but cannot heal.

As American society has become more secular, we've lost these ancient mechanisms for restoration. Cancel culture offers no clear path forward for the canceled. There is no process of atonement, no ritual of forgiveness, no community that welcomes back the penitent. Cancel culture creates a population of permanent outcasts—and nothing, at least not in this world, should be permanent.

The tragic irony is that secular societies have actually maintained and even amplified the religious demand for moral purity while at the same time divesting themselves of religious frameworks for mercy and reconciliation. This is a loss not for believers alone but for society as a whole. Whether you are religious or not, there is a better way.

Building a Culture of Covenant

So what might a culture of covenant look like in practice? First, it recognizes that rightful accountability need not mean permanent exclusion. It creates clear processes for addressing harmful behavior while providing pathways for reconciliation and reintegration. It acknowledges the complexity of human beings and the potential for growth and change.

Second, it emphasizes the primary importance of community in holding individuals accountable. Rather than anonymous mobs on social media, accountability should come from individuals who are in direct relationship with the accused—people who know their character, their history, and their potential for growth. This kind of intimate accountability is more likely to be both just and merciful.

Third, it prioritizes restoration over retribution. The end goal is not to punish for punishment's sake but to heal breaches in the community and help individuals learn from their mistakes. This does not mean that there are no consequences for harmful behavior but rather that those consequences are oriented toward healing and growth rather than mere punishment.

Finally, it recognizes the profound limits of human knowledge and judgment. As both Islamic and Christian traditions teach, ultimate judgment belongs to God alone. Our human judgments are always provisional, partial, and subject to revision. Spiritual humility prevents us from the kind of moral certainty that leads to the excesses of cancel culture.

Christian theologian Miroslav Volf argues that true reconciliation requires "both the will to embrace and the will to give space."[31] Exclusion is easy, but covenant demands the harder work of creating community across difference. The former is cheap, the latter quite costly.

How might we disagree with one another while still honoring our covenantal bonds? The Jewish concept of *machloket l'shem shamayim* is quite helpful on this point. This phrase is often translated (and beautifully so) as "conflict for the sake of heaven." Within this framework, debates are motivated not by self-interest, ego, or the will to power. They are motivated by a selfless and communal pursuit of truth. When debaters place their relationship and the truth above their self-interest, debate can rightly be considered holy. We can put it another way: When you are able to disagree in a way that actually strengthens your relationship, you know you are getting close to a conflict for the sake of heaven.

These principles don't apply just to private religious communities. They are not to be considered inside the church, mosque, or synagogue and then quickly forgotten once we return to our public lives. They can and should inform what we do and say in the public square—how we debate and disagree, how we share our views, and how we try to persuade. We may also choose not to persuade at all and instead sit with difference and accept it for what it is, because it's probably not going away, nor should it. These principles of engagement are essential to the health of a pluralistic democracy.

Both Islam and Christianity, despite their many differences, share a recognition of human fallibility and the need for reconciliation. They offer wisdom for building a more humane and just society—one that can hold individuals accountable without dehumanizing them. The tragedy is that we've discarded these ancient resources at the moment we need them the most—when globalization is churning and weaponizing human difference. In this critical moment, secular society has kept the human impulse to judge and exclude while throwing away the frameworks that might help us find our way back to one another. In doing so, it has impoverished not just our public discourse but our souls.

In an age of increasing polarization and moral certitude, these ancient traditions remind us of the complexity of human beings and the limitations of human judgment. They call us to a humility that says, "I might be wrong," and a generosity that says, "You might have something to teach me."

This doesn't mean abandoning our moral convictions or our commitment to justice. It does mean, however, that we should pursue these ends within the framework of covenant—a recognition of the sacred ties that bind.

In the end, the path from cancel culture to covenant is both religious and political. It is about building a society that can hold together amid profound disagreement, that can name harm without demonizing the harmful, and that can create both time and space for growth, change, and reconciliation. This is the promise of covenant—it is a promise that our religious traditions have been pursuing for millennia and that we would do well to recover today.

7

Schools of Democracy

KEY TAKEAWAY

Good citizens aren't born; they're formed in small schools of democracy that teach people to lead, serve, and compromise. The good news is that these schools of democracy already exist. They're often found in houses of worship and other religious institutions.

Imagine two women heavily invested in religious institutions. Aisha is a Muslim living in New York, and Marie is a Christian living in Chicago.

Aisha teaches history and English at a small Islamic school in the Bronx. She's a great teacher, loved by students and parents alike. In her small school, Aisha wears many hats. She leads the curriculum committee, briefs the school board, organizes fundraisers, and handles student development and discipline.

Serving in all these capacities is challenging. Aisha needs to connect and collaborate with parents—some Muslim families are quite conservative, others more progressive. While she loves her job, it's hard. Sometimes kids don't cooperate; sometimes parents get mad. Sometimes she fails to convince the board, and they make decisions she deeply disagrees with. But over the years, Aisha has slowly become a respected leader not only in her school but also in the neighborhood at large. When a seat on the neighborhood council opens up, her fellow teachers and parents encourage her to run for it.

Marie, on the other hand, is a successful Christian businesswoman from suburban Chicago preparing for retirement. Her pastor encourages her to find some way to serve her community during her retirement. Marie decides to volunteer at a Christian thrift store serving a struggling downtown neighborhood. In an effort to connect with the clientele, Marie learns how to work the cash register. At workday's end, Marie bonds with her fellow Christians in the back as they fold clothes and process inventory. When they discover her business background, they ask Marie to join the board and serve as the treasurer. In her new position, Marie applies for grants and city permits. She also coordinates with the local neighborhood council. After a year of service, Marie makes a passionate case to the board that they should open a second store nearby.

On paper, Marie brings valuable business skills to the thrift store. That said, when asked about her service, Marie replies that she receives much more than she gives. She admits that the thrift store has humbled her in various ways. A white, Christian woman from the suburbs, Marie had rarely interacted with people who were not white, Christian, or upper-middle class. Every day in the thrift store she serves Muslims from Somalia, Pentecostals from Nigeria, Hindus from India, and Buddhists from Sri Lanka. Marie has also learned a variety of hard political lessons. Advocating for the thrift store at the neighborhood council, she learned that the city's political and economic leaders often overlook poor communities' needs.

This wealthy businesswoman had pictured a retirement on a sunny Florida beach, but now, because of this little Christian thrift store, she is engaged in the long, hard work of urban reform.

Where Citizens Learn Democracy

The United States needs more Maries and more Aishas. This is not a controversial statement. The question is where they will come from.

A healthy democracy requires citizens with various desires, virtues, and skills. They need to be informed, patient, selfless, courageous, engaged, and open to compromise.

When we consider the enormity of the democratic deficit in American public life, Aisha's and Marie's stories feel quite small and almost quaint. But they reveal an urgent truth we hope to uncover through the course of this chapter.

As we've seen, an individual leader can tear a nation's democratic fabric relatively quickly. Repairing and restoring that fabric takes a lot of time—and a lot of people. But as we will see in this chapter, repairing a democracy takes more than just individuals. It also takes institutions. Without the combination of institutions and individuals who are willing to serve and compromise, debate and engage, a democratic culture will wither and die. Individuals and their institutions make up the critical cords that bind a democracy together.

This leads to a second point. Aisha's and Marie's stories of transformation and the institutions they serve are decidedly religious. Hidden from view, Aisha's and Marie's lives of service and institutional engagement are animated by the communal practices of prayer, worship, and scriptural study. Every morning, Aisha and her fellow teachers stop at the local mosque next to their school. There, with women from around the neighborhood, they kneel together in prayer. Every evening, Marie and her fellow volunteers go to the back of the thrift store to sing and pray together as they fold clothes and close down the store for the night.

Aisha and Marie both believe that God has called them to serve their communities. Contrary to popular belief, their religions don't make Marie and Aisha want to escape their cities and go to heaven. Their religious practices drive them to engage their cities even more.

The United States is filled with a rich diversity of religious charities, schools, and organizations that serve the democratic fabric of America. Whether you accept their religious convictions or not, you actually benefit from their presence, their service, and even their prayer.

But these women are not accidents. Aisha and Marie were "made." They were slowly formed, cultivated, and grown within the context of religious communities and organizations, where they developed attributes of courage and compromise, listening and patience, strength and humility. While institutional religion gets a bad rap today, religious institutions made all the difference for Aisha and Marie.

When it comes to institutional religion, Gen Z and millennials are increasingly out. Only about 50 percent of them ever attend church, synagogue, or mosque, and only around 30 percent of them pray on a daily basis.[1] But they're not becoming atheists. Instead, they are trading in institutional forms of religion for more individual forms of spirituality. While institutional religion in America is suffering, the spirituality industry is booming. Entrepreneurs of personal empowerment, life coaching, and self-actualization have set up shop all over America, while churches, charities, and religious nonprofits are crumbling.

Imagine an alternative history. Imagine for a moment that Aisha had left her mosque and school and Marie had left her church and thrift store. Imagine that these religious institutions had become too cumbersome and constraining for Aisha and Marie. What if they had decided to do yoga instead? Would the yoga studio have taught Aisha and Marie to sacrifice their personal ambitions for the good of the neighborhood? Would a seminar on mindfulness have taught Aisha and Marie to engage their cities, join the neighborhood council, fold clothes, or run a cash register?

A number of studies that trace the deterioration of American religious life should give us pause before we celebrate the decline of institutional religion. In fact, data consistently suggest that people who belong to religious institutions behave in ways that benefit democracy.

- One study shows that people who hold religious beliefs and attend religious services are more likely to volunteer in *non-religious* contexts over the course of their adult lives. The author of the study suggests that religious institutions are feeder systems of volunteering for the broader society.[2]
- According to one sociological study, "frequency of religious service attendance on average has a positive impact on generalized [trust] and perceived cooperativeness."[3]
- Other studies find certain spillover effects of religious institutions. Even if you yourself are not religious, simply living in the proximity of strong religious institutions can make a difference in how you treat fellow citizens. One study found that

"individuals living in devout countries were more likely to help strangers even if they themselves were not religious."[4] A survey of fifty-three countries found that, while churchgoers volunteer more than nonreligious people on average, nonreligious people living in devout societies were more likely to volunteer than nonreligious people in secular societies.[5]

- A study of Americans' social participation suggests that "if nonreligious people have close friends with religious affiliations, they are more likely to volunteer for religious and nonreligious causes."[6]
- A study titled "God Is Watching You" reports that the mere mention of God activates individuals to acts of generosity.[7]

While all this evidence is encouraging, religious institutions are not monolithic, nor are they flawless. They do not universally produce civic trust or engagement; some of them actively inhibit such things. Do religious institutions promote prosocial and democratic behavior? Sociologists are quick to note that it depends.

- One study found that participation in fundamentalist churches increases levels of distrust in outsiders, while participation in more moderate ones can lead to increases in trust.[8]
- A study found that evangelical, black, and mainline Protestant churches encourage different types of sociality. Participants in mainline or black churches are more likely to connect with outsiders by getting involved with non-Christian organizations and activities. Participants in evangelical churches, meanwhile, are more likely to connect with outsiders by getting involved in evangelical institutions.[9]
- According to another study, individualistic forms of spirituality do not produce the same results as more communal or institutional forms of religion. The authors conclude that "while social religiosity or belonging (services attendance, church membership) predicts more trust, individual religiosity or believing (prayer, closeness and belief in God) predicts lower trust."[10]

Participating in religious communities isn't just good for the health of our democracy; it's actually good for our literal health. People who get involved in institutional religion are, statistically speaking, more likely to live longer and healthier lives. Weekly participation in religious institutions is associated with a 26 percent drop in "all-cause mortality," a 34 percent decline in heavy drinking, and a 29 percent drop in smoking.[11] The same study found that religious participation is also shown to decrease feelings of depression, anxiety, despair, and loneliness.

Readers who aren't connected to institutional religion will no doubt experience this chapter differently than those who are religious. For secular readers and those who participate in forms of personal spirituality, our goal is not to guilt you or to convince you to join a Christian or Islamic institution. Rather, we want to invite you to reflect on the unseen democratic contributions that these religious institutions are making to your local community. There is often an unstated assumption that religion is bad for democracy. But the statistics point to a more complex reality. Religious institutions might not be for you, but you still might consider their hidden benefits.

As we've said, citizens like Aisha and Marie do not fall out of the sky. They emerge from the soil of healthy religious organizations. If you are unlikely to join a religious organization, we invite you to consider the following question: Where can you learn to both persuade and compromise, speak up and serve, fight and forgive?

Our agenda is different for religious readers. We hope to both encourage and warn you. We encourage you to avoid an isolated or individualistic approach to religion. Our respective faiths are personal, yes. But they are also profoundly communal. No Muslim is an island. There is no such thing as a solitary Christian. Isolated from communities of faith, individual Muslims and Christians can go down some dark political paths.[12] And this leads to our warning. Secular critics are correct that institutional religion can be bad, even really bad. Mosques and Islamic schools can indeed encourage insularity and close-mindedness; so, too, can Christian camps, churches, and political organizations. Religious organizations are not an unmitigated good in American public life. We can clearly see from sociological data and our own lived experiences that participation in a religious organization will not automatically make a person a good and virtuous citizen. Not all religious institutions are created alike.

How can Christian and Islamic institutions avoid becoming dens of extremism, distrust, and polarization? How can they cultivate citizens for democratic life? Our proposed solution is not to make them more secular, liberal, or modern. Churches and mosques should not try to mimic their local DNC chapter or the Sierra Club. After all, secularizing a religious institution destroys the spiritual roots that give it vitality, strength, and purpose.

In the pages that follow, we hope to uncover religious wisdom in both Christianity and Islam for how Americans can build institutions that cultivate something the United States so desperately needs: more Maries and more Aishas.

How to Make a Citizen

In 1831, America's democratic experiment was alive and kicking. But for most of Europe, the dream of democracy was quickly slipping away. Large swaths of the continent were mired in either open political conflict or authoritarian domination. And yet, on the other side of the Atlantic, the democratic institutions of the new American nation seemed to be surviving and even thriving.

It was in that year that a ship arrived in the New York harbor carrying a French scholar and aristocrat named Alexis de Tocqueville. A liaison from the French government, Tocqueville had received research funding to study America's prison systems. The true purpose of his visit, however, had not been revealed. What truly interested Tocqueville was a single question: Why had the institutions of democracy flourished in the United States when they had floundered in Europe?

Tocqueville's understanding of democracy was notoriously vague. More than a mere system of voting and representation, democracy, Tocqueville argued, was a sort of national spirit, a habit, a way of life, a culture. Democracy was a spirit that a nation would either learn and cultivate—or undermine and snuff out. Democracy, in other words, is more cultural than political. It requires not just systems of government but individuals who are skilled in self-government.

Upon investigation, Tocqueville concluded that America's unique democratic spirit was being actively cultivated through a vast collection of communities and institutions. He argued that America's small-town halls, churches, and voluntary associations were the true birthplace of American democracy. Americans, he argued, "associate":

> Americans of all ages, of all conditions, of all minds, constantly unite . . . to celebrate holidays, establish seminaries, build inns, erect churches, distribute books, send missionaries to the Antipodes; in this way they create hospitals, prisons, schools. . . .
>
> What political power would ever be able to be sufficient for the innumerable multitude of small enterprises that the American citizens carry out every day with the aid of the association? . . . The more [government] puts itself in the place of associations, the more individuals, losing the idea of associating, will need it to come to their aid. These are causes and effects that engender each other without stopping.[13]

Tocqueville concluded that "religion . . . must be considered as the first of their political institutions."[14] He argued that religious and civic institutions were the societal spaces in which Americans learned the hard lessons of governance.

Consider, if you will, the political training of a farmer in a small colonial town Tocqueville might have met. As the farmer made a case for a new policy at the town hall, he learned how to organize, articulate, and advocate for his beliefs. Whether he won or lost, he was reminded—through the institution—that he had a voice and that his voice mattered. Likewise, as an elder in his local church, the farmer learned how to deal with a pastor who is difficult or dictatorial. He had to discuss with the other elders a peaceful and just way to confront such a pastor. In these small religious and political institutions, American individuals learned to speak up, debate, compromise, and build their common political and religious life together.

Today, the sociological heirs of Alexis de Tocqueville continue to make his case. They argue that small voluntary associations, clubs, and civil society organizations play an integral role in weaving together the fabric of democratic life.

In his bestseller *Bowling Alone*, political scientist Robert Putnam argues for the political importance of institutions and civil society. He specifically notes that "faith communities in which people worship together are arguably the single most important repository of social capital in America."[15] As citizens participate in these religious communities, they have the opportunity to develop social skills, learn basic manners, build civic trust, and become acclimated to the inevitable imperfections of politics. Those imperfections require a unique combination of both vigorous debate and gracious compromise.

According to Putnam, it is through participating in formal institutions and informal networks that citizens learn how to cooperate and serve the common good and develop other practical skills for civic life. Putnam notes that citizens grow emotionally and intellectually by engaging with others. Institutions and the interactions therein also safeguard individuals from being drawn into extremist movements, which often prey on those who feel disconnected and alone. Putnam writes, "Community bonds keep individuals from falling prey to extremist groups that target isolated and untethered individuals. Studies of political psychology over the last forty years have suggested that people divorced from community, occupation, and association are first and foremost among the supporters of extremism."[16]

Sociologists read the stories of Marie and Aisha in ways that ordinary observers do not. While the rest of us might be inspired by their acts of charity, courage, and civic engagement, sociologists are more interested in the institutions that produced these inspiring individuals.

Sociologists would argue that as Aisha and Marie engage in religious institutions, they are developing something that is absolutely critical for American democracy, even if they themselves might not realize it. When Aisha keeps going back to her school board—even when they reject her proposals and she loses debates—she is developing political resilience, civic trust, and communal solidarity. As her bonds with her community and its institutions thicken, Aisha is accruing something sociologists call "social capital."[17]

As Aisha invests her time and talents in the mosque, the school, and the neighborhood, she is developing forms of social capital that both "bond" and "bridge" her fellow Muslims.[18] She is helping her fellow Muslims strengthen ties with other Muslims in the mosque and school. She is also helping them form bridges with non-Muslims as she engages the local neighborhood council.

The same is true for Marie. She is bonding with her fellow Christians when she prays with them in the back of the thrift store. She is also forming bridges with the diverse non-Christian clientele at the thrift store when she serves at the register. Putnam writes, "Bonding social capital constitutes a kind of sociological superglue, whereas bridging social capital provides a sociological WD-40. Bonding social capital, by creating strong in-group loyalty, may also create strong out-group antagonism. . . . For that reason we might expect negative external effects to be more common with this form of social capital. Nevertheless, under many circumstances both bridging and bonding social capital can have powerfully positive social effects."[19]

Media has shone a spotlight on hardline forms of religion that bond internally but fail to bridge externally. Religious extremists, populists, and authoritarians tend to cultivate environments of isolation, loneliness, and despair. Research shows that when Muslims and Christians are isolated and disconnected from work, family, community, worship, and organizational life, they are more likely to answer the siren song of extremism.[20]

This, again, is where religious institutions and communities play such an important role of spiritual and social formation. When Marie bonds with her fellow Christians in the thrift store and Aisha bonds with her fellow Muslims in the school, they are developing a needed sense of identity and belonging. As Marie and Aisha become more certain of who they are and to whom they belong, they become strong and healthy. They receive a sort of inoculation against the political diseases of alienation, isolation, and fear.[21] This makes sense. If you are connected to a local community with whom you have deep levels of trust and commitment, political movements that tell you "No one cares about you but me!" will not be persuasive.

Imagine that late one night Marie and Aisha are on their respective laptops, and they come across a religious fanatic. Aisha is invited to join a global Muslim struggle against nonbelievers. Marie is asked to join a nationwide Christian nationalist crusade. Aisha and Marie are being invited to find their purpose and identity in a political struggle that's digital, abstract, and detached from their local communities.

It is not guaranteed that Aisha and Maria will resist the digital call to political arms. But sociological studies tell us that being grounded in strong, local faith institutions will make these women less likely to join an online extremist movement. They will have the tools and relationships to resist the temptation. After all, Marie and Aisha already have something solid. They have an identity, a community, and a purpose. They have a neighborhood to serve and a difference to make. They don't have time for a digital crusade or jihad. Chances are they don't have much time even for a fight on social media either. Aisha and Marie have too much good work to do right here on the ground.

Here, we anticipate a rebuttal. Do these institutions really need to be *religious*? Couldn't Aisha have built the same social trust and capital working for New York public schools? Does she really need to go to the mosque? Does she really need an Islamic school? Likewise, do we really need *Christian* thrift stores? Couldn't Marie just serve as a social worker for the city government of Chicago? Does she really need to sing hymns every night in the back of the store? Can't secular organizations and government services replace these religious institutions? Can't the government serve as the school of democracy?

Alternatively, what if Aisha and Maria convinced their religious institutions to give up their theological boundaries and become open-minded centers of spiritual inclusivity? Couldn't these spiritual organizations serve their community all the same?

Maybe, but this is unlikely for several reasons.

First, religion constitutes the lifeblood of these institutions. An overwhelming range of America's charities, organizations, and private schools name religion as their raison d'être. Faith is their origin, essence, and end.

Second, as we saw earlier, participants in religious institutions will—statistically speaking—give and volunteer more than their secular neighbors.[22] Religious participants are even more likely to volunteer at, give to, and lead in secular charities.[23]

Third, the political transformation Marie experienced while serving at the thrift store cannot be easily separated from her communal prayer and singing in the back room. If Marie had prayed alone in her suburban home and never volunteered in the thrift store, would she have changed? It just might be that stronger citizens are built through the combination of spiritual and civic practice.

Fourth, sociologists are quick to point out that secular and religious organizations are not created equal. One study demonstrates how religious organizations offer the poor and disenfranchised more opportunities to develop social skills and capital than their secular counterparts. It concludes that "houses of worship are superior to their two main competitors (i.e., the workplace setting and non-political civic organizations, such as the Rotary Club) in bringing transferable civic skills to the more disenfranchised. The workplace and non-political civic organizations tend to reward those who already have human capital and are middle-class."[24] Elsewhere, a similar argument is made that religious institutions "play an unusual role in the American participatory system by providing opportunities for the development of civic skills to those who would be otherwise resource poor."[25]

Sociologists have also begun to note what Tocqueville suspected all the way back in 1831: Religious institutions can serve as schools of democracy, training citizens in the practices of democratic life. Inside a church or mosque, humility, love, and patience aren't merely theories. They are actual ways of life that people are invited to practice. In religious communities, individual citizens can learn to share a meal, resolve a dispute, start a business, find a job, save a marriage, confront a deadbeat dad, and deal with an authoritarian leader. Such civic virtues can be practiced in small ways and—over time—achieve meaning, thickness, and sustainability in the life of a citizen.

Sociologists of Islam in America are beginning to uncover the extremely important role that Muslim institutions play in the formation of healthy Muslim citizens. While the political beliefs of individual Muslims certainly matter, the more crucial factor is the provision of Muslim spaces where individual Muslims can grow, deepen, and amplify their public voice. Anthropologist Andrew Shryock sees Muslim institutions as "zones of communal discipline, where citizenship is crafted and tested."[26] Rather than viewing Muslim institutions with suspicion, Shryock encourages us to view Muslim spaces as providing integral paths toward a fuller sense of belonging and citizenship.

Imagine a young Syrian refugee who fled to the United States during his country's civil war. He's isolated and cut off from his home culture, family, faith, language, and history. He's unemployed, uninvolved, and alone. In every way, this young man is disoriented and vulnerable. Muslim organizations, sports clubs, and mosques are some of the best-equipped institutions to support him as he begins acclimating to American public life. The various institutions connected to the man's religious identity can provide a sense of belonging and purpose in a strange new land. His faith can serve as a reservoir of strength, hope, and community during the disruptive experience of resettlement.

Jocelyne Cesari, an observer of Muslim immigration, argues that "one of the most common denominators of these young people attracted to jihadist movements and causes is not their socioeconomic level, but rather their displaced status."[27] Surveying young men most vulnerable to extremism, Cesari notes that their trajectories "all point to a kind of nomadism, a permanent mobility in the countries and cultures of the West."[28] Those most vulnerable to the temptations of extremism are not the poor but the lonely and the disconnected.

The connections the young Syrian refugee makes in Islamic institutions can help him find a job, find a partner, and even begin to make an honorable name for himself. Importantly, while Islamophobic voices try to tell this young Syrian that it is impossible to be both a Muslim and an American, Islamic communities can offer a rich communal space where this young man can decide for himself what it means to be both a Muslim and an American. In time, equipped with a job, a community, and a solid sense of self, this young Syrian will be empowered to actually contest and resist the Islamophobia in America that will attempt to define and demonize him.

The irony, of course, is painfully clear. Despite their immense civic benefits, Muslim institutions are often attacked by fearful and suspicious politicians and citizens. Despite their psychological, economic, and democratic benefits, these same organizations are routinely surveilled and demonized. In the name of safety and security, Islamophobes target the very Muslim community centers that actually contribute to the social flourishing of society.

The Liberal Need for Illiberal Communities

Your authors are big fans of freedom. We love the liberty to choose, to speak, to assemble, and to worship. Freedom is great. There is a lot to love about liberal amounts of choice. That said, it's possible to have too much of a good thing.

Psychologist Barry Schwartz coined the term *the paradox of choice* to describe the unhappiness we experience when our choices seem limitless.[29] When there are too many options, we become paralyzed, never quite knowing if we're living as we should.

Human beings, it turns out, actually benefit from having some real constraints—and even some real friction and pain for the choices we make. When we have to struggle against genuine resistance, when our decisions carry weight and consequence, we are forced to clarify what truly matters to us. The ease and convenience of modern life, for all its comfort, can leave us spiritually untethered—always choosing but never committing, always moving but never arriving at any destination that feels like home.

A liberated market can offer limitless wealth but no moral limits on how to spend it. A liberated internet can offer limitless digitized experiences of sexuality but no moral limits on how that sexuality should be expressed. A liberated public square can offer a forum for the limitless expression of anger, fear, or hatred but no moral limits on how those emotions should be communicated.

Without a moral compass or a pluralistic collection of different moral compasses, limitless individual choice can quickly overwhelm a person—and a society. The freedom to pursue wealth can become the burden to get ahead. The freedom to speak can become the burden to say the socially acceptable thing. The freedom to assemble can become the burden to join the right tribe. The freedom to drink can become the burden of alcoholism. The freedom to divorce can become the burden of fatherlessness. And so on. Many of these freedoms are great, but the burdens are not.

While liberty in these public spaces is wonderful, individuals require some sort of container, some level of moral direction, discipline, and—yes—constraint to navigate these spaces of freedom well. Contemporary scholars who study choice are increasingly confirming what time-tested religions have always known: When it comes to freedom and limitless choice, sometimes more is less.

Coming from communities of faith, we have learned that what the heart desires is not always good for the soul. This is why the goal of belonging to our local mosque or church is not the infinite expansion of our personal choice, freedom, or autonomy. Self-actualization and self-empowerment are not the final ends of a Muslim or Christian school. A Christian charity is not trying to turn people into materialistic consumers. A Muslim marriage is not designed to increase one's sexual choices.

For our religious traditions, freedom is a means to other, more important ends. Religion gives us clarity into what those substantive ends might be. As Tocqueville writes, "While the law allows the American people to do everything [they can amend the Constitution after all], there are things which religion prevents them from imagining and forbids them to dare." He goes on to make a powerful point: "I doubt that man can ever bear complete religious independence and full political liberty at the same time; and I am led to think that, if he does not have faith, he must serve, and, if he is free, he must believe."[30]

So what should be done? How do we escape the tyranny of choice? How do we begin to limit ourselves and reintroduce healthy forms of constraint?

Authoritarianism is one solution. Simply take away people's choice en masse. We could make a host of draconian laws against sexual, financial, and social freedoms that are bad for us. Aside from being unjust and evil, autocratic systems are famously unsustainable and brittle as a form of governance. Moreover, authoritarianism fails to provide people with any sort of internal moral direction or constraint beyond fear of reprisal. True internal virtue is possible only if we have the freedom to reject it. This is at the heart of God's test of believers: You have the right to make the wrong choice.

Libertarianism is on the opposite end of the spectrum. Libertarians emphasize personal responsibility above all else. Individuals are instructed to gird their loins, to take charge of their lives. It's up to you to stay informed, speak, buy, and choose for yourself. You are autonomous. The captain of your own fate. You are your own. There is no such thing as society. So make good choices—whatever that might mean to you.

The problem here is that human beings are not completely rational, autonomous, or independent. They are not the captains of their own fate. They are emotional and social animals. They live and thrive in groups, families, and organizations. Moreover, humans are not impervious to the society around them. They're deeply dependent creatures. Individuals are, in a very important sense, vulnerable. The market, the state, the culture, and the forces of globalization and technology are so much more powerful and influential than any fully "self-actualized" individual could ever hope to be.

Christianity and Islam offer their followers a way beyond modernity's false binary of libertarianism and authoritarianism. As we will see, their alternative path is not intellectual or ideological; it's institutional. Their primary offering is not a set of authoritarian rules or a limitless freedom. Instead, they offer both freedom and constraint within the context of community.

Christianity: From Movement to Institution

Christianity began as a small religious movement on the shores of Galilee in the form of conversations and meals between friends and fishermen. It was far from an institutional religion. Jesus gave his famous Sermon on the Mount without a planning committee or an advance team. As he traveled the region and gained followers, he had no security detail, no marketing taskforce, no charitable foundation. When the crowds around Jesus started to get hungry, no soup kitchen was organized. Jesus just fed them. When someone was sick, no one set up a hospital. Jesus just healed them.

Christianity started out as a spiritual movement, but it quickly took on an institutional form. As we read in the book of Acts, to honor Christ's ethic of sharing, his disciples organized formal offerings for the poor. Later on, they set up charities and poorhouses. Later still, they built welfare systems on a national scale. To honor Christ's healing of the sick, his followers organized formal care for the old and the sick throughout the Roman Empire. Monasteries took in the sick and disabled. Eventually, Christians created the first hospitals. To honor Christ's practice of teaching, Christians established schools of formal learning. Eventually, Christians established colleges, seminaries, and universities.

What began as a social movement quickly became a web of social institutions.

Driven by a desire to effectively organize their efforts, Christians established a kaleidoscopic diversity of social institutions in the centuries to follow. They set up orphanages, monasteries, libraries, work-training programs, guilds, unions, and city councils. A thousand years before the modern welfare state, medieval Christians established institutions to address needs in health care, education, business, work, justice, the arts, media, and so on.

Many of America's most important organizations began as overtly Christian institutions. Everything from Ivy League colleges to labor unions, the Red Cross, the YMCA, the United Way, the Boy and Girl Scouts, Habitat for Humanity, and Doctors Without Borders were all founded by Christians inspired by deeply held Christian beliefs. Whether you appreciate these institutions or not, chances are they have directly or indirectly benefited your community. One could not write America's democratic story without them.

Christianity has a rich legacy of building communal institutions for the common good. But that legacy is now in danger. Americans today are less likely to come together to organize, build, and invest in their institutions. Rather than reimagining and reinvesting in their institutions for a new day, these citizens either ignore or actively tear down their institutions.

Sociologists have been observing these trends of individualism over institutions for decades. Putnam's *Bowling Alone* famously tracks the decline of communal bowling leagues as an indicator of the death of America's institutional life. In an individualistic age, participation rates in labor unions, neighborhood councils, churches, and charities have all been falling. The death of associations should concern Americans, Putnam argues, because they "instill in their members habits of cooperation and public-spiritedness, as well as the practical skills necessary to partake in public life."[31] Without these institutions to ground and embed people in something greater than themselves, political extremism—and the polarization that results—becomes more common, confirming that "people divorced from community, occupation, and association are first and foremost among the supporters of extremism."[32]

Robert Bellah and his team of sociologists tracked similar trends in their influential work *Habits of the Heart: Individualism and Commitment in American Life*. The book describes the ways in which individualism undermines the social and civic fabric of American public life. Bellah and his coauthors argue that too many Americans have accepted a myopic understanding of what it means to be free. In essence, they've accepted a "vision of freedom as freedom from the demands of others."[33]

> Clearly, the meaning of one's life for most Americans is to become one's own person, almost to give birth to oneself. . . . It involves breaking free from family, community, and inherited ideas. Our culture does not give us much guidance as to how to fill the contours of this autonomous, self-responsible self. . . . It is hard to find in it the kind of story or narrative . . . many cultures have used to link private and public . . . the life of the individual to the life of society and the meaning of the cosmos.[34]

This individualistic approach to freedom "limits the ways in which people think" and "provides no vocabulary . . . to coordinate cooperative action with others."[35]

The authors posit that Americans need to revive what they call "communities of memory," which historically have been "an important way in which individuals are led into public life."[36] These communities provide individuals with powerful "examples of men and women who have embodied and exemplified the meaning of the community. . . . [These stories] carry a context of meaning that can allow us to connect our aspirations to a larger whole and see our efforts as being, in part, contributions to the common good."[37]

Historically, such formative communities of memory have included neighborhoods, clubs, universities, unions, cities, and, even for short and fleeting periods, the nation as a whole. However, in the United States, religion has been, by far, the most formative and influential community of memory.

Without these communities of memory, citizens begin to search for meaning in their careers, on social media, through consumerism, and—finally—through cultural and political combat. While these activities might hold off loneliness and despair for a short time, they do not provide the thick sense of belonging that democracy requires. Bellah explains that "Americans are fairly ingenious in finding *temporary* ways to counteract the harsher consequences of our damaged social ecology."[38] But these temporary forms of retail therapy do not last.

The West started down the path of individualism in the eighteenth century with the Industrial Revolution and the Enlightenment. The shift was gradual and then sudden. Citizens increasingly came to see the increase of choice and the reduction of constraint as the key to individual flourishing. The autonomous individual, so the story went, could not fully self-actualize until they shook off all the political, cultural, religious, sexual, and familial constraints that held them down. Rising from the ashes of social restriction, the modern self would emerge empowered, rational, free, democratic, and peaceful.

We know how this story ends.

8

Praying for Democracy

KEY TAKEAWAY

Democratic renewal requires more than better arguments; it requires a transformation in how citizens feel about one another and their differences. Prayer operates at this deeper level, cultivating the humility and resilience that democratic life demands.

Thoughts and prayers.

This phrase rightly draws scorn when mass shootings occur and politicians offer a grieving community nothing but spiritual sentiments. Desperate citizens receive platitudes instead of public action. If politicians want to appear spiritual and empathetic while avoiding public responsibility, they go with "thoughts and prayers."

In a moment of profound tragedy and searching, prayer—an ancient and transformative religious practice—is sullied by the cynicism, hypocrisy, and dysfunction of modern politics. In a moment when it is needed the most, holy prayer is reduced to a manipulative political device. It's no surprise that people scoff at calls for the nation to "return to prayer."

But what if this reflexive dismissal of prayer has led us to overlook how this ancient practice might actually alleviate a serious crisis within the heart of a democracy? Moreover, what if our political dysfunctions stem in part from our attempt to do politics without the spiritual practices of listening and reflection, patience and humility, vulnerability and confession?

Martin Luther King Jr. said, "Prayer is a marvelous and necessary supplement of our feeble efforts, but it is a dangerous and callous substitute."[1] Many modern Americans point to this sentiment to discount prayer as a replacement for "real" public action. But we are drawn to King's initial comment: Prayer is both marvelous and necessary.

In this chapter, we explore the surprising, unexpected, and even unintended benefits of prayer for democracy. More specifically, we outline how Muslim and Christian practices of prayer can cultivate postures of humility, patience, resilience, empathy, and courage—qualities American public life desperately needs.

But let's be clear on a few things. First, prayer doesn't fix everything. There are tons of jerks out there who pray. Christian fundamentalists pray. Muslim extremists pray. Abusive husbands pray. Prayer is not a panacea. It is not a silver bullet. That is not our argument. Instead, we intend to outline how prayer, when rightly understood and practiced, can change people for the better.

Second, ancient prayers were not designed for modern democracy. Centuries ago, when the first Muslims and Christians knelt to pray, none of them were using prayer to become more democratic. Neither Jesus nor Muhammad taught his followers to pray so that they would become more tolerant, humble, or resilient. Prayer was not designed to help us vote or debate, protest or campaign. Speaking more personally, we both pray every day, but helping democracy is never our motivation. God is the reason we pray, not democracy. If we become better listeners through prayer, if we grow in empathy or patience, that is a by-product of our time on our knees. It is not the purpose.

Third, some of our readers may find prayer a rather strange and superstitious practice. When moderns encounter something that is both ancient and religious, they often seek the safety of higher ground. They start by distancing themselves from the religious subject. From an elevated vantage point of science and rationality, they attempt to inspect and examine the religious subject with supposed objectivity. We want to invite you to step down from this elevated position and stand alongside your religious neighbors. This final chapter will be much more rewarding if you allow yourself to consider how maybe—just maybe—the political noise in our present moment could benefit from some time spent in silence and reflection. Who knows? Kneeling quietly for a few minutes a day might be good for a political culture that loves to stick out its chest and bellow.

From this more humble position, we hope that readers might discover a series of surprising paradoxes about the political nature of prayer. Consider the following paradoxes. Muslims and Christians believe that when we close our eyes in prayer, we can somehow see the world better. We believe that when we put our work down, we can somehow become more useful. We believe that when we take on a humble posture of vulnerability, weakness, and submission, we can somehow receive strength, dignity, and honor. And we believe that when we lower ourselves, we are somehow lifted up. It is difficult to explain, but G. K. Chesterton did it well when he said that when an ancient man prayed, he "felt taller when he bowed" and "freer when he bent."[2]

Fourth and finally, it should be noted that we don't entirely agree about prayer. There are very real—and very important—differences between Islam and Christianity on the subject. Broadly speaking, when Muslims pray, they tend to emphasize the importance of following an established schedule, content, and bodily practice for their prayers. Christians, on the other hand, tend to assume a more informal, spontaneous, and relational posture in prayer. Broadly speaking, Muslims value the use of the Arabic language in prayer, whereas Christians readily pray in their native languages. A Muslim prays directly to God, whereas Christians believe they should approach God in the name of Jesus and through the power and direction of the Holy Spirit. Christians believe that Jesus stands with them as they pray and that the Holy Spirit actually prompts and enables them to pray even when they falter in their faith. Muslims tend to kneel as an obedient response to God's command. Christians tend to pray as a grateful response to God's good gifts. These (and many other) differences between these traditions are worthy of serious reflection. But this is not our task today.

Amid their differences, the prayers of Muslims and Christians share a key ingredient: They have the surprising capacity to bear some unexpected democratic fruit. As we will see, Muslim and Christian prayers can nurture humility, personal reflection, and examination; they can challenge social divisions and hierarchies; they can cultivate gratitude and civic solidarity. Each of these virtues plays an important role that benefits democratic society.

Prayer Helps the Politically Exhausted

Faced with a 24/7 news cycle, the feeling of never doing enough, and frequent political storms, many believers turn to prayer as their anchor. There's profound wisdom in this.

When we pray, we turn off our devices and the frenetic social media feeds that only compound our feelings of anxiety, depression, and resignation. We close our eyes, quiet our hearts, and enter into a posture of silence and reflection, dependence and release.

Empirical evidence suggests that these prayerful postures contribute something remarkable to the human psyche and to our way of being in the world. A 2009 randomized controlled trial by physician Peter Boelens and his colleagues found that participants who took part in weekly prayer showed significant improvements in depression and anxiety—effects that persisted for at least a year.[3] The study's methodology was rigorous: Seventy-four participants with clinical depression or anxiety were randomly assigned to receive either six weekly one-hour prayer sessions or no intervention, with standardized psychological assessments at baseline, post-intervention, and follow-up. The results weren't subtle. Those who prayed showed marked increases in daily spiritual experiences and optimism alongside decreased psychological distress.

The study was strikingly specific. The prescribed prayer wasn't a spiritually vague period of personal meditation or mindfulness. It was a structured exercise involving specific moments of gratitude, confession, and intercession. Participants were instructed to pray for others as well as themselves, to express thanksgiving for positive aspects of their lives, and to seek forgiveness for their failures.

This multifaceted and structured approach to prayer—combining self-reflection, regard for others, and humility—mirrors postures that lead to being a good democratic citizen. Democracy is demanding. Healthy democracies require citizens equipped with the capacity for listening and speaking, gratitude and complaint, vulnerability and resilience. These are the exact qualities that prayer is designed to cultivate.

A 2016 analytical review of clinical studies found that frequent prayer was associated with significant positive outcomes for mental health.[4] Ten studies on anxiety and related conditions showed a significant benefit associated with prayer. On average, individuals who prayed regularly experienced lower anxiety levels, better coping skills, and greater optimism. Another study revealed that the practice of prayer was associated with greater pain tolerance.[5] When it comes to politics, that might come in handy.

In another study, researchers conducted a series of innovative experiments testing whether prayer could reduce social aggression after provocation.[6] The design was clever. Participants each wrote a personal essay. They then received harsh criticism (e.g., "This is one of the worst essays I have ever read.") Then participants were randomly assigned to either pray for their critic or simply think about them. Participants then played a competitive game in which they could freely inflict uncomfortable noise blasts on their opponents. Those who did not pray but merely thought about their critics inflicted significantly longer and louder noise blasts against their competitors (a standard measure of aggressive behavior). According to the study, the difference between a person's thoughts and their prayers is quite large. In short, if someone offers you their "thoughts and prayers," opt for the latter.

Interestingly, these researchers found that such prayer activities were effective regardless of how religious the participants were—even nonreligious participants showed reduced social aggression when they prayed. Prayer's social benefits appear to stem in part from the redirection of attention—away from a preoccupation with personal grievance and toward a concern for others. Prayer seems to give us humans a way to regulate our hostile emotions through what psychologists call "cognitive reappraisal." Rather than suppressing anger, prayer transforms it by shifting the participant's perspective from self-centered grievance to compassion for neighbors—even critics.

These aren't isolated findings. A growing body of research suggests that prayer practices correlate with enhanced emotional regulation, increased civic participation, greater empathy, and improved social cohesion across cultural contexts. The *Journal for the Scientific Study of Religion* published research showing that private prayer was associated with greater participation in civic action groups, particularly those focusing on individual needs and community support. The researchers conclude that "by encouraging concern for others, prayer lays a foundation upon which voluntary associations can be firmly developed."[7]

To be clear, prayer won't necessarily make people more politically active. Prayer, it appears, affects something more fundamental: the internal capacity of a citizen to see beyond themselves and their grievances, to feel connected to and implicated in the lives of others, and to engage others with humility. Coincidentally, these are precisely the qualities that are essential for democratic life.

The democratic puzzle has always been a question of how to inoculate citizens against the political diseases of hate, fear, selfishness, cynicism, and tribalism. How can we help citizens see their neighbors, their enemies, and their political environment in a different and better light?

Prayer, we argue, offers at least part of an answer.

Beyond Secular Rationalism

How do we revive a dying democracy?

Modern advocates for democracy love to raise awareness. They assume that education is the solution to democratic life. If they just educate the public about democracy, if they just teach children about civil rights, if they just provide more information about what government does, then citizens will become more democratic. The problem, they assume, is a lack of information.

But it doesn't work that way, does it?

As anyone who's spent more than five minutes on social media knows, more information can easily make things worse. More often than not, people harvest new data only to confirm their biases. We don't go to social media looking for just any information; we go there looking for more data to confirm our beliefs, not challenge them.

Political theorist William Connolly illustrates the dead end of civic education and awareness campaigns. He argues that they "fail to grasp the ways visceral modes of appraisal affect political thinking below the conscious register of reasons and argument alone."[8] This is academic speak for something we all intuit: People don't just *think* their way into politics; they *feel* their way into it. Democracy is less about the things we know and more about the things that excite, terrify, and titillate us. Democracy is less about what we know in our brains and more about what we feel in our guts and bones. If democracy is less about our knowledge and more about our feelings, then our discussions about its revival need to move—somehow—from our heads to our hearts.

Democratic renewal requires an emotional and (dare we say) spiritual transformation. We need the elusive capacity to accept difference, to hold tension, to sit with uncertainty, to engage with people who see the world differently without losing our minds.

Prayer operates precisely at this foundational level. It shapes not just what we think but how we feel about the disturbing differences that confront us in the public square. And maybe that's exactly what we need.

In regard to the many diseases that infect our democratic spirit, prayer bypasses the symptoms and goes to the source—the political fears and anxieties that are festering inside of us. Prayer functions at a deeper register, what we might call the pre-rational level of politics.

Before you begin a political fight online, a regular morning practice of prayer will have already been at work on your mind and heart. Before you start pounding on your keyboard, your prayerful posture will have already impacted the posture you assume toward your supposed enemies. Muslims speak of prayer practices creating *taqwa*—a God-consciousness that shows up as a heightened moral sensitivity. Christians talk about prayer helping them to die to self (Gal. 2:20). Having died to themselves, they might actually be able to hear voices other than their own. In prayer, a Christian might slowly begin to reimagine their political opponent as their political neighbor. Through prayer, a Muslim might receive a strange new sensitivity toward those with whom they're debating.

Prayer appears to address a deep emotional issue that secular political theorists struggle to account for: Before a culture of democratic debate can develop, citizens must *desire* conversation over control. They must *desire* peace over power.[9] This is not a matter of the head. It's one of the heart or even the guts.

Here again, prayer becomes politically relevant, because prayer focuses on this "lower" level of political desire. The evidence suggests that regular contemplative practices can develop the internal capacities that democracy requires—namely, the ability to regulate our emotions when provoked, humility about our own limitations, genuine concern for community well-being, and the rare ability to see opponents as fellow human beings deserving of respect despite profound disagreement.

When it comes to the tenuous future of democracy in the West, these aren't nice-to-have extras. They're the critical foundation that makes everything else in democracy possible.

The Politics of Prayer

The political implications of prayer are easy to see when you know what to look for.

I (Shadi) was in Egypt during the Arab Spring uprisings. I was walking the streets of Cairo, observing and documenting the widespread political calls for democratic reform. One day amid the protests, I decided to enter a local mosque to pray.

There in long rows, Egyptian citizens from different social classes and political movements—doctors, street vendors, government bureaucrats—knelt together in prayer. A millionaire businessman would have prostrated right next to his doorman. A supporter of the Muslim Brotherhood would have knelt right next to someone who supported the military. And they wouldn't have known. And it would not have mattered, at least not in that moment. There, in prayer, the political divisions and economic hierarchies that rigidly structured and stratified Egyptian society briefly fell away.[10] That one communal prayer did not fix or save Egyptian democracy, but it did offer those citizens a moment of solidarity, a break from the division, and a chance to experience a form of connection with their neighbor.

Something political was happening on the floor of that mosque. Kneeling in prayer, diverse and divided citizens practiced an Islamic form of liberty, equality, and fraternity. In that mosque, I observed the paradoxical power of prayer. After those citizens took a submissive posture—faces on the ground—they seemed to depart with strength, courage, and self-assurance. Shoulder to shoulder in prayer, Cairo's citizens could briefly imagine a way of being together amid their differences.

As mentioned before, from time to time, cynical politicians will use the word *prayer* to appear pious while eschewing their political responsibility to take action. Prayer, they imagine, has no material or public consequence; it is merely private and personal. This is almost entirely wrong.

When we close our eyes to pray, we are not escaping the public square. We're not running away from our political problems or responsibilities; we're trying to rearticulate, reimagine, and reengage them in a new way—God's way. Rightly understood, prayer is not about retreating from the world but about reengaging it. Prayer is about reexamining and restoring our relationships—with God, with other people, with the world around us.

Here we see another critical paradox: We are better prepared to engage our political responsibilities if we put them down for a little while in prayer. Standing up from a time of prayer, we can walk away with a deeper sense of the public responsibilities that surround and bind us.

If politicians are looking to avoid political responsibility, we don't recommend prayer—at least not the real kind.

Prayer as Democratic Practice

Five times daily, Muslims turn their faces toward Mecca and perform a choreographed series of movements: standing, bowing, prostrating, sitting. The motions matter as much as the words. Hamza Yusuf, Muslim scholar and founding president of America's first accredited Islamic undergraduate college, notes, "Bowing and prostrating express humility, the sense that before the vastness of God and God's creation, we are truly small."[11] In congregational prayer, the Prophet Muhammad instructed that there should be no gaps in the prayer lines, that believers should stand so close that their shoulders touch. These bodily motions and spiritual practices have social and political implications for Muslim citizens.

As another Islamic scholar observes, "Spirituality is about praying with our hands, not just our lips."[12] In other words, prayer is not merely about uttering a series of holy words or ideas but also about doing good in the world. Islamic prayer takes the abstract ideas of equality, solidarity, and humility and inscribes them into bodies and souls as Muslims bow and bend alongside one another.

Christian prayer is not often recognized as a social practice in the same way Muslim prayer is. This is due in part to the enduring legacy of Augustine. Augustine has been widely recognized as "inventing the inner self" through the deep and prayerful self-examination we see in his *Confessions*.[13] However, Augustine's written instructions on prayer emphasize the social dynamics and postures necessary for proper prayer. He states that the foundation for all prayer is a posture of desolation, or emptiness before God.[14] Riches and social status mean nothing before God, and they pale in comparison to the eternal pleasures that are found in God's presence (Ps. 16:11). In other words, prayer levels the economic and political hierarchies of a praying community.

The Rule of St. Benedict, from the sixth century, outlines prayer practices for monks in monastic communities. It adds much detail to the personal and the political power of prayer. For monks, communal prayer creates the social conditions for living in community. A day of social harmony among the monks demands a morning of prayer. The monks have to "first pray together, so that they may associate in peace."[15]

James K. A. Smith's work on liturgical formation provides a theological framework for the social and civic power of prayer. Smith argues that regular rituals like prayer can slowly begin to "shape our loves." Prayer can accomplish this by training citizens in the unfamiliar (and uncomfortable) postures of attention, gratitude, and service.[16] Christian prayers for neighbors, enemies, and political leaders constitute what Smith calls "counter-formative" practices. If social media is slowly forming our hearts for destructive rage, prayer can counter-form our hearts for peaceful and productive exchange. If social media directs our hearts to tribal grievances and echo chambers, prayer can focus our hearts on compassion for those we might otherwise wish to ignore or even crush.

But does all this praying translate into real and measurable effects on democratic behavior? The evidence suggests it just might. Nancy Ammerman's extensive fieldwork on twenty religious congregations across the country revealed "a very strong link between organized religious participation and the presence of a sacred consciousness in everyday life," including in civic engagement.[17] But the mechanism matters more than the correlation. Ammerman's research demonstrated that religious institutions and practices create what she calls "moral communities" that extend the civic concern of the participants beyond their immediate families to broader circles of care.[18]

The Islamic concept of *ummah* provides insight into prayer's ability to bridge differences—how prayer can cultivate someone's sense of connection and solidarity outside their immediate tribe. While *ummah* is often translated as "community," the term actually implies something broader—a person's internal sense of shared responsibility that transcends ethnic, national, and class divisions. The Islamic practice of praying for the welfare of all believers, including those whom one has never met, develops what we might call "imaginative solidarity." In a democracy as large and unwieldy as our own, imaginative solidarity across great distances and divides is absolutely essential.

Democracy Is for Losers (and So Is Prayer)

The concession speech might be the most underrated democratic tradition there is. Learning to lose is one of the hardest and most demanding lessons a politician can learn. The decline of the concession speech in recent years is a symptom of a worrying disease at the heart of our democracy: the inability to lose well.

Political defeat is hard. In recent years, voters have increasingly found that when their side loses, it's difficult to accept. Watching a candidate fall short, seeing policies dismantled, and confronting the harsh reality that democracy sometimes produces outcomes we find troubling can test a citizen's soul in ways that abstract theories of pluralism can only gesture at.

Democracy demands that political movements know when they've been defeated and—more important—accept that defeat. But losing is hard.

Given this reality, how should we emotionally process our political defeats? What should we do when the political forces that we abhor triumph? As it turns out, comedian Tina Fey tackled this question in a sketch on *Saturday Night Live*. She asked, How should my fellow Democrats respond to the electoral triumph of Donald Trump as well as the rise of white nationalist rallies across the country like those in Charlottesville?

Fey offered a humorous, if deeply sad, response. She recommended that her fellow Democrats process their defeat by ritualistically stuffing their faces with massive sheet cakes. Drown your political sorrows in frosting and sugar. What should you do with your feelings of political anxiety and depression? How should you process your defeat? Talk to a cake about it.[19]

For both of us, democracy is a long training in defeat and disappointment. Every political defeat reveals the yawning chasm between our political longings and the harsh reality of the world as it is. Staring into this chasm, we can respond to defeat in one of three ways: rage, resignation, or prayer. We've found the third option to be the most productive.

If we're doing it right, prayer reminds us every single day that we are not in charge. When we ask God almighty to jump, he does not respond "How high?" Muslims and Christians regularly make requests to God that will not be answered immediately or positively. In prayer, we have to regularly sit with the fact that we can neither fully comprehend nor control how God will respond. The outcome belongs to God alone. In prayer, we remember and rehearse our finitude. We cannot control God or our fellow citizens. God alone sees the whole board. Prayer, in this sense, is a daily concession speech.

In the days that followed her cake-eating joke, Fey was publicly excoriated. Those on the right mocked her political defeat and gloried in her liberal tears. Those on the left argued that the only acceptable response to political defeat is to get up and fight all the harder. Her critics sadly missed a deeper truth about the complex realities of loss and defeat.

Human beings are complex emotional creatures. The proper human response to political defeat is not simply fight or flight. Complex citizens require complex modes of processing their loss. Tears and resignation will not do, nor will endless rage posting and political combat. Political losers require something more than cake eating. They need a formative practice through which they can process their defeats and the complex emotions and questions that accompany them. In prayer, we find just such a practice. As Mormon writer Diana Brown puts it, "We're so prone to want to check out when life doesn't go the way we think it should and to busy ourselves with blaming others. Religion invites us to reckon with things as they actually are."[20] Neither cake nor self-pity nor rage will suffice.

A tough political defeat can trigger in the loser an either-or, fight-or-flight reflex. "Let's storm the Capitol!" and "I'm moving to Canada!" are visceral responses that are simplistic and limited. Prayer offers political losers a more complex and multifaceted way to process political defeats. Losing an election need not register as either a cosmic injustice or a divine judgment. When our side loses, rather than immediately assuming our opponents cheated or the system failed, we can prayerfully ask a series of uncomfortable questions that we might wish to avoid. Did my side fail to make an effective case in the election? Did we fail to listen to our opponents? Do we need to reconsider our policies and posture in some way? The democratic capacity to accept defeat and earnestly reflect on it with wisdom requires the humility to imagine the unimaginable—our side might have gotten something wrong.

Political Rage and Prayerful Lament

Some losers respond to defeat with resignation, depression, and copious amounts of cake eating; others opt for rage. But where should modern citizens express their rage? As town hall meetings die out, Americans are increasingly likely to take their anger and frustration to social media.

Rage posting has transformed social media into a wasteland of chaotic emotions and anonymous hostility. One study from researchers at Yale University illustrates social media's unique ability to not only funnel moral outrage but also amplify it.[21]

Social media is a quick and convenient outlet for our political rage, but it struggles to transform that rage into anything constructive or productive. It is no surprise that, in the age of social media, practices of open democratic dialogue are on the decline.[22] Here we encounter a dark paradox. Through social media, American citizens feel both incredibly connected and incredibly isolated at the same time. As a medium for political discourse, social media is simultaneously personal and anonymous, vulnerable and brutal.

A healthy democracy will regularly train citizens to reckon with political loss and disappointment. If you do democracy long enough, you will taste defeat. This raises questions: Where will you carry your despair and disappointment? Who will bear these burdens at your side? Citizens go to social media looking for companionship in victory and defeat, and yet it does not satisfy. It just seems to make things worse.

Defeat is a prominent theme in the Hebrew Scriptures, especially in the book of Psalms. Of the 150 psalms, 65 are focused on lament and despair. In these various songs and prayers, the Israelites process their defeats and disappointments by crying out to God with rage and sadness. Together they plead to God that things should be different. They ask why their enemies triumph.

After the Israelites have been conquered and are living as slaves in exile—talk about a political defeat—they bring their ire directly to God.

They even ask God for a gruesome retribution against their Babylonian enemies:

> Daughter Babylon, doomed to destruction,
> happy is the one who repays you
> according to what you have done to us.
> Happy is the one who seizes your infants
> and dashes them against the rocks. (Ps. 137:8–9)

Some mistakenly think passages like these justify baby killing in the face of defeat—not so. Rather, they show that readers of the Psalms are allowed to carry their trauma and despair directly to God. Readers of the Psalms don't have to rage post online. They can share their frustration and rage with God almighty.

How much difference is there between social media outrage and prayerful lament? A lot, actually.

When Christians lament, God can absorb their rage in ways that social media cannot. An online news feed is disjointed, frayed, and weak. While social media will focus and even amplify your anger, prayerful lament can transform that anger into something productive. Christian ethicist and activist Emilie Townes puts it this way: "Laments mark the beginning of the healing process when we open ourselves up to look at the situations we find ourselves in and our own complicity in them as well as the ways in which we are victimized by them."[23] The raw honesty of prayerful lament can be the beginning of a citizen's journey toward acknowledging and processing. If social media transforms our political losses into a chronic state of grievance and victimhood, prayerful lament turns our losses into a transformative experience of personal reflection and healing.

Social media outrage also has a well-documented performative element. In a competition for clicks and engagement, citizens attempt to outdo one another in their righteous anger against their foes. In the privacy of a prayer room, all such competition and performance is removed. It's just you and God. There are no followers to gain. Solitary prayer offers citizens a gift. A release from political performance. An opportunity to be honest and vulnerable. This is part of why Jesus advises his followers, "When you pray, go into your room, close the door and pray to your Father, who is unseen. Then your Father, who sees what is done in secret, will reward you" (Matt. 6:6).

In secret prayer, citizens are radically free—not to perform their rage but to process it. When you're rage posting for your followers, it can be difficult to see straight. When you enter the privacy of prayer, you might just notice a few things that you would otherwise miss. Perhaps this political defeat is a divine wake-up call, a way of reminding us that we can't do things alone. Perhaps we need to learn that there is more to life than politics. Perhaps our political team was not the team we've been waiting for. Perhaps we are the ones who need to change.

Even if prayer does not provide the answer for our political defeat, it can still provide a gentle and powerful reminder that we are not alone and that one day all will be made right. Justice and judgment will come, but they are not ours to deliver and the time is not now. One of the Quran's best-known verses captures this divine assurance amid human uncertainty: "You may dislike something although it is good for you, or like something although it is bad for you: God knows and you do not" (Q 2:216).

Prayerful Submission and Political Power

Both Muslim and Christian approaches to prayer invite humans to submit to divine will. Prayer is not about our greatness and glory; it's about God's. Muslims begin every prayer cycle with *Allahu akbar* (God is greater), a humbling declaration that we, as mere mortals, are nothing in the face of the divine. Likewise, Christians also submit to God in prayer, placing their will beneath his. Their most important prayer, the Lord's Prayer, contains a very submissive political statement: "*Your* kingdom come" (not ours), "*your* will be done" (not ours). In prayers like this, Christians assume a humble political posture. They follow Christ's example of emptying himself, acknowledging that they are completely dependent on God.

Here, you might say it sounds as if prayerful submission will lead to political submission. If we start bowing to God, won't we also bow to a tyrant?

This language of prayerful submission and dependence troubles our modern sensibilities. We've been taught to value empowerment, confidence, and individual agency above all else. How can submissive prayers foster powerful democratic citizens? Won't quiet prayers lead to quietism?

Not necessarily.

Consider the sails on a ship. In a way, they appear soft, weak, and malleable. They are incredibly submissive to the direction of the wind, flipping from one side of the ship to the other. However, in their submissiveness, these sails are uniquely capable of catching the power of the wind. Filled with the power of the wind, these supposedly submissive sails become incredibly stiff and powerful. The ship flies through the water, and the various currents and tides try in vain to hold it back. The ship will not submit to their forces precisely because its sails have submitted to the wind.[24]

Submissiveness in prayer will not necessarily produce submissiveness in politics. In fact, it can actually produce quite the opposite. The answer lies in distinguishing between submission to human authority and submission to divine authority.

Imagine you start every morning declaring that God alone is great. Imagine you repeatedly declare that God alone owns your heart and your life. Now imagine that a politician comes along and says, "I'm the greatest. I'm the highest. You need me. I can save you. I can make you great again." When politicians make a run at God's throne, those who regularly submit to that throne should be particularly sensitive to the fact that they are trespassing.

"Should be" is the operative phrase, of course. When American evangelicals submitted themselves to Donald Trump's play at the divine throne, it was not simply an indictment of their political judgment; it was an indictment of their prayer. Prayer, rightly practiced, should put all human authorities in their proper place.

Abraham Lincoln exemplified the prayerful posture of humility during the Civil War when he insisted that the chief political question was not "Is God on our side?" but "Are we on God's side?"[25] Once we recognize through prayer that God is enthroned, we can begin to ask uncomfortable but necessary political questions: God, am I truly on your side? Am I truly seeking your political will and not my own? These sorts of questions have a way of immunizing citizens against the diseases of political selfishness, overconfidence, and idolatry. In politics, it is common to confuse our cause with God's cause. A regular practice of submissive prayer guards against that confusion.

Prayerful Action

Before the automobile, the camel was of central importance to the mobility and even survival of those living in the Middle East. If your camel was stolen or it wandered away, you were in deep trouble. It's no surprise, therefore, that the Prophet Muhammad used the camel as a central image in some of his teachings.

In one, the camel is used to reconcile a perceived tension between human submission and human action. A bedouin in the desert leaves his camel untied and unattended. The Prophet Muhammad is dismayed: Why is the man doing this? The man replies, "I put my trust in God." The Prophet responds by telling him to "tie your camel first and then trust in God."[26] In other words, do both. You have a human responsibility to secure your camel as best you can. You also have a responsibility to trust that God will take care of both the camel and you. As you walk away from your camel, you should experience a freedom that can be found in a combination of both prayerful submission and prayerful action. Archbishop Anthony Bloom writes, "A prayer makes sense only if it is lived. Unless they are 'lived,' unless life and prayer become completely interwoven, prayers become a sort of polite madrigal which you offer to God at moments when you are giving time to Him."[27]

How can democratic citizens be politically active while also accepting that there are political realities beyond their comprehension and control? Ancient prayer offers modern citizens a way in which this supposed tension can be resolved. Christian theologian Reinhold Niebuhr illustrates this point beautifully in his now-famous serenity prayer: "God, grant me the serenity to accept the things I cannot change, the courage to change the things I can, and the wisdom to know the difference."[28]

The prayerful life of a citizen is one in which action and submission are interwoven. We don't live two separate lives, one life of frenetic political activity, passion, and rage, and another life of despair, resignation, and cake eating. In the prayerful life, we are integrated citizens of humility and responsibility. We bow in self-reflective silence and submission, and we stand in a power and a will that are not our own.

Post-Christian Prayer?

We anticipate another objection: The United States is an increasingly secular society, and the practice of prayer is on the decline. In essence, how can prayer be a political solution if we don't really do it anymore?

This objection betrays a misunderstanding of both the problem and the potential solution. First, the United States remains far more religious than most Western democracies.[29] Second, and more importantly, the democratic benefits of prayer don't require universal adoption. Even if only a minority of citizens engage in prayer, it would still affect the political landscape.

What about various practices of mindfulness, yoga, and meditation? Could they work just as well? Can dark retreats (where all external sensory input is eliminated) and mindfulness exercises also help citizens cultivate the civic humility we so desperately need?

It's no surprise that we have reservations about these forms of spirituality. That said, America is desperate. Our frayed political culture stands in tremendous need of silence and solidarity. While we would strongly commend our respective traditions of prayer to America, at this point, anything is better than nothing.

If Christian or Muslim prayers are not for you, there is evidence that alternative meditative practices can also benefit democratic society. In one MIT-affiliated study, middle schoolers who participated in a daily mindfulness practice experienced lower stress levels and fewer negative feelings compared to their peers. Brain scans even showed reduced activation of the amygdala, the brain's fear center, indicating that the students were calmer in the face of stress.[30] The same study reported that students who exhibited more mindfulness demonstrated improved academic performance and fewer disciplinary issues.[31]

So, if Christian and Muslim forms of prayer feel like too much of a stretch for you, we encourage you to seek out a regular practice of humility and gratitude and a structured time for personal reflection and examination. But we also offer a word of caution: While some yoga and mindfulness programs include some of these elements, they are often individualistic. In other words, they emphasize personal empowerment and rarely foster social solidarity, reconciliation, and forgiveness. These programs also normally serve a very specific socioeconomic class of Americans. It's rare to find mindfulness spaces in poor neighborhoods. Yoga studios rarely bring rich and poor together. This might help us understand why America's churches and mosques open charities and soup kitchens while yoga studios do not.

Offering a Practice, Not a Solution

We want to be clear: Prayer isn't a political cure-all. It is not the solution to our democratic crisis. It will not fix everything. But it does offer a way of navigating the disappointments of life in a democracy. Prayer slowly trains us in the capacities we so desperately need for living with political uncertainty.

As we reflect again on Shadi's experience in the Cairo mosque standing shoulder to shoulder with his fellow Muslims in prayer, what should strike us is how this communal ritual could mend and renew social bonds between citizens—not through a shared ideology but through a shared practice. These citizens may have voted for different parties, held different views on economic policy, or disagreed about foreign policy questions. But in this sacred moment of collective prostration, these citizens enacted a more fundamental solidarity and equality than their politics ever could.

American democracy needs more such moments—moments when citizens practice humility, acknowledge their limitations, and recognize their interdependence. Prayer is a powerful practice for creating these moments. Whether Americans will embrace this ancient practice as a response to polarization remains to be seen. But at minimum, we should take seriously what prayer teaches us about the kinds of democratic citizens we can—and perhaps must—become: humble enough to accept defeat, strong enough to resist injustice, and wise enough to know that, in democracy as in life, we see through a glass darkly.

A Deeper Democratic Hope

We began this book with a simple but unsettling observation: America has been losing its religion, and the result has been greater division, not less.

The expectation was that as traditional faith receded from public life, something better would take its place: a more rational politics, a more tolerant culture, a calmer, more deliberative public square where citizens could sit together and work things out like adults. That was the expectation.

The reality has been something else entirely. As churches empty, politics hasn't become more reasonable but rather more desperate. Americans didn't stop needing the things religion once provided—meaning, belonging, a sense that their lives mattered in some ultimate way—they just started looking for those things in the wrong places.

We've tried to make sense of this predicament over the course of eight chapters, and we've done so not by offering a neat political program or a policy agenda for democratic renewal. We've done something different and perhaps more radical. We've gone back—way back—to the ancient reservoirs of two of the world's oldest and most enduring religions, Christianity and Islam, and we've asked a provocative question: What if the cure for our democratic sickness isn't less religion but more?

If that question makes you uncomfortable, good. It should. We've been uncomfortable with it ourselves at times. The case for more religion in public life is not the sort of argument that earns you applause in the green rooms of cable news or at faculty cocktail parties. People hear "more religion" and they think theocracy, they think the Taliban, they think the January 6 insurrectionists waving crosses as they storm the Capitol. And they're not wrong to worry. Those things are real.

But here's what we keep coming back to. The choice was never between religion and no religion. The choice was between religion that knows itself as religion and religion that doesn't, between a faith that is self-aware of its own passions and pieties, and one that isn't. Some of the most zealous practitioners of political faith in America today are often the ones who would never set foot in a church or mosque. They don't think of themselves as religious. But watch how they behave: the purity tests, the excommunications, the moral panics, and the conviction that they alone have a monopoly on the truth. Strip away the language and what you're left with is a familiar structure—one that looks an awful lot like the religious fundamentalism these same people claim to oppose.

The difference is that traditional religion, at its best, comes equipped with internal checks on its own worst impulses. It has centuries of hard-won wisdom about the dangers of self-righteousness, the limits of human knowledge, and the ever-present temptation to mistake your own will for God's. Our secular political religions have no such safeguards. They are often all zeal and zero humility, all judgment and no mercy. That is what makes them dangerous—not that they care too much but that they care without any self-awareness that they might be wrong.

In this book, we've drawn on our respective traditions to address eight challenges facing democratic life. We've argued that conflict is inevitable and that pretending otherwise makes things worse. We've made the case that epistemological humility—the recognition that our knowledge is partial, provisional, and shaped by our limitations—is a sign not of weakness but of wisdom. We've suggested, perhaps controversially, that the concept of hell has something important to teach a society that longs for swift and immediate justice in the here and now. Sometimes, it's better to wait. We've explored how something we call *covenant* offers a richer, more relational model for political life than the purity-driven exclusion that dominates so much of our discourse. We've looked at how religious institutions function as training grounds for citizenship. And we have ended with prayer, which might sound like an odd prescription for political renewal but is, we believe, one of the most underrated civic practices available.

These are not solutions. We want to be clear about that, because the temptation to present religion as a solution is itself part of the problem. Religion is not a tool. It is not a means to an end. You don't go to church or mosque because it will make you a better citizen, even if it might. You go because you have faith, even if you can't fully articulate how this faith works. The democratic benefits of faith are, in this sense, a by-product. They emerge not from the instrumentalization of religion but from the genuine practice of it.

This distinction matters. When religion becomes a political instrument—when it's reduced to a cudgel for winning elections or rallying a base—it ceases to be religion in any meaningful sense. We've seen this happen across the American political landscape, where faith has been hollowed out and repurposed as a vehicle for tribal identity. The label remains but without the substance. This isn't more religion. It's less religion with a lot more volume.

We are an odd pair, the two of us. A Muslim political scientist and a Christian theologian who disagree on quite a lot. We don't share the same view of God, salvation, scripture, or the afterlife. We don't vote the same way. We don't always see eye to eye on policy, and we certainly don't agree on some of the more contentious questions roiling American politics. In a culture that increasingly sorts people into teams and demands that you choose sides, our friendship is, frankly, a little weird.

But that's the point. Or at least part of it.

The fact that we've managed to write a book together—arguing, debating, pushing back, and occasionally getting on each other's nerves—without resolving our deepest disagreements is itself a modest proof of concept. We didn't set out to find common ground in the way that phrase is usually meant. We didn't water down our respective convictions to arrive at some bland consensus. If anything, our years of conversation have made us more rooted in our own traditions, not less. Engaging seriously with someone who sees the world differently has a way of sharpening your understanding of what you actually believe and why.

This is what we mean when we talk about the strangeness of religion being a gift. In a culture that prizes sameness and comfort, encountering someone whose fundamental commitments are genuinely different from your own—not superficially different but deeply, irreducibly so—can be disorienting. But that disorientation can be productive. It forces you to examine your assumptions. It reminds you that your way of seeing the world is not the only way. And it gives you practice in the difficult democratic art of coexisting with people you think are wrong about important things.

One of the recurring themes of this book has been the distinction between certainty and confidence—and where each properly belongs. We are both certain about the fundamentals of our respective faiths. Shadi believes the Quran is the word of God. Matthew believes in the person of Jesus Christ. These are not negotiable positions for either of us, and we do not hold them tentatively. But here is the critical move: Our certainty about the truth of our faiths does not translate into certainty about every political judgment we make in their name.

We are certain that God is just. We are far less certain that we know exactly what justice requires in any given policy debate. It is precisely because we believe our faiths are true that we take seriously their warnings against confusing our political preferences with the will of God. When you are grounded in what you believe, you can afford to listen to someone who believes differently, because your faith is not so fragile that a good counterargument will shatter it. You can sit with discomfort. You can tolerate ambiguity on political questions without feeling that your entire worldview has collapsed.

This is harder than it sounds. Our political culture rewards certainty about everything—not just about God but about tax policy, immigration, whether wars should be waged, or the moral worth of the other party's voters. To say "I'm not sure how my faith applies here" is to invite accusations of weakness, naivete, or capitulation. But the great thinkers of both our traditions understood that political certainty is a dangerous drug—dangerous because it tempts us to claim a totalizing perspective that belongs to God alone, not to us, and certainly not to our preferred political party.

Here is one of the many things we have learned from each other. In the Islamic tradition, the gap between divine knowledge and human understanding is not a minor caveat—it is foundational. A Muslim can be wholly certain that the Quran is true and still recognize that no single human being has an exclusive claim on its political implications. For a Muslim to claim that kind of interpretive certainty is to commit a theological trespass of the highest order. Christianity arrives at a similar conclusion by a different route: Creation is marked by brokenness, and our attempts to understand and apply God's truth to the political realm are always impacted by who we are and where we stand. Both traditions, in their own way, are telling us the same uncomfortable thing about our politics, which is that you are not as right as you think you are. This is not a call for religious relativism. It is an invitation to intellectual honesty about political life—the kind of honesty that makes genuine conversation possible, and without which democracy is just organized shouting.

There is a line from earlier in this book that we keep returning to: "Neither of us believes that the other's religion is true." When we first wrote that sentence, it felt risky to put it on the page. In most interfaith contexts, the polite thing to do is to emphasize common ground, to focus on shared values, to sand down the edges of real disagreement until everyone can nod along comfortably. We didn't want to do that. We wanted to be honest, not because honesty is a virtue we're particularly good at practicing but because dishonesty about our differences would have undermined everything this book is trying to say.

And yet here we are, at the end of a project that has taken years of conversation, argument, and the more than occasional sharp exchange. We haven't converted each other. We haven't even come close. But something else has happened, something harder to name. Through the act of taking each other's traditions seriously—not as curiosities to be studied but as living reservoirs of wisdom that make real claims about the world—we've arrived at a kind of mutual regard that doesn't require agreement. Call it deep disagreement held in deeper respect. It's what years of working and writing together actually feels like.

We're under no illusions. Religion may not save democracy, even if we think it *can*. We chose the title of this book as a question, not an answer, because we don't have an answer—at least not a tidy one. What we have are resources, practices, and hard-won wisdom from ancient traditions that have been grappling with deep human differences for far longer than the secular modern West. Our religious resources are imperfect, as everything interpreted through humans is imperfect. They've been misused and abused, wielded as instruments of oppression and exclusion. We know this. We've said this. We'll say it again.

But the fact that religion can be misused does not mean it has nothing to offer. The question is not whether our faith traditions have ever been complicit in injustice. Of course they have. The question is whether they also contain deep resources and power for resisting that exact same injustice, for cultivating the kinds of citizens who can sustain democratic life over the long haul. We believe they do—not because we're naive about religion's failures but because we've seen its capabilities up close.

We think the answer to our democratic crisis involves cultivating democratic virtues that have fallen out of fashion: patience, humility, the willingness to lose gracefully, the ability to hold strong convictions without being consumed by them. These capacities don't come from reading the right op-ed, listening to the right podcast, or getting the right education. They have to be practiced, ritualized, and embodied in rich moral communities that have been doing this work for a very long time.

When healthy, Christianity and Islam shape and form people in precisely those capacities that democratic life requires: the humility to acknowledge that you might be wrong, the courage to stand up for what you believe is right, the patience to endure political outcomes you didn't want, and the hope that things can get better even when the evidence is discouraging.

Hope is the operative word here, not optimism. That's different. Optimism is the belief that things will probably work out. Hope is the stubborn refusal to give up even when they probably won't. Democracy can't endure on optimism; it needs an almost dogmatic hope. Democracy demands that citizens keep believing in the possibility of persuasion even when their fellow citizens seem so far out of reach. Hope does not come easy in an age of political exhaustion, cynicism, and mutual contempt. It runs against every human instinct that we have. But hope is exactly what democracy demands. And this is precisely what our respective traditions have to offer.

When we started writing this book, the political landscape in the United States was already fractured. By the time we finished, it had gotten worse. Elections came and went, each one supposedly the most consequential in American history. Political violence moved from the unthinkable to the unsurprising. Trust in institutions continued its long decline. The feeling that America was coming apart wasn't paranoia; it was simply the truth.

And yet.

We remain convinced that the resources for democratic renewal are closer at hand than many realize. These don't require a new political party, leader, or revolutionary movement. They don't demand that we all agree or even like one another. What this democratic renewal will require is something at once more modest and more radical, a willingness to draw on wisdom that is older than our current crisis.

We recognize that not every reader will find this persuasive. Some will close this book thinking that two religious guys gave it a nice try but ultimately asked too much. Fair enough. We're not in the business of forcing anyone to believe anything. That would defeat the purpose.

But we'd ask this much. Before you dismiss our argument, consider the alternative. Consider what a politics without any transcendent reference point actually looks like—a politics in which human beings are the final measure of all things, in which there's no authority higher than the state, no accountability beyond the next election cycle, no basis for human dignity other than whatever consensus happens to hold at the moment. We don't need to imagine such a political culture; we're living it.

Our faith traditions can push back against this. They can insist that human dignity is our due, not because we say so but because God says so. They insist that every human being has inherent worth, not because of how they vote or the virtues they happen to signal but because of who made them. They insist that justice matters, that mercy is possible, and that a final accounting is coming regardless of whether our earthly courts manage to deliver one. As we've said repeatedly, the fact that final accounting comes later—in the next life—should, ideally, allow us to "chill" in the here and now.

You don't have to be religious to benefit from living in a society where many of your fellow citizens are religious. That's one of religion's underappreciated gifts to democratic life. Even the nonreligious benefit from a moral ecology in which people act as though their behavior matters in some ultimate sense. It can be a profoundly good thing to live, work, and vote alongside citizens who believe that they will be held accountable for their actions by a higher power.

We end where we began, with a friendship that shouldn't work but does. A Muslim and a Christian who disagree profoundly on questions that matter enormously to both of us. We've spent years in conversation, and we're no closer to agreement on the big theological questions than when we started.

Rather than requiring agreement, democracy requires something harder: the willingness to live with disagreement, to make room for people who see the world differently, and to resist the urge to resolve the tension prematurely by silencing or converting the other side.

That might not sound like much. In an age that demands grand solutions and transformative visions. It can feel small. But we've come to believe that "enough to keep going" is precisely what democracy needs most. Not a utopian vision of how things should be but the gritty, unglamorous determination to keep showing up, to keep talking to people you disagree with, to keep praying for those who wrong you, to keep failing and trying again.

Democracy, after all, is a training in disappointment. Every political season brings with it the hope that this time things will be different, and every political season ends with the reminder that they mostly aren't. The question is what you do with that disappointment. Do you let it curdle into cynicism? Do you let it harden into rage? Or do you find a way to hold it, to sit with it, to let it develop rather than destroy you?

In the Islamic tradition, there is a concept called *sabr*, often translated as "patience" but meaning something closer to endurance or the capacity to persist in the face of hardship without losing hope or giving in to despair. The Quran speaks repeatedly of *sabr* as among the highest virtues, promising that "God is with those who are patient" (Q 2:153). Christianity has its own parallel: the theological virtue of hope, which is not optimism but something sturdier—the stubborn insistence that redemption remains possible even when all visible evidence argues otherwise.

Hope is not a strategy. It is something far greater. Hope is a way of being human and a way of remaining human in a political environment that is anything but. We have not offered you, dear reader, a "strategy" for saving democracy. Instead, we've offered ways of being human in a world that doesn't always cooperate with our plans. These are, if you like, postures that neither surrender to chaos nor pretend it isn't there.

We will keep looking together. That, in the end, may be the most democratic thing religion has to teach us: how to live with what we cannot fully know, how to act on what we cannot prove, and how to remain in community with people whose deepest convictions we do not share.

The hour is late. But the door is still open.

Acknowledgments

While only two names appear on the front of this book, a substantial network of generous individuals and institutions stands behind it. Our unique friendship and partnership have been nurtured by a forward-thinking community of generous colleagues, organizations, and foundations.

Our deep thanks to the Templeton Religion Trust for their early support of our research on religion, democracy, and pluralism. In addition to encouraging our writing, the Trust has enabled us to launch the Templeton Pluralism Fellowship, which gathers emerging Muslim and Christian scholars working at the intersection of faith, politics, and pluralism. Leading this cohort of emerging thought leaders has been a tremendously encouraging and rewarding experience for both of us.

Our thanks as well to our institutional home, Georgetown University, and the gifted team at the Alwaleed Center for Muslim-Christian Understanding. Our colleagues there—Nader Hashemi, Jonathan Stupple, and Rachel Collins in particular—have blessed us with incredible hospitality, support, and encouragement in this work.

Several other institutions dedicated to faith, democracy, and pluralism are deserving of special recognition. The Center for Public Justice brought us together for the first time for a joint event in 2018, and they've been consistent supporters of our work in faith and politics ever since. The Fetzer Institute has offered invaluable assistance to these various projects through their mission to address social problems through the cultivation of rich spiritual resources. *Comment Magazine* and its editor Anne Snyder approached us early on wanting to invest and participate in this project through producing our podcast *Zealots at the Gate* and extending these conversations throughout North America. We're deeply grateful to her for taking a chance on this project and to our producers Matt and Allie Crummy for their steady encouragement and support.

Several universities, think tanks, and organizations have invited us to speak or consult on these issues. In doing so, they've created invaluable spaces for us to challenge and develop our thinking. We're particularly grateful for Neighborly Faith, Faith Angle Forum, the Aspen Institute's Religion and Society Program, Veritas Forum, Interfaith America, the Danforth Center on Religion and Politics at Washington University–St. Louis, Theological University Utrecht, and the Institute on Religion and Democracy.

For helping to bring this book to fruition we would like to thank our editor Katelyn Beaty and our agent Bridget Matzie for the consistent encouragement, counsel, and advice. Our research assistants Yusuf Lenfest, Gregory Conarroe, Meg Jenista, and Rachel Collins each provided an incredible amount of support. Far more than simply running down references and quotes, each one of them provided valuable critiques and insights during the writing process. This project simply wouldn't have been possible without them.

On a personal note, I (Shadi) would like to thank some of the people who have been instrumental in shaping my own thinking on religion and pluralism, including Mustafa Akyol, Samuel Kimbriel, Jonathan Brown, Ovamir Anjum, Hadia Mubarak, Eboo Patel, Andrew March, Mohammad Fadel, Asifa Quraishi-Landes, and Anver Emon.

I (Matthew) would also like to thank several friends and colleagues who have shaped my thinking in these same areas: John Inazu, Jonathan Chaplin, Robert Joustra, Asma Uddin, Kevin Den Dulk, George Harinck, Richard Mouw, Michael Wear, Kristen Deede Johnson, Luke Bretherton, Micah Watson, Elaine Ecklund, and James K. A. Smith.

Finally, we would like to offer a word of special thanks to Chris Seiple, who invited us into his home years ago and spoke a strong word of encouragement and advice into how we might enrich and extend these conversations on pluralism to a broader public audience. His early and consistent support throughout this project is deeply appreciated. We are not alone in this indebtedness to Chris Seiple; he has been an incredible supporter of so many of us working in this space for so many years.

Notes

Preface

1. "Political Polarization in the American Public," Pew Research Center, June 12, 2014, https://www.pewresearch.org/politics/2014/06/12/section-3-political-polarization-and-personal-life/.

2. Jim Davis, Michael Graham, and Ryan P. Burge, *The Great Dechurching: Who's Leaving, Why Are They Going, and What Will It Take to Bring Them Back?* (Zondervan Reflective, 2023), 12.

Introduction

1. Gregory A. Smith, Alan Cooperman, Becka A. Alper, et al., "Decline of Christianity in the U.S. Has Slowed, May Have Leveled Off," Pew Research Center, February 26, 2025, https://www.pewresearch.org/religion/2025/02/26/decline-of-christianity-in-the-us-has-slowed-may-have-leveled-off/.

2. Barack Obama, "Keynote Address at the 2004 Democratic National Convention," Boston, MA, July 27, 2004, https://www.presidency.ucsb.edu/documents/keynote-address-the-2004-democratic-national-convention.

3. Jeffrey M. Jones, "U.S. Church Membership Falls Below Majority for First Time," Gallup, March 29, 2021, https://news.gallup.com/poll/341963/church-membership-falls-below-majority-first-time.aspx.

4. Steven Bullivant, *Nonverts: The Making of Ex-Christian America* (Oxford University Press, 2022), 5–9.

5. Smith, Cooperman, Alper, et al., "Decline of Christianity."

6. See Robert Hunt, "Public Missiology and Anxious Tribalism," *Missiology: An International Review* 44, no. 2 (2016): 129–41.

7. Ezra Klein and Ross Douthat, "Ross Douthat on Trump, Mysticism, and Psychedelics," *New York Times*, April 25, 2025, https://www.nytimes.com/2025/04/25/opinion/ezra-klein-podcast-ross-douthat.html.

8. Ross Douthat (@DouthatNYT), "A thought sent back in time to the theocracy panic of 2005: If you dislike the religious right, wait till you meet the post-religious

right," Twitter (now X), February 29, 2016, https://x.com/DouthatNYT/status/704462319074594816.

9. "Trump Posts an Image of Himself as Pope," *New York Times*, May 6, 2025, https://www.nytimes.com/2025/05/03/us/politics/trump-pope-photo.html.

10. Robert Wuthnow, *Why Religion Is Good for American Democracy* (Princeton University Press, 2021), 6.

11. "Non-Religious Voters Wield Clout, Tilt Heavily Democratic," *Associated Press*, December 3, 2022, https://whyy.org/articles/non-religious-voters-wield-clout-tilt-heavily-democratic/.

12. Ryan Burge, "2024 Election Post-Mortem: Evangelicals," Graphs About Religion, April 21, 2025, https://www.graphsaboutreligion.com/p/2024-election-post-mortem-evangelicals.

13. "Evangelical Protestants," Pew Research Center, accessed February 11, 2026, https://www.pewresearch.org/religious-landscape-study/religious-tradition/evangelical-protestant/.

14. Gregory A. Smith, "More White Americans Adopted Than Shed Evangelical Label During Trump Presidency, Especially His Supporters," Pew Research Center, September 15, 2021, https://www.pewresearch.org/short-reads/2021/09/15/more-white-americans-adopted-than-shed-evangelical-label-during-trump-presidency-especially-his-supporters/.

15. John F. Helliwell, Richard Layard, Jeffery D. Sachs, Jan-Emmanuel De Neve, Lara B. Aknin, and Shun Wang, eds., *World Happiness Report 2024* (University of Oxford Wellbeing Research Centre, 2024), 24–26, https://worldhappiness.report/ed/2024/.

16. Michael J. Roche and Nicolas C. Jacobson, "Elections Have Consequences for Student Mental Health: An Accidental Daily Diary Study," *Psychological Reports* 122, no. 2 (2019): 451–64; American Psychological Association, *Stress in America: Coping with Change*, February 15, 2017, https://www.apa.org/news/press/releases/stress/2016/coping-with-change.pdf, 1–6; "2020 Presidential Election a Source of Significant Stress for More Americans than 2016 Presidential Race," American Psychological Association, October 7, 2020, https://www.apa.org/news/press/releases/2020/10/election-stress; and "Political Breaking Point: Over 60% Say 2024 Election Is Damaging Their Mental Health," StudyFinds, October 25, 2024, https://studyfinds.org/political-breaking-point-2024/.

17. Christopher H. Achen and Larry M. Bartels, *Democracy for Realists: Why Elections Do Not Produce Responsive Government* (Princeton University Press, 2017), 232.

18. John Gray, *Two Faces of Liberalism* (Polity Press, 2000), 4.

19. "Political Polarization in the American Public," Pew Research Center, June 12, 2014, https://www.pewresearch.org/politics/2014/06/12/section-3-political-polarization-and-personal-life/.

20. Kevin B. Smith, Matthew V. Hibbing, and John R. Hibbing, "Friends, Relatives, Sanity, and Health: The Costs of Politics," *PLoS ONE* 14, no. 9 (2019): 11.

21. Publius Decius Mus (Michael Anton), "The Flight 93 Election," Claremont Review of Books, September 5, 2016, https://claremontreviewofbooks.com/digital/the-flight-93-election/.

22. Kevin B. Smith, "Politics Is Making Us Sick: The Negative Impact of Political Engagement on Public Health During the Trump Administration," *PLoS ONE* 17, no. 1 (2022), https://journals.plos.org/plosone/article?id=10.1371/journal.pone.0262022.

23. Smith, "Politics Is Making Us Sick," 3. See also Melissa J. Hagan, Michael R. Sladek, Linda J. Luecken, and Leah D. Doane, "Event-Related Clinical Distress in College Students: Responses to the 2016 U.S. Presidential Election," *Journal of American College Health* 68 no. 1 (2018): 21–25; Isabel Musse and Rodrigo Schneider, "The Effect of Presidential Election Outcomes on Alcohol Drinking," *SSRN* (March 16, 2022): 3; and Shevaun D. Neupert, Jennifer A. Bellingtier, and Emily L. Smith, "Emotional Reactivity Changes to Daily Stressors Surrounding the 2016 U.S. Presidential Election," *Current Psychology* 40 (2021): 2832–42.

24. Centers for Disease Control and Prevention, "U.S. Teen Girls Experiencing Increased Sadness and Violence," CDC Newsroom, February 13, 2023, https://www.cdc.gov/media/releases/2023/p0213-yrbs.html.

25. Richard Reeves, *Of Boys and Men: Why the Modern Male Is Struggling, Why It Matters, and What to Do About It* (Brookings Institution, 2022).

26. Helliwell et al., *World Happiness Report 2024*, 15.

27. Catherine Gimbrone, Lisa M. Bates, Seth J. Prins, and Katherine M. Keyes, "The Politics of Depression: Diverging Trends in Internalizing Symptoms Among US Adolescents by Political Beliefs," *PLoS ONE* 17, no. 1 (2022), https://doi.org/10.1016/j.ssmmh.2021.100043.

28. Kyle Orton (@KyleWOrton), "Fascinating thread. Opens a whole new reading list. It meshes with a line of thought I'm increasingly unable to shake: namely that tolerance might not be possible from the secular world, tinged as it is with utopianism and a drive for final victories (over 'hatred' etc.)," Twitter (now X), November 9, 2018, https://twitter.com/KyleWOrton/status/1061067839342370817.

29. Quoted in Shadi Hamid, "America Without God," *The Atlantic*, April 2021, https://www.theatlantic.com/magazine/archive/2021/04/america-politics-religion/618072/.

30. "Religion's Relationship to Happiness, Civic Engagement and Health Around the World," Pew Research Center, January 31, 2019, https://www.pewresearch.org/religion/2019/01/31/religions-relationship-to-happiness-civic-engagement-and-health-around-the-world/.

31. Robert D. Putnam and David E. Campbell, *American Grace: How Religion Divides and Unites Us* (Simon & Schuster, 2010), 472.

32. Joseph Kip Kosek, *Acts of Conscience: Christian Nonviolence and Modern American Democracy* (Columbia University Press, 2009), 7.

33. Putnam and Campbell, *American Grace*, 71.

34. William T. Cavanaugh, *The Myth of Religious Violence* (Oxford University Press, 2009), 15.

35. Putnam and Campbell, *American Grace*, 54.

36. See Alan Bullock, *Hitler: A Study in Tyranny*, abridged ed. (HarperPerennial, 1962), 219.

37. Gregory A. Smith et al., "Decline of Christianity in the U.S. Has Slowed, May Have Leveled Off," Pew Research Center, February 26, 2025, https://www.pewresearch.org/religion/2025/02/26/decline-of-christianity-in-the-us-has-slowed-may-have-leveled-off/.

Chapter 1 We Can't Quit Religion

1. Bob Dylan, "Gotta Serve Somebody," track 1 on *Slow Train Coming*, Columbia Records, 1979.

2. John Lennon, "Imagine," track 1 on *Imagine*, Apple Records, 1977.

3. Neil Rothschild, "Young Dems More Likely to Despise the Other Party," *Axios*, December 8, 2021, https://www.axios.com/2021/12/08/poll-political-polarization-students.

4. Wendy Wang, "The Partisan Marriage Gap Is Bigger Than Ever," *The Hill*, October 27, 2020, https://thehill.com/opinion/white-house/522987-the-partisan-marriage-gap-is-bigger-than-ever/.

5. Abraham Kuyper, *Ons Program* (J. H. Kruyt, 1879), 53.

6. Phil Zuckerman, John T. Jost, Kevin D. Wilson, and Daniel T. M. Kinkaid, "The Nonreligious as Political and Moral Counterweights," *Personality and Social Psychology Review* 14, no. 1 (2010): 49, https://doi.org/10.1177/1088868309353759.

7. Jared Friedman and Anthony I. Jack, "What Makes You So Sure? Dogmatism, Fundamentalism, Analytic Thinking, Perspective Taking and Moral Concern in the Religious and Nonreligious," *Journal of Religion and Health* 57, no. 1 (February 2018): 50.

8. Friedrich Wilhelm Nietzsche, *The Gay Science*, trans. Walter Kaufmann (Vintage Books, 1974), 181.

9. Abraham Kuyper, *Lectures on Calvinism* (Eerdmans, 1931), 23.

10. Kuyper, *Lectures on Calvinism*, 87.

11. *The Guardian* newspaper reported that an overwhelming majority of "MPs voted 494–36 in favour of banning 'conspicuous' religious symbols in the schools." See Jon Henley, "French MPs Vote for Veil Ban in State Schools," *The Guardian*, February 11, 2004, https://www.theguardian.com/world/2004/feb/11/schools.schoolsworldwide.

12. Aala Abdelgadir and Vasiliki Fouka, "Political Secularism and Muslim Integration in the West: Assessing the Effects of the French Headscarf Ban," *American Political Science Review* 114, no. 3 (2020): 707–23.

13. Abraham Kuyper, "Sphere Sovereignty," in *Abraham Kuyper: A Centennial Reader*, ed. James D. Bratt (Eerdmans, 1998), 486.

14. Abraham Kuyper, *Encyclopedia of Sacred Theology: Its Principles*, trans. J. Hendrik de Vries (Charles Scribner's Sons, 1898), 152.

15. Kuyper, *Encyclopedia of Sacred Theology*, 132.

16. Kuyper, *Lectures on Calvinism*, 131.

17. Abraham Kuyper, *Our Program*, ed. and trans. Harry Van Dyke (Lexham, 2015), 32.

Chapter 2 Conflict Is Inevitable

1. J. B. Bury, *The Idea of Progress: An Inquiry into Its Origin and Growth* (The Floating Press, 2009), 15.

2. See Talal Asad, *Formations of the Secular: Christianity, Islam, Modernity* (Stanford University Press, 2003).

3. Saba Mahmood, *Religious Difference in a Secular Age: A Minority Report* (Princeton University Press, 2016), 1.

4. Mark Murray, "'Anger on Their Minds': NBC News Poll Finds Sky-High Interest and Polarization Ahead of Midterms," *NBC News*, October 23, 2022, https://www.nbcnews.com/meet-the-press/first-read/anger-minds-nbc-news-poll-finds-sky-high-interest-polarization-ahead-m-rcna53512.

5. "Amid Campaign Turmoil, Biden Holds Wide Lead on Coronavirus, Unifying the Country," Pew Research Center, October 9, 2020, https://www.pewresearch.org/politics/2020/10/09/amid-campaign-turmoil-biden-holds-wide-leads-on-coronavirus-unifying-the-country/.

6. Bury, *Idea of Progress*, 15.

7. Chantal Mouffe, *Agonistics: Thinking the World Politically* (Verso, 2013), 2–3.

8. Chantal Mouffe, *The Democratic Paradox* (Verso, 2009), 93.

9. Mouffe, *Democratic Paradox*, 17.

10. Mouffe, *Agonistics*, 5.

11. Mouffe, *Agonistics*, 7.

12. See Jacques Derrida, "Hostipitality," *Angelaki* 5, no. 3 (2000): 3–18.

13. For the most authoritative and influential exploration of "creative destruction," see Joseph A. Schumpeter, *Capitalism, Socialism, and Democracy* (Routledge Classics, 2010).

14. Robert Wuthnow, *Why Religion Is Good for Democracy* (Princeton University Press, 2022), 17–18.

15. Abraham Kuyper, "Calvinism: Source and Stronghold of Our Constitutional Liberties," in *Abraham Kuyper: A Centennial Reader*, ed. James Bratt (Eerdmans, 1998), 390.

16. Abraham Kuyper, *Lectures on Calvinism* (Eerdmans, 1931), 44–45.

17. Kuyper, *Lectures on Calvinism,* 44–45.

18. Kuyper, "Calvinism," 390.

19. Abraham Kuyper, *Our Program: A Christian Political Manifesto*, trans. Harry Van Dyke (Lexham, 2015), 37.

20. Kuyper, *Our Program*, 37.

21. Kuyper, *Our Program*, 37.

22. On Muhammad's role in the founding of Islam, see Shadi Hamid, *Islamic Exceptionalism: How the Struggle Over Islam Is Reshaping the World* (St. Martin's Press, 2016), 45–49.

23. Andrew March, "Genealogies of Sovereignty in Islamic Political Theology," Yale Law School, Public Law Working Paper no. 268, p. 3, https://papers.ssrn.com/sol3/papers.cfm?abstract_id=2166953.

24. John Voll, *Islam: Continuity and Change in the Modern Era* (Syracuse University Press, 1994), 351.

25. Sahih Muslim 2749, book 50, hadith 13, Sunnah.com, accessed April 2, 2026, https://sunnah.com/muslim/50.

Chapter 3 God Only Knows

1. Brian Wilson with Ben Greenman, *I Am Brian Wilson: A Memoir* (Da Capo Press, 2016).

2. Brian Wilson, "God Only Knows," single by *The Beach Boys*, Capitol, 1966.

3. Kevin Vallier, *Must Politics Be War? Restoring Our Trust in the Open Society* (Oxford University Press, 2019), 46.

4. Slavoj Žižek, "Some Politically Incorrect Reflections on Violence in France and Related Matters," in *The Universal Exception*, ed. Rex Butler and Scott Stephens (Continuum, 2007), 308–9 (emphasis original).

5. Lesslie Newbigin, *The Gospel in a Pluralist Society* (Eerdmans, 1989), 33.

6. Abū Nuʿaym al-Iṣfahānī, *Ḥilyat al-Awliyāʾ wa-Ṭabaqāt al-Aṣfiyāʾ*, vol. 9, ed. Muḥammad Ibrāhīm al-Bannā, Muḥammad Aḥmad ʿAbd al-ʿAzīz, and Yūsuf al-Baqʿūrī (Dār al-Kutub al-ʿIlmiyyah, 1985), 123.

7. Anne Lamott, *Plan B: Further Thoughts on Faith* (Penguin, 2006), 256–57.

8. On this, see Khaled Abou El Fadl, *Speaking in God's Name: Islamic Law, Authority and Women* (Oneworld Publications, 2001), 24.

9. On apophatic theology, or the tradition of describing God by what God is not, see Rowan Williams, "Negative Theology: Some Misunderstandings," *Modern Theology* 40, no. 1 (January 2024): 243–55.

10. Ibn al-Qayyim, *Iʿlām al-Muwaqqiʿīn*, vol. 4 (Dar ibn al-Jawzi, 2002), 470.

11. An explanation of the basic idea behind this maxim can be found in Aḥmad b. Muḥammad al-Zarqā, *Sharḥ al-Qawā'id al-Fiqhiyyah*, ed. Muṣṭafā Aḥmad al-Zarqā, 4th ed. (Dār al-Qalam, 1996), 227–29.

Chapter 4 Make Politics Mundane Again

1.Tim Reid, Gabriella Borter, and Michael Martina, "'You Are No Longer My Mother': A Divided America Will Struggle to Heal After Trump Era," *Reuters*, November 3, 2020, https://cloudflare.egyptindependent.com/you-are-no-longer-my-mother-how-the-election-is-dividing-american-families/.

2. Jonathan Haidt, *The Righteous Mind: Why Good People Are Divided by Politics and Religion* (Pantheon Books, 2012), 239.

3. Haidt, *Righteous Mind*, 25.

4. "The Partisan Divide on Political Values Grows Even Wider," Pew Research Center, October 5, 2017, https://www.pewresearch.org/politics/2017/10/05/the-partisan-divide-on-political-values-grows-even-wider/.

5. Alysse ElHage, "Marriages Between Democrats and Republicans Are Extremely Rare," Institute for Family Studies, January 30, 2020, https://ifstudies.org/blog/marriages-between-democrats-and-republicans-are-extremely-rare.

6. Lynn Vavreck, "Americans Tend to Be Married to Their Political Party," UCLA Newsroom, February 3, 2020, https://newsroom.ucla.edu/stories/ucla-faculty-voice-americans-tend-to-be-married-to-their-political-party.

7. Sarah Marx, "Political Preferences Increasingly Influence Migration Patterns: Redfin," *HousingWire*, February 7, 2024, https://www.housingwire.com/articles/political-preferences-increasingly-influence-migration-patterns-redfin/.

8. Hannah Robbins, "Poll: Nearly Half of Americans Think Members of the Opposing Political Party Are 'Evil,'" Johns Hopkins University Hub, October 27, 2024, https://hub.jhu.edu/2024/10/27/snf-agora-poll-september-2024/.

9. See Justin Martyr, "The First Apology," in *The Fathers of the Church: A New Translation*, trans. Thomas B. Falls (The Catholic University of America Press, 1965), 38–39.

10. Muḥammad ʿAbduh, *Risālat al-Tawḥīd*, ed. and trans. Ishaq Musa'ad and Kenneth Cragg (al-Manar, 1897; repr., Allen & Unwin, 1966).

11. Barbara Walters, interview by Piers Morgan on *Piers Morgan Live* (CNN), December 10, 2013, quoted in Jonathon M. Seidl, "Piers Morgan: 'We Thought That [Obama] Was Going to Be the Next Messiah,'" Blaze Media, December 18, 2013,

https://www.theblaze.com/news/2013/12/18/barbara-walters-to-piers-morgan-we-thought-that-obama-was-going-to-be-the-next-messiah.

12. Barack Obama, "Democratic Nomination Victory Speech," St. Paul, MN, American Rhetoric, June 3, 2008, https://www.americanrhetoric.com/speeches/barackobamademocraticnominationvictoryspeech.htm.

13. St. Augustine of Hippo, *The City of God*, trans. Henry Bettenson (Penguin Books, 2003), 70–80.

14. See Christopher J. H. Wright, *Here Are Your Gods: Faithful Discipleship in Idolatrous Times* (InterVarsity, 2020).

15. Augustine, *The City of God*, trans. Henry Bettenson (Penguin Classics, 2003), book 19, chap. 13.

16. Augustine, *City of God*, book 14, chap. 28.

17. As discussed in Haidt, *Righteous Mind*, 30.

18. Abdolkarim Soroush, "Abdolkarim Soroush," Berkley Center for Religion, Peace, and World Affairs, Georgetown University, accessed March 11, 2026, https://berkleycenter.georgetown.edu/people/abdolkarim-soroush.

19. Khaled Abou El Fadl, *The Great Theft: Wrestling Islam from the Extremists* (HarperSanFrancisco, 2005), 23–25.

20. Sayyid Qutb, *Milestones*, ed. and trans. A. B. al-Mehri (The Mother Mosque Foundation, 2006), 60.

21. Sayyid Qutb, *Milestones*, 60.

22. Muqtedar Khan, "Syed Qutb—John Locke of the Islamic World," Brookings Institution, July 28, 2003, https://www.brookings.edu/articles/syed-qutb-john-locke-of-the-islamic-world/.

23. Khan, "Syed Qutb."

Chapter 5 The Case for Hell

1. Megan Brenan, "Belief in Five Spiritual Entities Edges Down to New Lows," Gallup, July 20, 2023, https://news.gallup.com/poll/508886/belief-five-spiritual-entities-edges-down-new-lows.aspx.

2. Gregory A. Smith, Alan Cooperman, Becka A. Alper, et al., "Religious and Spiritual Beliefs," Pew Research Center, February 26, 2025, https://www.pewresearch.org/religion/2025/02/26/religious-and-spiritual-beliefs/#belief-in-hell.

3. See Shadi Hamid, "Hell Is Necessary," *Wisdom of Crowds* (Substack), May 20, 2024, https://wisdomofcrowds.live/p/hell-is-necessary.

4. Hannah Arendt, *Between Past and Future: Eight Exercises in Political Thought* (Penguin, 2006), 133.

5. Robert Golding, "Making Sense of Hell," *Themelios*, The Gospel Coalition, accessed June 25, 2025, https://www.thegospelcoalition.org/themelios/article/making-sense-of-hell/.

6. Anas ibn Mālik, in *Musnad Aḥmad*, reports that the Prophet asked Jibrīl why Mikāʾīl never laughed, to which Jibrīl replied, "He has not laughed since Hell was created." Aḥmad ibn Ḥanbal, *Musnad Aḥmad*, vol. 3 (Dār al-Maʿrifah, n.d.), hadith 13343.

7. Rachel Falconer, *Hell in Contemporary Literature: Western Descent Narratives Since 1945* (Edinburgh University Press, 2005).

8. Vinson Cunningham, "How the Idea of Hell Has Shaped the Way We Think," *The New Yorker*, January 21, 2019, https://www.newyorker.com/magazine/2019/01/21/how-the-idea-of-hell-has-shaped-the-way-we-think.

9. Derek Thompson, "The News Media's Dangerous Obsession with 'Fake Facts,'" *The Ringer*, June 7, 2024, https://www.theringer.com/2024/06/07/media/news-media-dangerous-obsession-with-fake-facts-negativity-bias.

10. In the forty-three-year period between 1946 and 1988, the number of battlefield deaths hovered at around 182,000 annually, marking a drastic decrease from the era dominated by two world wars. After the Cold War ended, the period from 1989 to 2021 saw significantly fewer deaths per year—approximately 51,000, representing a more than 70 percent decrease. "Data Page: Deaths in State-Based Conflicts by Region," part of the following publication: Bastian Herre, Lucas Rodés-Guirao, and Max Roser, "War and Peace" (2024), data adapted from Uppsala Conflict Data Program, geoBoundaries, Peace Research Institute Oslo, https://archive.ourworldindata.org/20250909-093708/grapher/deaths-in-state-based-conflicts-by-region.html, archived September 9, 2025.

11. Alan E. Bernstein, *Hell and Its Rivals: Death and Retribution Among Christians, Jews, and Muslims in the Early Middle Ages* (Cornell University Press, 2017), 2–3.

12. Thomas Hobbes, *Leviathan*, ed. Edwin Curley (Hackett, 1994), 1.13.

13. Hobbes, *Leviathan*, 2.17–18.

14. Hobbes, *Leviathan*, 2.28.

15. Hobbes, *Leviathan*, 3.38–42.

16. Hobbes, *Leviathan*, 1.12.

17. Hobbes, *Leviathan*, 1.13; 2.17.

18. Christopher S. McClure, *Hobbes and the Artifice of Eternity* (Cambridge University Press, 2016), i.

19. See Lisa R. Holliday, "Will Satan Be Saved? Reconsidering Origen's Theory of Volition in *Peri Archon*," *Vigiliae Christianae* 63 (2009): 3.

20. See Daniel De Smet, "Ismaʿili-Shiʿi Visions of Hell," in *Locating Hell in Islamic Traditions*, ed. Christian Lange (Brill, 2016), 241–67. For the original source, see Ḥamīd al-Dīn al-Kirmānī, *Kitāb Rāḥat al-ʿaql*, ed. M. Ghālib (Oxford University Press, 1983).

21. Martin Luther King Jr., "Address at the National Cathedral," Washington, DC, March 31, 1968, quoted in Clayborne Carson et al., *The Papers of Martin Luther King, Jr.*, vol. 7, *To Save a Soul and a Nation, January 1959–December 1960* (University of California Press, 1998), 125.

22. Barack Obama, speech at the Democratic National Convention, Denver, CO, August 28, 2008, American Rhetoric, https://www.americanrhetoric.com/speeches/barackobama2008dnc.htm.

23. F. J. C. Hearnshaw, *The Social and Political Ideas of Some Great Mediaeval Thinkers* (Barnes & Noble, 1928), 180.

24. James V. Schall, "Displacing Damnation: The Neglect of Hell in Political Theory," *The Thomist* 44, no. 1 (1980): 36.

Chapter 6 From Cancel Culture to Covenant Culture

1. Conor Friedersdorf, "The Perils of Writing a Provocative Email at Yale," *The Atlantic*, May 26, 2016, https://www.theatlantic.com/politics/archive/2016/05/the-peril-of-writing-a-provocative-email-at-yale/484418/.

2. Pilar Blitvich, *Pragmatics, (Im)Politeness, and Intergroup Communication: A Multi-Layered Discursive Analysis of Cancel Culture* (Cambridge University Press, 2024), 1.

3. Greg Lukianoff and Rikki Schlott, *The Canceling of the American Mind: Cancel Culture Undermines Trust and Threatens Us All—but There Is a Solution* (Simon & Schuster, 2023), 112.

4. Paul du Quenoy, *Cancel Culture: Tales from the Front Lines* (Academica Press, 2021), ii. See also Julia Manchester, "64 Percent View 'Cancel Culture' as Threat of Freedom," The Hill, March 29, 2021, https://thehill.com/homenews/campaign/545387-64-percent-say-they-view-cancel-culture-as-a-threat-to-their-freedom-poll/.

5. For a helpful examination of the ways that theological and political conservatives have adopted the identitarian methods of the "woke left," see Neil Shenvi, "What Is the 'Woke Right'?," Neil Shenvi—Apologetics, accessed November 10, 2025, https://shenviapologetics.com/what-is-the-woke-right/.

6. While the vast majority of studies focus on the negative impacts of exclusion, some studies examine potential benefits. See, for example, Elaine O. Cheung and Wendi L. Gardner, "The Way I Make You Feel: Social Exclusion Enhances the Ability to Manage Others' Emotions," *Journal of Experimental Social Psychology* 60 (2015): 59–75.

7. Hannah Arendt, *The Origins of Totalitarianism*, 2nd ed. (Allen & Unwin, 1958), 465–66.

8. Philip G. Zimbardo, *The Lucifer Effect: Understanding How Good People Turn Evil* (Random House, 2007).

9. Reinhold Niebuhr, *Moral Man and Immoral Society* (Westminster John Knox, 2016).

10. Niebuhr, *Moral Man and Immoral Society*, 91.

11. Geoff Nunberg, "As Fissures Between Political Camps Grow, 'Tribalism' Emerges as the Word of 2017," NPR, December 6, 2017, https://www.npr.org/transcripts/568583263.

12. Robert D. Putnam and David E. Campbell, *American Grace: How Religion Divides and Unites Us* (Simon & Schuster, 2010), 34.

13. Jared Diamond, *Guns, Germs, and Steel: The Fates of Human Societies* (Norton, 1997), 74.

14. Michael W. Young, *The Makhuwa of Mozambique: Culture and Society* (Routledge, 2005), 112–13.

15. Dennis Prager, "America, Not Keith Ellison, Decides What Book a Congressman Takes His Oath On," *The Dennis Prager Show*, November 28, 2006, https://www.townhall.com/columnists/dennisprager/2007/01/05/ellison-and-the-quran-n1018011.

16. See "Muslim Civil Rights Group Condemns GOP Senators' Treatment of Muslim Court Pick," *HuffPost*, December 16, 2023, https://www.huffpost.com/entry/muslim-judicial-nominee-adeel-mangi-republicans_n_657c8262e4b08e9b410a2ae3; and Kathrina (Kasia) Szymborski Wolfkot, "Treatment of First Muslim Federal Appellate Nominee Has Damaged Our Institutions," Brennan Center for Justice, April 5, 2024, https://www.brennancenter.org/our-work/analysis-opinion/treatment-first-muslim-federal-appellate-nominee-has-damaged-our.

17. Riyad as-Salihin 1732, Sunnah.com, accessed April 2, 2026, https://sunnah.com/riyadussalihin:1732.

18. Al-Bukhārī, *Ṣaḥīḥ al-Bukhārī* (Damascus: 1423/2002), Kitāb al-adab, Bāb 44, no. 6045.

19. Patricia Crone, *Medieval Islamic Political Thought* (Edinburgh University Press, 2004), 56–58.

20. Ibn Taymiyya, *Majmūʿ al-Fatāwā*, ed. ʿAbd al-Raḥmān ibn Muḥammad ibn Qāsim, 37 vols. (Maṭābiʿ al-Riyāḍ, 1961–67), 12:524.

21. Abū Ḥāmid al-Ghazālī, *Fayṣal al-Tafriqa Bayna al-Islam wa al-Zandaqa*. For an excellent analysis and translation, see Sherman A. Jackson, *On the Boundaries of Theological Tolerance in Islam* (Oxford University Press, 2002).

22. Al-Ghazālī, *Faḍāʾiḥ al-Bāṭiniyya*, ed. ʿAbd al-Raḥmān Badawī (Muʾassasat Dār al-Kutub al-Thaqāfa, 1964).

23. See, for example, Ibn Rajab al-Ḥanbalī, *The Compendium of Knowledge and Wisdom*, trans. Abdassamad Clarke (Turath Publishing, 2007).

24. Ibn Rajab al-Ḥanbalī, *Jāmiʿ al-ʿulūm wa-l-ḥikam*, 2 vols., ed. Shuʿayb al-Arnāʾūṭ and Ibrāhīm Bājis (Muʾassasat al-Risālah, 2001).

25. Al-Bayhaqī, *Shuʿab al-Īmān*, ed. Muḥammad al-Saʿīd Zaghlūl (Dār al-Kutub al-ʿIlmiyya, 1990), 6:323.

26. Dietrich Bonhoeffer, *Life Together* (HarperCollins, 1954), 38.

27. Martin Luther King Jr., "Loving Your Enemies," sermon delivered at Dexter Avenue Baptist Church, Montgomery, AL, November 17, 1957, The Martin Luther King Jr. Research and Education Institute, accessed March 30, 2026, https://kinginstitute.stanford.edu/king-papers/documents/loving-your-enemies-sermon-delivered-dexter-avenue-baptist-church.

28. Gregory of Nyssa, *Homilies on Ecclesiastes*, ed. Stuart George Hall (De Gruyter, 1993), 74.

29. W. Christopher Stewart, Chris Seiple, and Dennis R. Hoover, "Toward a Global Covenant of Peaceable Neighborhood: Introducing the Philosophy of Covenantal Pluralism," *The Review of Faith & International Affairs* 18, no. 4 (2020): 1–17.

30. Stewart, Seiple, and Hoover, "Toward a Global Covenant," 9.

31. Miroslav Volf, *Exclusion and Embrace: A Theological Exploration of Identity, Otherness, and Reconciliation* (Abingdon, 1996), 18.

Chapter 7 Schools of Democracy

1. "Religion Holds Steady in America," Pew Research Center, December 8, 2025, https://www.pewresearch.org/religion/2025/12/08/religion-holds-steady-in-america/?utm_source=chatgpt.com.

2. Joseph B. Johnston, "Religion and Volunteering over the Adult Life Course," *Journal for the Scientific Study of Religion* 52, no. 4 (December 2013): 733–52.

3. Ozan Aksoy and Dingeman Wiertz, "The Impact of Religious Involvement on Trust, Volunteering, and Perceived Cooperativeness: Evidence from Two British Panels," *European Sociological Review* 40, no. 1 (February 2024): 143.

4. Matthew R. Bennett and Christopher J. Einolf, "Religion, Altruism, and Helping Strangers: A Multilevel Analysis of 126 Countries," *Journal for the Scientific Study of Religion* 56, no. 2 (June 2017): 323.

5. Stijn Ruiter and Nan Dirk De Graaf, "National Context, Religiosity, and Volunteering: Results from 53 Countries," *American Sociological Review* 71, no. 2 (April 2006): 206.

6. Chaeyoon Lim and Carol Ann MacGregor, "Religion and Volunteering in Context: Disentangling the Contextual Effects of Religion on Voluntary Behavior," *American Sociological Review* 77, no. 5 (October 2012): 750–51.

7. Azim F. Shariff and Ara Norenzayan, "God Is Watching You: Priming God Concepts Increases Prosocial Behavior in an Anonymous Economic Game," *Psychological Science* 18, no. 9 (2007): 803–9.

8. Joseph P. Daniels and Marc von der Ruhr, "Trust in Others: Does Religion Matter?," *Review of Social Economy* 68, no. 2 (June 2010): 163–86.

9. Kraig Beyerlein and John R. Hipp, "From Pews to Participation: The Effect of Congregation Activity and Context on Bridging Civic Engagement," *Social Problems* 53, no. 1 (February 2006): 97–117.

10. Rubia R. Valente and Adam Okulicz-Kozaryn, "Religiosity and Trust: Evidence from the United States," *Review of Religious Research* 63 (2021): 345.

11. Ying Chen, Eric S. Kim, and Tyler J. VanderWeele, "Religious-Service Attendance and Subsequent Health and Well-Being Throughout Adulthood: Evidence from Three Prospective Cohorts," *International Journal of Epidemiology* 49, no. 6 (December 2020), https://academic.oup.com/ije/article/49/6/2030/5892419.

12. See, for example, Michaela Pfundmair, Natasha R. Wood, Andrew Hales, and Eric D. Wesselmann, "How Social Exclusion Makes Radicalism Flourish: A Review of Empirical Evidence," *Journal of Social Issues* 80 (2024): 341–59; Kipling D. Williams, Andrew H. Hales, and Corinna Michels, "Social Ostracism as a Factor Motivating Interest in Extreme Groups," in *Current Directions in Ostracism, Social Exclusion, and Rejection Research*, ed. Selma C. Rudert, Rainer Greifeneder, and Kipling D. Williams (Routledge, 2019), 18–31; Arie W. Kruglanski, Xiaoyan Chen, Mark Dechesne, Shira Fishman, and Edward Orehek, "Fully Committed: Suicide Bombers' Motivation and the Quest for Personal Significance," *Political Psychology* 30, no. 3 (2009): 331–57; and Andrew H. Hales and Kipling D. Williams, "Marginalized Individuals and Extremism: The Role of Ostracism in Openness to Extreme Groups," *Journal of Social Issues* 74, no. 1 (2018): 75–92.

13. Alexis de Tocqueville, *Democracy in America*, vol. 1, English ed., ed. Eduardo Nolla, trans. James T. Schleifer (Liberty Fund, 2012), 896, 900.

14. Tocqueville, *Democracy in America*, 475.

15. Robert Putnam, *Bowling Alone: The Collapse and Revival of American Community* (Simon & Schuster, 2000), 66.

16. Putnam, *Bowling Alone*, 338.

17. Putnam states that the term *social capital* has been "independently invented at least six times over the course of the twentieth century." *Bowling Alone*, 19.

18. Putnam identifies the most important distinction in forms of social capital to be the difference between "bonding" and "bridging." Bonding forms of social capital are inclusive and inner-facing, which reinforce exclusive communal identities. He identifies "ethnic fraternal organizations, church-based women's reading groups, and fashionable country clubs" as examples. Bridging forms of social capital seek to bring people together across social differences. As examples he identifies "the civil rights movement, many youth service groups, and ecumenical religious organizations." *Bowling Alone*, 22–23.

19. Putnam, *Bowling Alone*, 23.

20. See Sarah Lyons-Padilla, Michele J. Gelfand, Hedieh Mirahmadi, Mehreen Farooq, and Marieke Van Egmond, "Belonging Nowhere: Marginalization and Radicalization Risk Among Muslim Immigrants," *Behavioral Science and Policy* 1, no. 2 (October 2015): 1–12; Pfundmair, Wood, Hales, and Wesselmann, "How Social Exclusion Makes Radicalism Flourish"; and Emma A. Renström, Hanna Bäck, and Holly M. Knapton, "Exploring a Pathway to Radicalization: The Effects of Social Exclusion and Rejection Sensitivity," *Group Processes & Intergroup Relations* 23, no. 8 (2020): 1204–29.

21. See Aksoy and Wiertz, "Impact of Religious Involvement"; Beyerlein and Hipp, "From Pews to Participation"; Deborah L. Hall, Adam B. Cohen, Kaitlin K. Meyer, Allison H. Varley, and Gene A. Brewer, "Costly Signaling Increases Trust, Even Across Religious Affiliations," *Psychological Science* 26, no. 9 (2015): 1368–76; and Valente and Okulicz-Kozaryn, "Religiosity and Trust."

22. See Aksoy and Wiertz, "Impact of Religious Involvement." See also Bennett and Einolf, "Religion, Altruism, and Helping Strangers."

23. See John A. Coleman, "Religious Social Capital: Its Nature, Social Location, and Limits," in *Religion as Social Capital: Producing the Common Good*, ed. Corwin Smidt (Baylor University Press, 2003), 35; and Johnston, "Religion and Volunteering."

24. Coleman, "Religious Social Capital," 35.

25. Sidney Verba, Kay Lehman Schlozman, and Henry E. Brady, *Voice and Equality: Civic Volunteerism in American Politics* (Harvard University Press, 1995), 18–19.

26. Andrew Shryock, "On Discipline and Inclusion," in *Being and Belonging: Muslims in the United States Since 9/11*, ed. Katherine Pratt Ewing (Russell Sage, 2008), 206.

27. For a Christian perspective on the growing debates over Muslim presence in the West, see Matthew Kaemingk, *Christian Hospitality and Muslim Immigration in an Age of Fear* (Eerdmans, 2018), especially his engagement with the work of Jocelyn Cesari.

28. Jocelyne Cesari, *When Islam and Democracy Meet: Muslims in Europe and in the United States* (Palgrave Macmillan, 2004), 102.

29. Barry Schwartz, *The Paradox of Choice: Why More Is Less*, rev. ed. (HarperCollins, 2016).

30. Tocqueville, *Democracy in America*, 745.

31. Putnam, *Bowling Alone*, 338.

32. William Kornhauser, *The Politics of Mass Society* (Free Press, 1959), 73.

33. Robert N. Bellah, Richard Madsen, William M. Sullivan, Ann Swidler, and Steven M. Tipton, *Habits of the Heart: Individualism and Commitment in American Life*, 3rd ed. (University of California Press, 2008), 24.

34. Bellah et al., *Habits of the Heart*, 83.

35. Bellah et al., *Habits of the Heart*, 290, 24.

36. Bellah et al., *Habits of the Heart*, 157.

37. Bellah et al., *Habits of the Heart*, 153.

38. Bellah et al., *Habits of the Heart*, 294 (emphasis added).

Chapter 8 Praying for Democracy

1. Martin Luther King Jr., "Draft of Chapter XV, 'The Answer to a Perplexing Question,'" The Martin Luther King Jr. Research and Education Institute, accessed March 30, 2026, https://kinginstitute.stanford.edu/king-papers/documents/draft-chapter-xv-answer-perplexing-question.

2. G. K. Chesterton, *The Everlasting Man* (John Lane, 1905), 124.

3. Peter A. Boelens, Roy R. Reeves, William H. Replogle, and Harold G. Koenig, "A Randomized Trial of the Effect of Prayer on Depression and Anxiety," *International Journal of Psychiatry in Medicine* 39, no. 4 (2009): 377–92; Peter A. Boelens, Roy R. Reeves, Harold G. Koenig, and William H. Replogle, "The Effect of Prayer on Depression and Anxiety: Maintenance of Positive Influence One Year After Prayer Intervention," *International Journal of Psychiatry in Medicine* 43, no 1 (2012): 85–98.

4. J. W. Anderson and P. A. Nunnelley, "Private Prayer Associations with Depression, Anxiety and Other Health Conditions: An Analytical Review of Clinical Studies," *Postgraduate Medicine* 128, no. 7 (September 2016): 635–41.

5. Jessie Dezutter, Amy Wachholtz, and Josef Corveleyn, "Prayer and Pain: The Mediating Role of Positive Re-Appraisal," *Journal of Behavioral Medicine* 34, no. 6 (2011): 542–49.

6. Ryan H. Bremner, Sander L. Koole, and Brad J. Bushman, "'Pray for Those Who Mistreat You': Effects of Prayer on Anger and Aggression," *Personality and Social Psychology Bulletin* 37, no. 6 (2011): 830–37.

7. Matthew T. Loveland, David Sikkink, Daniel J. Myers, and Benjamin Radcliff, "Private Prayer and Civic Involvement," *Journal for the Scientific Study of Religion* 44, no. 1 (2005): 12.

8. William E. Connolly, *Neuropolitics: Thinking, Culture, Speed* (University of Minnesota Press, 2002), 32.

9. See Amos Yong, "Hospitality and Religious Others: An Orthopathic Perspective," in *A Charitable Orthopathy: Christian Perspectives on Emotions in Multifaith Engagement*, ed. John W. Morehead and Brandon C. Benziger (Pickwick, 2020), 167–78. James K. A. Smith has drawn from St. Augustine to recognize the importance of rightly ordered love/desire in shaping belief and practice. See James K. A. Smith, *Desiring the Kingdom: Worship, Worldview, and Cultural Formation* (Baker Academic, 2009). For a more accessible entry into Smith's project, see his *You Are What You Love: The Spiritual Power of Habit* (Brazos, 2016). While there are fewer sources from the Muslim perspective, owing to the Islamic world's relatively new relationship to democracy, a good place to start is Muhammad Khalid Masud, Armando Salvatore, and Martin van Bruinessen, eds., *Islam and Modernity: Key Issues and Debates* (Edinburgh University Press, 2009).

10. Shadi's experience of a habitual, communal practice as the basis for the cultural and moral formation of group identity resonates with Pierre Bourdieu's notion of *habitus*. Bourdieu argues that practices engage people bodily to ingrain certain dispositions, postures, and embodied norms (such as an accent) within them. See Pierre Bourdieu, *The Logic of Practice*, trans. Richard Nice (Stanford University Press, 1990). According to the logic of *habitus*, Shadi's experience in the mosque helps illustrate that prayer is an example of a practice that forms an egalitarian community where one may not have existed previously.

11. Hamza Yusuf, *Purification of the Heart* (Starlatch, 2004), 89.

12. Tariq Ramadan, *In the Footsteps of the Prophet* (Oxford University Press, 2007), 156.

13. Phillip Cary, *Augustine's Invention of the Inner Self: The Legacy of a Christian Platonist* (Oxford University Press, 2003).

14. St. Augustine, "Letter 130: To Proba," in *The Fathers of the Church: Saint Augustine, Letters Volume II (83–130)*, trans. Sister Wilfrid Parsons (The Catholic University of America Press, 2008), 376–401.

15. Benedict of Nursia, *The Rule of Saint Benedict*, ed. Timothy Fry, in *The Rule of Saint Benedict in English* (Liturgical Press, 1981), chap. 20.

16. Smith, *Desiring the Kingdom*, 58.

17. Nancy Tatom Ammerman, *Congregation and Community* (Rutgers University Press, 1997), 368.

18. Ammerman, *Congregation and Community*, 354.

19. Tina Fey, "Weekend Update," *Saturday Night Live Weekend Update: Summer Edition*, NBC, August 17, 2017.

20. As quoted in Shadi Hamid, "A Muslim's Guide to Accepting Electoral Defeat," *The Washington Post*, November 18, 2024.

21. William J. Brady, Killian McLoughlin, Tuan N. Doan, and Molly J. Crockett, "How Social Learning Amplifies Moral Outrage Expression in Social Networks," *Science Advances* 7, no. 33 (August 2021), https://www.science.org/doi/10.1126/sciadv.abe5641.

22. Jason M. Shepard and Kathleen B. Culver, "Culture Wars on Campus: Academic Freedom, the First Amendment, and Partisan Outrage in Polarized Times," *San Diego Law Review* 55 (2018): 87–158.

23. Emilie M. Townes, "Lament and Hope: Defying This Hot Mess," *Reflections* (Fall 2019), https://reflections.yale.edu/article/resistance-and-blessing-women-ministry-and-yds/lament-and-hope-defying-hot-mess.

24. Richard Foster uses the sail as a powerful metaphor for prayerful submission in *Prayer: Finding the Heart's True Home* (HarperCollins, 1992), 65.

25. Abraham Lincoln, "Second Inaugural Address," March 4, 1865, in *Collected Works of Abraham Lincoln*, ed. Roy P. Basler (Rutgers University Press, 1953), 8:333–37.

26. This hadith is so widely known that it is part of the common lexicon of Muslims and many non-Muslims alike, even beyond the Arab world. The full hadith reads: "Anas ibn Malik reported: A man said, 'O Messenger of Allah, should I tie my camel and trust in Allah, or should I leave her untied and trust in Allah?' The Prophet, peace and blessings be upon him, said, 'Tie her and trust in Allah.'" Sunan al-Tirmidhi 2517, book 37, hadith 103.

27. Anthony Bloom, *Beginning to Pray* (Paulist Press, 1970), 59.

28. Reinhold Niebuhr, in *Book of Prayers and Services for the Armed Forces* (Federal Council of the Churches of Christ in America, 1944).

29. "Religion Holds Steady in America," Pew Research Center, December 8, 2025, https://www.pewresearch.org/religion/2025/12/08/religion-holds-steady-in-america/?utm_source=chatgpt.com.

30. Anne Trafton, "Two Studies Reveal Benefits of Mindfulness for Middle School Students," *MIT News*, August 26, 2019, https://news.mit.edu/2019/mindfulness-mental-health-benefits-students-0826.

31. Trafton, "Two Studies."

MATTHEW KAEMINGK is a Christian ethicist and public theologian. He serves as professor of public theology at Theological University Utrecht and senior research fellow at Georgetown University. Kaemingk is an award-winning author and frequent public speaker for universities, think tanks, and religious organizations exploring the intersection between religion, politics, and deep difference. He is the author and editor of several books on faith and public life, including *Christian Hospitality and Muslim Immigration in an Age of Fear* and *Reformed Public Theology*. He received his MDiv from Princeton Theological Seminary and his PhD from the Vrije Universiteit Amsterdam, where he was a Fulbright Scholar.

Connect with Matthew:

@matthew_kaemingk   @matthewkaemingk

SHADI HAMID is a columnist for and member of the editorial board at *The Washington Post* and a research professor of Islamic Studies at Fuller Theological Seminary. Previously, he was a senior fellow at the Brookings Institution and a contributing writer at *The Atlantic*. Hamid is the author of several books, including most recently *The Problem of Democracy*. His previous book *Islamic Exceptionalism: How the Struggle Over Islam Is Reshaping the World* was shortlisted for the 2017 Lionel Gelber Prize for best book on foreign affairs. His book *The Case for American Power* was recently released by Simon & Schuster. He is also the cofounder of *Wisdom of Crowds*, a podcast, newsletter, and debate platform. Hamid received his BS and MA from Georgetown University's School of Foreign Service and his PhD in political science from Oxford University, where he was a Marshall Scholar.

Connect with Shadi:

shadihamid20   @shadihamid

@shadihamid2   @shadihamid